93 3-22-79

ON THE ENGLISH POETS.

LECTURES

ON

THE ENGLISH POETS.

BY WILLIAM HAZLITT.

Third Edition.

EDITED BY HIS SON.

NEW YORK / RUSSELL & RUSSELL

REPRODUCED FROM THE THIRD EDITION PUBLISHED IN 1841
REISSUED, 1968, BY RUSSELL & RUSSELL
A DIVISION OF ATHENEUM HOUSE, INC.
L. C. CATALOG CARD NO: 68-25032
PRINTED IN THE UNITED STATES OF AMERICA

TO

BARRY CORNWALL,

WHOM THE AUTHOR OF THESE LECTURES

ESTEEMED AS A MAN

AND ADMIRED AS A POET,

This Volume is Dedicated.

CONTENTS.

------•------

The articles in the Appendix on Wordsworth and on Milton are taken from " The Round Table." That on Pope, Lord Byron, and Mr. Bowles, from " The London Magazine, for 1821."

LECTURES

THE ENGLISH POETS.

———◆———

LECTURE I.—INTRODUCTORY.

ON POETRY IN GENERAL.

The best general notion which I can give of
poetry is that it is the natural impression
of any object or event, by its vividness exciting an involuntary movement of imagination
and passion, and producing, by sympathy, a
certain modulation of the voice, or sounds,
expressing it.

In treating of poetry, I shall speak first of
the subject-matter of it, next of the forms of
expression to which it gives birth, and afterwards of its connection with harmony of sound.

Poetry is the language of the imagination
and the passions. It relates to whatever gives
immediate pleasure or pain to the human mind.
It comes home to the bosoms and businesses of

men ; for nothing but what so comes home to
them in the most general and intelligible shape
can be a subject for poetry.   Poetry is the
universal language which the heart holds with
nature and itself. He who has a contempt for
poetry cannot have much respect for himself,
or for any thing else. It is not a mere frivolous
accomplishment (as some persons have been
led to imagine), the trifling amusement of a
few idle readers or leisure hours—it has been
the study and delight of mankind in all ages.
Many people suppose that poetry is something
to be found only in books, contained in lines
of ten syllables, with like endings : but where-
ever there is a sense of beauty, or power, or
harmony, as in the motion of a wave of the sea,
in the growth of a flower, that " spreads its
sweet leaves to the air, and dedicates its beauty
to the sun,"—*there* is poetry, in its birth. If
history is a grave study, poetry may be said to
be a graver : its materials lie deeper, and are
spread wider.   History treats, for the most
part, of the cumbrous and unwieldly masses
of things, the empty cases in which the affairs
of the world are packed, under the heads of
intrigue or war, in different states, and from
century to century : but there is no thought or
feeling that can have entered into the mind of
man, which he would be eager to communi-

cate to others, or which they would listen to with delight, that is not a fit subject for poetry. It is not a branch of authorship : it is " the stuff of which our life is made." The rest is " mere oblivion," a dead letter : for all that is worth remembering in life is the poetry of it. Fear is poetry, hope is poetry, love is poetry, hatred is poetry ; contempt, jealousy, remorse, admiration, wonder, pity, despair, or madness, are all poetry. Poetry is that fine particle within us that expands, rarefies, refines, raises our whole being : without it " man's life is poor as beasts'." Man is a poetical animal : and those of us who do not study the principles of poetry act upon them all our lives, like Moliere's *Bourgeois Gentilhomme*, who had always spoken prose without knowing it. The child is a poet, in fact, when he first plays at hide-and-seek, or repeats the story of Jack the Giant-killer ; the shepherd-boy is a poet, when he first crowns his mistress with a garland of flowers ; the countryman, when he stops to look at the rainbow ; the city-apprentice, when he gazes after the Lord-Mayor's show; the miser, when he hugs his gold ; the courtier, who builds his hopes upon a smile ; the savage, who paints his idol with blood ; the slave, who worships a tyrant, or the tyrant, who fancies himself a god ; — the vain, the ambitious, the

proud, the choleric man, the hero and the
coward, the beggar and the king, the rich and
the poor, the young and the old, all live in a
world of their own making ; and the poet does
no more than describe what all the others think
and act.   If his art is folly and madness, it is
folly and madness at second hand.   " There
is warrant for it."   Poets alone have not " such
seething brains, such shaping fantasies, that
apprehend more than cooler reason" can.

> " The lunatic, the lover, and the poet,
> Are of imagination all compact.
> One sees more devils than vast hell can hold ;
> The madman.   While the lover, all as frantic,
> Sees Helen's beauty in a brow of Egypt.
> The poet's eye, in a fine frenzy rolling,
> Doth glance from heav'n to earth, from earth to heav'n ;
> And, as imagination bodies forth
> The forms of things unknown, the poet's pen
> Turns them to shape, and gives to airy nothing
> A local habitation and a name.
> Such tricks hath strong imagination."

If poetry is a dream, the business of life is
much the same. If it is a fiction, made up of
what we wish things to be, and fancy that they
are, because we wish them so, there is no other
nor better reality. Ariosto has described the
loves of Angelica and Medoro: but was not
Medoro, who carved the name of his mistress
on the barks of trees, as much enamoured of
her charms as he ? Homer has celebrated the

anger of Achilles : but was not the hero as mad as the poet ? Plato banished the poets from his Commonwealth, lest their descriptions of the natural man should spoil his mathematical man, who was to be without passions and affections, who was neither to laugh nor weep, to feel sorrow nor anger, to be cast down nor elated by any thing. This was a chimera, however, which never existed but in the brain of the inventor ; and Homer's poetical world has outlived Plato's philosophical Republic.

Poetry then is an imitation of nature, but the imagination and the passions are a part of man's nature. We shape things according to our wishes and fancies, without poetry ; but poetry is the most emphatical language that can be found for those creations of the mind " which ecstacy is very cunning in." Neither a mere description of natural objects, nor a mere delineation of natural feelings, however distinct or forcible, constitutes the ultimate end and aim of poetry, without the heightenings of the imagination. The light of poetry is not only a direct but also a reflected light, that, while it shews us the object, throws a sparkling radiance on all around it : the flame of the passions, communicated to the imagination, reveals to us, as with a flash of lightning, the inmost recesses of thought, and penetrates our whole being. Poetry represents forms chiefly as they suggest other forms; feelings, as they suggest forms or other feelings. Poetry puts a spirit of life and motion into the universe. It describes the flowing, not the fixed. It does not define the limits of sense, nor analyze the distinctions of the understanding, but signifies the excess of the imagination beyond the actual or ordinary impression of any object or feeling. The poetical impression of any object is that uneasy, exquisite sense of beauty or power that cannot be contained within itself; that is impatient of all limit; that (as flame bends to flame) strives to link itself to some other image of kindred beauty or grandeur; to enshrine itself, as it were, in the highest forms of fancy, and to relieve the aching sense of pleasure by expressing it in the boldest manner, and by the most striking examples of the same quality in other instances. Poetry, according to Lord Bacon, for this reason, " has something divine in it, because it raises the mind and hurries it into sublimity, by conforming the shows of things to the desires of the soul, instead of subjecting the soul to external things as reason and history do." It is strictly the language of the imagination; and the imagination is that faculty which represents

objects, not as they are in themselves, but as
they are moulded, by other thoughts and feelings, into an infinite variety of shapes and combinations of power. This language is not the
less true to nature because it is false in point
of fact ; but so much the more true and natural, if it conveys the impression which the
object under the influence of passion makes on
the mind. Let an object, for instance, be
presented to the senses in a state of agitation
or fear—and the imagination will distort or
magnify the object, and convert it into the
likeness of whatever is most proper to encou-
rage the fear. " Our eyes are made the fools "
of our other faculties. This is the universal
law of the imagination,

> " That if it would but apprehend some joy,
> It comprehends some bringer of that joy :
> Or in the night, imagining some fear,
> How easy is each bush suppos'd a bear !"

When Iachimo says of Imogen,

> "————The flame o' th' taper
> Bows toward her, and would under-peep her lids
> To see the enclosed lights "—

this passionate interpretation of the motion of
the flame to accord with the speaker's own
feelings is true poetry. The lover, equally
with the poet, speaks of the auburn tresses of
his mistress as locks of shining gold, because

the least tinge of yellow in the hair has, from
novelty and a sense of personal beauty, a
more lustrous effect to the imagination than
the purest gold. We compare a man of gigantic stature to a tower : not that he is any
thing like so large, but because the excess of
his size beyond what we are accustomed to expect, or the usual size of things of the same
class, produces by contrast a greater feeling of
magnitude and ponderous strength than another
object of ten times the same dimensions. The
intensity of the feeling makes up for the dis-
proportion of the objects. Things are equal
to the imagination, which have the power of
affecting the mind with an equal degree of
terror, admiration, delight, or love. When
Lear calls upon the heavens to avenge his
cause, " for they are old like him," there is
nothing extravagant or impious in this sublime
identification of his age with theirs ; for there
is no other image which could do justice to
the agonising sense of his wrongs and his
despair !

Poetry is the high-wrought enthusiasm of
fancy and feeling. As, in describing natural
objects, it impregnates sensible impressions
with the forms of fancy, so it describes the
feelings of pleasure or pain, by blending
them with the strongest movements of passion,

and the most striking forms of nature. Tragic
poetry, which is the most impassioned species
of it, strives to carry on the feeling to the
utmost point of sublimity or pathos, by all
the force of comparison or contrast; loses the
sense of present suffering in the imaginary
exaggeration of it; exhausts the terror or pity
by an unlimited indulgence of it; grapples
with impossibilities in its desperate impatience of restraint; throws us back upon the
past, forward into the future; brings every
moment of our being or object of nature in
startling review before us; and, in the rapid
whirl of events, lifts us from the depths of
woe to the highest contemplations on human
life. When Lear says, of Edgar, " Nothing
but his unkind daughters could have brought
him to this;" what a bewildered amazement,
what a wrench of the imagination, that cannot
be brought to conceive of any other cause of
misery than that which has bowed it down,
and absorbs all other sorrow in its own ! His
sorrow, like a flood, supplies the sources of
all other sorrow. Again, when he exclaims
in the mad scene, " The little dogs and
all, Tray, Blanche, and Sweetheart, see,
they bark at me !" it is passion lending occasion to imagination to make every creature
in league against him, conjuring up ingra-

titude and insult in their least looked-for and most galling shapes, searching every thread and fibre of his heart, and finding out the last remaining image of respect or attachment in the bottom of his breast, only to torture and kill it! In like manner, the " So I am" of Cordelia gushes from her heart like a torrent of tears, relieving it of a weight of love and of supposed ingratitude, which had pressed upon it for years. What a fine return of the passion upon itself is that in Othello—with what a mingled agony of regret and despair he clings to the last traces of departed happiness—when he exclaims,

———"Oh now, for ever
Farewell the tranquil mind. Farewell content ;
Farewell the plumed troops and the big war,
That make ambition virtue ! Oh farewell !
Farewell the neighing steed, and the shrill trump,
The spirit-stirring drum, th' ear-piercing fife,
The royal banner, and all quality,
Pride, pomp, and circumstance of glorious war :
And O, you mortal engines, whose rude throats
Th' immortal Jove's dread clamours counterfeit,
Farewell ! Othello's occupation's gone !"

How his passion lashes itself up and swells and rages like a tide in its sounding course, when, in answer to the doubts expressed of his returning love, he says,

"Never, Iago. Like to the Pontic sea,
Whose icy current and compulsive course

Ne'er feels retiring ebb, but keeps due on
To the Propontic and the Hellespont :
Even so my bloody thoughts, with violent pace,
Shall ne'er look back, ne'er ebb to humble love,
Till that a capable and wide revenge
Swallow them up."—

The climax of his expostulation afterwards
with Desdemona is at that line,

" But there, where I had garner'd up my heart,
To be discarded thence !"

One mode in which the dramatic exhibition
of passion excites our sympathy without
raising our disgust is that, in proportion as it
sharpens the edge of calamity and disappointment, it strengthens the desire of good.   It
enhances our consciousness of the blessing,
by making us sensible of the magnitude of
the loss.   The storm of passion lays bare and
shews us the rich depths of the human soul :
the whole of our existence, the sum total of
our passions and pursuits, of that which we
desire, and that which we dread, is brought
before us by contrast ; the action and re-action
are equal ; the keenness of immediate suffering
only gives us a more intense aspiration after,
and a more intimate participation with, the
antagonist world of good ; makes us drink
deeper of the cup of human life ; tugs at
the heart-strings ; loosens the pressure about

them ; and calls the springs of thought
and feeling into play with tenfold force.

Impassioned poetry is an emanation of the
moral and intellectual part of our nature, as
well as of the sensitive---of the desire to know,
the will to act, and the power to feel; and
ought to appeal to these different parts of
our constitution, in order to be perfect. The
domestic or prose tragedy, which is thought
to be the most natural, is in this sense the
least so, because it appeals almost exclusively
to one of these faculties, our sensibility. The
tragedies of Moore and Lillo, for this reason,
however affecting at the time, oppress and lie
like a dead weight upon the mind, a load of
misery which it is unable to throw off : the
tragedy of Shakspeare, which is true poetry,
stirs our inmost affections ; abstracts evil from
itself by combining it with all the forms of
imagination, and with the deepest workings
of the heart, and rouses the whole man within us.

The pleasure, however, derived from tragic
poetry is not any thing peculiar to it as poetry,
as a fictitious and fanciful thing. It is not an
anomaly of the imagination. It has its source
and ground-work in the common love of
strong excitement. As Mr. Burke observes,
people flock to see a tragedy ; but, if there

were a public execution in the next street,
the theatre would very soon be empty. It is
not then the difference between fiction and
reality that solves the difficulty. Children
are satisfied with the stories of ghosts and
witches in plain prose : nor do the hawkers of
full, true, and particular accounts of murders
and executions about the streets find it necessary to have them turned into penny ballads,
before they can dispose of these interesting and
authentic documents. The grave politician
drives a thriving trade of abuse and calumnies
poured out against those whom he makes his
enemies for no other end than that he may
live by them. The popular preacher makes
less frequent mention of heaven than of hell.
Oaths and nicknames are only a more vulgar
sort of poetry or rhetoric. We are as fond of
indulging our violent passions as of reading a
description of those of others. We are as
prone to make a torment of our fears as to
luxuriate in our hopes of good. If it be asked,
Why we do so ? the best answer will be, Because we cannot help it. The sense of power
is as strong a principle in the mind as the
love of pleasure. Objects of terror and pity
exercise the same despotic control over it as
those of love or beauty. It is as natural to
hate as to love, to despise as to admire,

to express our hatred or contempt, as our love
or admiration.

> " Masterless passion sways us to the mood
> Of what it likes or loathes."

Not that we like what we loathe ; but we like
to indulge our hatred and scorn of it ; to dwell
upon it, to exasperate our idea of it by every
refinement of ingenuity and extravagance of
illustration ; to make it a bugbear to ourselves,
to point it out to others in all the splendour
of deformity, to embody it to the senses, to
stigmatise it by name, to grapple with it in
thought, in action, to sharpen our intellect, to
arm our will against it, to know the worst we
have to contend with, and to contend with it
to the utmost. Poetry is only the highest
eloquence of passion, the most vivid form of
expression that can be given to our conception
of any thing, whether pleasurable or painful,
mean or dignified, delightful or distressing.
It is the perfect concidence of the image and
the words with the feeling we have, and of
which we cannot get rid in any other way,
that gives an instant " satisfaction to the
thought." This is equally the origin of wit
and fancy, of comedy and tragedy, of the
sublime and pathetic. When Pope says of
the Lord Mayor's shew,—

" Now night descending, the proud scene is o'er,
But lives in Settle's numbers one day more ;"

—when Collins makes Danger, " with limbs
of giant mould,"

————"Throw him on the steep
Of some loose hanging rock asleep ;"

when Lear calls out, in extreme anguish,

" Ingratitude, thou marble-hearted fiend,
How much more hideous shew'st thou in a child
Than the sea-monster !—"

—the passion of contempt in the one case, of
terror in the other, and of indignation in the
last, is perfectly satisfied. We see the thing
ourselves, and shew it to others as we feel it
to exist, and as, in spite of ourselves, we are
compelled to think of it. The imagination,
by thus embodying and turning them to shape,
gives an obvious relief to the indistinct and
importunate cravings of the will.—We do not
wish the thing to be so; but we wish it to
appear such as it is. For knowledge is conscious power; and the mind is no longer, in
this case, the dupe, though it may be the
victim, of vice or folly.

Poetry is, in all its shapes, the language of
the imagination and the passions, of fancy and
will. Nothing, therefore, can be more absurd
than the outcry which has been sometimes

raised by frigid and pedantic critics, for reducing the language of poetry to the standard
of common sense and reason : for the end and
use of poetry, both at the first and now,
was and is " to hold the mirror up to nature,"
seen through the medium of passion and imagination, not divested of that medium by means
of literal truth or abstract reason.   The painter of history might as well be required to represent the face of a person who has just trod
upon a serpent with the still-life expression of
a common portrait, as the poet to describe the
most striking and vivid impressions which
things can be supposed to make upon the
mind in the language of common conversation.
Let who will strip nature of the colours and
the shapes of fancy, the poet is not bound to
do so ; the impressions of common sense and
strong imagination, that is, of passion and indifference, cannot be the same, and they must
have a separate language to do justice to either.
Objects must strike differently upon the mind,
independently of what they are in themselves,
as long as we have a different interest in them,
as we see them in a different point of view,
nearer or at a greater distance (morally or phy-
sically speaking) from novelty, from old acquaintance, from our ignorance of them, from
our fear of their consequences, from contrast,

from unexpected likeness. We can no more
take away the faculty of the imagination than
we can see all objects without light or shade.
Some things must dazzle us by their preternatural light ; others must hold us in suspense,
and tempt our curiosity to explore their obscurity. Those who would dispel these various
illusions, to give us their drab-coloured creation
in their stead, are not very wise. Let the
naturalist, if he will, catch the glow-worm,
carry it home with him in a box, and find it
next morning nothing but a little grey worm ;
let the poet or the lover of poetry visit it at
evening, when beneath the scented hawthorn
and the crescent moon it has built itself a
palace of emerald light. This is also one part of
nature, one appearance which the glow-worm
presents, and that not the least interesting ; so
poetry is one part of the history of the human
mind, though it is neither science nor philosophy. It cannot be concealed, however, that
the progress of knowledge and refinement has
a tendency to circumscribe the limits of the
imagination, and to clip the wings of poetry.
The province of the imagination is principally
visionary, the unknown and undefined : the
understanding restores things to their natural
boundaries, and strips them of their fanciful
pretensions. Hence the history of religious

and poetical enthusiasm is much the same ; and both have received a sensible shock from the progress of experimental philosophy. It is the undefined and uncommon that gives birth and scope to the imagination ; we can only fancy what we do not know. As in looking into the mazes of a tangled wood we fill them with what shapes we please, with ravenous beasts, with caverns vast, and drear enchantments, so, in our ignorance of the world about us, we make gods or devils of the first object we see, and set no bounds to the wilful suggestions of our hopes and fears.

> " And visions, as poetic eyes avow,
>   Hang on each leaf, and cling to every bough."

There can never be another Jacob's dream. Since that time the heavens have gone farther off, and grown astronomical. They have become averse to the imagination, nor will they return to us on the squares of the distances, or on Doctor Chalmers's Discourses. Rembrant's picture brings the matter nearer to us.—It is not only the progress of mechanical knowledge, but the necessary advances of civilization, that are unfavourable to the spirit of poetry. We not only stand in less awe of the preternatural world, but we can calculate more surely, and look with more indifference, upon

the regular routine of this. The heroes of
the fabulous ages rid the world of monsters
and giants. At present we are less exposed
to the vicissitudes of good or evil, to the incur-
sions of wild beasts or " bandit fierce," or to
the unmitigated fury of the elements. The
time has been that " our fell of hair would at
a dismal treatise rouse and stir as life were in
it." But the police spoils all ; and we now
hardly so much as dream of a midnight murder. Macbeth is only tolerated in this country for the sake of the music ; and in the
United States ȯf America, where the philosophical principles of government are carried
still farther in theory and practice, we find
that the Beggar's Opera is hooted from the
stage. Society, by degrees, is constructed
into a machine that carries us safely and insi-
pidly from one end of life to the other, in a
very comfortable prose style.

> " Obscurity her curtain round them drew,
> And siren Sloth a dull quietus sung."

The remarks which have been here made
would, in some measure, lead to a solution of
the question of the comparative merits of painting and poetry. I do not mean to give any
preference, but it should seem that the argu-

ment, which has been sometimes set up, that painting must affect the imagination more strongly, because it represents the image more distinctly, is not well founded. We may assume, without much temerity, that poetry is more poetical than painting. When artists or connoisseurs talk on stilts about the poetry of painting, they show that they know little about poetry, and have little love for the art. Painting gives the object itself ; poetry what it implies. Painting embodies what a thing contains in itself : poetry suggests what exists out of it, in any manner connected with it. But this last is the proper province of the imagination. Again, as it relates to passion, painting gives the event, poetry the progress of events : but it is during the progress, in the interval of expectation and suspense, while our hopes and fears are strained to the highest pitch of breathless agony, that the pinch of the interest lies.

> " Between the acting of a dreadful thing
> And the first motion, all the interim is
> Like a phantasma or a hideous dream.
> The mortal instruments are then in council ;
> And the state of man, like to a little kingdom,
> Suffers then the nature of an insurrection."

But by the time that the picture is painted, all is over. Faces are the best part of a pic-

ture ; but even faces are not what we chiefly
remember in what interests us most.—But it
may be asked then, Is there any thing better
than Claude Lorraine's landscapes, than
Titian's portraits, than Raphael's Cartoons,
or the Greek statues ? Of the two first I shall
say nothing, as they are evidently picturesque,
rather than imaginative. Raphael's Cartoons
are certainly the finest comments that ever
were made on the Scriptures. Would their
effect be the same if we were not acquainted
with the text ? But the New Testament
existed before the cartoons. There is one
subject of which there is no cartoon, Christ
washing the feet of the disciples the night before his death. But that chapter does not need
a commentary ! It is for want of some such
resting - place for the imagination that the
Greek statues are little else than specious
forms. They are marble to the touch and to
the heart. They have not an informing principle within them. In their faultless excellence
they appear sufficient to themselves. By their
beauty they are raised above the frailties of
passion or suffering. By their beauty they are
deified. But they are not objects of religious faith
to us, and their forms are a reproach to common humanity. They seem to have no sympathy with us, and not to want our admiration.

Poetry in its matter and form is natural imagery or feeling, combined with passion and fancy. In its mode of conveyance, it combines the ordinary use of language with musical expression. There is a question of long standing, in what the essence of poetry consists; or what it is that determines why one set of ideas should be expressed in prose, another in verse. Milton has told us his idea of poetry in a single line :—

> " Thoughts that voluntary move
> Harmonious numbers."

As there are certain sounds that excite certain movements, and the song and dance go together, so there are, no doubt, certain thoughts that lead to certain tones of voice, or modulations of sound, and change " the words of Mercury into the songs of Apollo." There is a striking instance of this adaptation of the movement of sound and rhythm to the subject, in Spenser's description of the Satyrs accompanying Una to the cave of Sylvanus.

> " So from the ground she fearless doth arise,
>   And walketh forth without suspect of crime.
> They, all as glad as birds of joyous prime,
>   Thence lead her forth, about her dancing round,
> Shouting and singing all a shepherd's rhyme ;
>   And with green branches strewing all the ground,
> Do worship her as queen with olive garland crown'd.

And all the way their merry pipes they sound,
    That all the woods and doubled echoes ring ;
And with their horned feet do wear the ground,
    Leaping like wanton kids in pleasant spring ;
So towards old Sylvanus they her bring,
    Who, with the noise awaked, cometh out."

Faery Queen, b. i. c. vi.

On the contrary, there is nothing either musical or natural in the ordinary construction of
language. It is a thing altogether arbitrary
and conventional. Neither in the sounds
themselves, which are the voluntary signs of
certain ideas, nor in their grammatical arrange-
ments in common speech, is there any principle of natural imitation, or correspondence to
the individual ideas, or to the tone of feeling
with which they are conveyed to others. The
jerks, the breaks, the inequalities, and harsh-
nesses of prose, are fatal to the flow of a poetical imagination, as a jolting road or a stum-
bling horse disturbs the reverie of an absent
man. But poetry makes these odds all even.
It is the music of language, answering to the
music of the mind, untying, as it were, " the
secret soul of harmony." Wherever any object takes such a hold of the mind as to make
us dwell upon it, and brood over it, melting
the heart in tenderness, or kindling it to a
sentiment of enthusiasm ;—wherever a movement of imagination or passion is impressed

on the mind, by which it seeks to prolong
and repeat the emotion, to bring all other objects into accord with it, and to give the same
movement of harmony, sustained and continuous, or gradually varied according to the occasion, to the sounds that express it—this is
poetry.   The musical in sound is the sustained and continuous ; the musical in thought is
the sustained and continuous also.   There is
a near connection between music and deep-
rooted passion.   Mad people sing.   As often
as articulation passes naturally into intonation
there poetry begins.   Where one idea gives a
tone and colour to others, where one feeling
melts others into it, there can be no reason
why the same principle should not be extended
to the sounds by which the voice utters these
emotions of the soul, and blends syllables and
lines into each other.   It is to supply the inherent defect of harmony in the customary
mechanism of language, to make the sound an
echo to the sense, when the sense becomes a
sort of echo to itself—to mingle the tide of
verse, " the golden cadences of poetry," with
the tide of feeling, flowing and murmuring as
it flows—in short, to take the language of the
imagination from off the ground, and enable
it to spread its wings where it may indulge
its own impulses—

" Sailing with supreme dominion
    Through the azure deep of air—"

without being stopped, or fretted, or diverted
with the abruptnesses and petty obstacles, and
discordant flats and sharps of prose, that poetry
was invented. It is to common language what
springs are to a carriage, or wings to feet. In
ordinary speech we arrive at a certain harmony
by the modulations of the voice : in poetry the
same thing is done systematically by a regular
collocation of syllables. It has been well observed, that every one who declaims warmly,
or grows intent upon a subject, rises into a
sort of blank verse or measured prose. The
merchant, as described in Chaucer, went on
his way " sounding always the increase of his
winning." Every prose-writer has more or
less of rhythmical adaptation, except poets,
who, when deprived of the regular mechanism
of verse, seem to have no principle of modulation left in their writings.

An excuse might be made for rhyme in the
same manner. It is but fair that the ear should
linger on the sounds that delight it, or avail itself of the same brilliant coincidence and unexpected recurrence of syllables, that have been
displayed in the invention and collocation of
images. It is allowed that rhyme assists the
memory ; and a man of wit and shrewdness

has been heard to say that the only four good
lines of poetry are the well-known ones which
tell the number of days in the months of the
year.

"Thirty days hath September," &c.

But if the jingle of names assists the memory,
may it not also quicken the fancy? and there
are other things worth having at our fingers'
ends besides the contents of the almanac.—
Pope's versification is tiresome, from its excessive sweetness and uniformity. Shakspeare's
blank verse is the perfection of dramatic
dialogue.

All is not poetry that passes for such : nor
does verse make the whole difference between
poetry and prose.   The Iliad does not cease
to be poetry in a literal translation ; and
Addison's Campaign has been very properly
denominated a Gazette in rhyme.   Common
prose differs from poetry, as treating for the
most part either of such trite, familiar, and irk-
some matters of fact as convey no extraordinary impulse to the imagination, or else of such
difficult and laborious processes of the understanding as do not admit of the wayward or
violent movements either of the imagination
or the passions.

I will mention three works which come as

near to poetry as possible without absolutely
being so, namely, the Pilgrim's Progress,
Robinson Crusoe, and the Tales of Boccaccio.
Chaucer and Dryden have translated some of
the last into English rhyme, but the essence
and the power of poetry was there before.
That which lifts the spirit above the earth,
which draws the soul out of itself with in-
describable longings, is poetry in kind, and
generally fit to become so in name, by being
" married to immortal verse." If it is of the
essence of poetry to strike and fix the imagination, whether we will or no, to make the eye
of childhood glisten with the starting tear, to
be never thought of afterwards with indifference, John Bunyan and Daniel Defoe may be
permitted to pass for poets in their way. The
mixture of fancy and reality in the Pilgrim's
Progress was never equalled in any allegory.
His pilgrims walk above the earth, and yet
are on it. What zeal, what beauty, what truth
of fiction! What deep feeling in the description of Christian's swimming across the water
at last, and in the picture of the Shining Ones
within the gates, with wings at their backs
and garlands on their heads, who are to wipe
all tears from his eyes! The writer's genius,
though not " dipped in dews of Castalie," was
baptised with the Holy Spirit and with fire.

The prints in this book are no small part of it.
If the confinement of Philoctetes in the island
of Lemnos was a subject for the most beautiful of all the Greek tragedies, what shall we say
to Robinson Crusoe in his?   Take the speech
of the Greek hero on leaving his cave, beautiful as it is, and compare it with the reflections
of the English adventurer in his solitary place
of confinement.   The thoughts of home, and
of all from which he is for ever cut off, swell
and press against his bosom, as the heaving
ocean rolls its ceaseless tide against the rocky
shore, and the very beatings of his heart become audible in the eternal silence that surrounds him.   Thus he says :

" As I walked about, either in my hunting, or for view-
ing the country, the anguish of my soul at my condition
would break out upon me on a sudden, and my very heart
would die within me to think of the woods, the mountains,
the deserts I was in ; and how I was a prisoner, locked up
with the eternal bars and bolts of the ocean, in an unin-
habited wilderness, without redemption. In the midst of the
greatest composures of my mind, this would break out upon
me like a storm, and make me wring my hands, and weep
like a child.   Sometimes it would take me in the middle of
my work, and I would immediately sit down and sigh, and
look upon the ground for an hour or two together, and this
was still worse to me, for if I could burst into tears or vent
myself in words, it would go off, and the grief, having exhausted itself, would abate."

The story of his adventures would not make

a poem like the Odyssey, it is true, but the
relator had the true genius of a poet.   It has
been made a question whether Richardson's
romances are poetry ; and the answer, perhaps,
is that they are not poetry, because they are not
romance.   The interest is worked up to an
inconceivable height ; but it is by an infinite
number of little things, by incessant labour
and calls upon the attention, by a repetition of
blows that have no rebound in them.   The sympathy excited is not a voluntary contribution,
but a tax.   Nothing is unforced and spontaneous.   There is a want of elasticity and
motion.   The story does not " give an echo
to the seat where love is throned." The heart
does not answer of itself like a chord in music.
The fancy does not run on before the writer
with breathless expectation, but is dragged
along with an infinite number of pins and
wheels, like those with which the Lilliputians
dragged Gulliver pinioned to the royal palace.--
Sir Charles Grandison is a coxcomb.   What
sort of a figure would he cut, translated into
an epic poem, by the side of Achilles ? Clarissa, the divine Clarissa, is too interesting by
half.   She is interesting in her ruffles, in her
gloves, her samplers, her aunts and uncles—
she is interesting in all that is uninteresting.
Such things, however intensely they may be

brought home to us, are not conductors to the
imagination. There is infinite truth and feeling in Richardson ; but it is extracted from a
caput mortuum of circumstances : it does not
evaporate of itself. His poetical genius is like
Ariel confined in a pine-tree, and requires an
artificial process to let it out.   Shakspeare
says—

> " Our poesy is as a gum
> Which issues whence 'tis nourished, our gentle flame
> Provokes itself, and, like the current, flies
> Each bound it chafes."*

I shall conclude this general account with
some remarks on four of the principal works
of poetry in the world, at different periods of
history—Homer, the Bible, Dante, and, let me
add, Ossian. In Homer, the principle of action

---

* Burke's writings are not poetry, notwithstanding the
vividness of the fancy, because the subject matter is abstruse
and dry, not natural, but artificial. The difference between
poetry and eloquence is that the one is the eloquence of the
imagination, and the other of the understanding. Eloquence
tries to persuade the will, and convince the reason : poetry
produces its effect by instantaneous sympathy. Nothing is a
subject for poetry that admits of a dispute. Poets are in
general bad prose-writers, because their images, though fine
in themselves, are not to the purpose, and do not carry on the
argument. The French poetry wants the forms of the imagination. It is didactic more than dramatic. And some
of our own poetry, which has been most admired, is only
poetry in the rhyme, and in the studied use of poetic
diction.

or life is predominant; in the Bible, the principle of faith and the idea of Providence ;
Dante is a personification of blind will ; and
in Ossian we see the decay of life, and the fag
end of the world. Homer's poetry is the
heroic: it is full of life and action : it is bright
as the day, strong as a river. In the vigour
of his intellect, he grapples with all the objects
of nature, and enters into all the relations of
social life. He saw many countries, and the
manners of many men ; and he has brought
them all together in his poem. He describes
his heroes going to battle with a prodigality
of life, arising from an exuberance of animal
spirits ; we see them before us, their number,
and their order of battle, poured out upon the
plain, " all plumed like ostriches, like eagles
newly bathed, wanton as goats, wild as young
bulls, youthful as May, and gorgeous as the
sun at midsummer," covered with glittering
armour, with dust and blood ; while the gods
quaff their nectar in golden cups, or mingle in
the fray ; and the old men assembled on the
walls of Troy rise up with reverence as Helen
passes by them. The multitude of things in
Homer is wonderful ; their splendour, their
truth, their force, and variety. His poetry is,
like his religion, the poetry of number and

form : he describes the bodies as well as the souls of men.

The poetry of the Bible is that of imagination and of faith : it is abstract and disembodied : it is not the poetry of form, but of power ; not of multitude, but of immensity. It does not divide into many, but aggrandizes into one. Its ideas of nature are like its ideas of God. It is not the poetry of social life, but of solitude : each man seems alone in the world, with the original forms of nature, the rocks, the earth, and the sky. It is not the poetry of action or heroic enterprise, but of faith in a supreme Providence, and resignation to the power that governs the universe. As the idea of God was removed farther from humanity and a scattered polytheism, it became more profound and intense, as it became more universal, for the Infinite is present to every thing : " If we fly into the uttermost parts of the earth, it is there also ; if we turn to the east or the west, we cannot escape from it." Man is thus aggrandised in the image of his Maker. The history of the patriarchs is of this kind ; they are founders of a chosen race of people, the inheritors of the earth ; they exist in the generations which are to come after them. Their poetry, like their religious creed, is vast, unformed, obscure, and infinite ;

a vision is upon it—an invisible hand is sus-
pended over it. The spirit of the Christian
religion consists in the glory hereafter to be
revealed ; but in the Hebrew dispensation,
Providence took an immediate share in the
affairs of this life. Jacob's dream arose out of
this intimate communion between heaven and
earth : it was this that let down, in the sight
of the youthful patriarch, a golden ladder
from the sky to the earth, with angels ascending and descending upon it, and shed a light
upon the lonely place, which can never pass
away. The story of Ruth, again, is as if all
the depth of natural affection in the human
race was involved in her breast. There are
descriptions in the book of Job more prodigal
of imagery, more intense in passion, than any
thing in Homer, as that of the state of his
prosperity, and of the vision that came upon
him by night. The metaphors in the Old
Testament are more boldly figurative. Things
were collected more into masses, and gave a
greater *momentum* to the imagination.

Dante was the father of modern poetry,
and he may therefore claim a place in this
connection. His poem is the first great step
from Gothic darkness and barbarism ; and the
struggle of thought in it to burst the thral-
dom in which the human mind had been so

D

long held, is felt in every page. He stood
bewildered, not appalled, on that dark shore
which separates the ancient and the modern
world ; and saw the glories of antiquity dawn-
ing through the abyss of time, while revelation
opened its passage to the other world.   He
was lost in wonder at what had been done
before him, and he dared to emulate it. Dante
seems to have been indebted to the Bible for
the gloomy tone of his mind, as well as for the
prophetic fury which exalts and kindles his
poetry ; but he is utterly unlike Homer. His
genius is not a sparkling flame, but the sullen
heat of a furnace.   He is power, passion, self-
will personified.   In all that relates to the
descriptive or fanciful part of poetry he bears
no comparison to many who had gone before,
or who have come after, him ; but there is a
gloomy abstraction in his conceptions which
lies like a dead weight upon the mind ; a be-
numbing stupor, a breathless awe, from the
intensity of the impression ; a terrible obscurity, like that which oppresses us in dreams ;
an identity of interest, which moulds every
object to its own purposes, and clothes all
things with the passions and imaginations of
the human soul,—that make amends for all
other deficiencies.   The immediate objects he
presents to the mind are not much in them-

selves; they want grandeur, beauty, and order; but they become every thing by the force of the character he impresses upon them. His mind lends its own power to the objects which it contemplates, instead of borrowing it from them. He takes advantage even of the nakedness and dreary vacuity of his subject. His imagination peoples the shades of death, and broods over the silent air. He is the severest of all writers, the most hard and impenetrable, the most opposite to the flowery and glittering; who relies most on his own power, and the sense of it in others, and who leaves most room to the imagination of his readers. Dante's only endeavour is to interest; and he interests by exciting our sympathy with the emotion by which he is himself possessed. He does not place before us the objects by which that emotion has been created; but he seizes on the attention, by shewing us the effect they produce on his feelings; and his poetry accordingly gives the same thrilling and overwhelming sensation which is caught by gazing on the face of a person who has seen some object of horror. The improbability of the events, the abruptness and monotony in the Inferno, are excessive: but the interest never flags, from the continued earnestness of the author's mind. Dante's great power is in combining internal feelings with external objects. Thus the gate of hell, on which that withering inscription is written, seems to be endowed with speech and consciousness, and to utter its dread warning, not without a sense of mortal woes. This author habitually unites the absolutely local and individual with the greatest wildness and mysticism. In the midst of the obscure and shadowy regions of the lower world, a tomb suddenly rises up with the inscription, " I am the tomb of Pope Anastasius the Sixth :" and half the personages whom he has crowded into the Inferno are his own acquaintance. All this perhaps tends to heighten the effect by the bold intemixture of realities, and by an appeal, as it were, to the individual knowledge and experience of the reader. He affords few subjects for picture. There is, indeed, one gigantic one, that of Count Ugolino, of which Michael Angelo made a bas - relief, and which Sir Joshua Reynolds ought not to have painted.

Another writer whom I shall mention last, and whom I cannot persuade myself to think a mere modern in the ground-work, is Ossian. He is a feeling and a name that can never be destroyed in the minds of his readers. As Homer is the first vigour and lustihead, Ossian is the decay and old age of poetry. He lives

only in the recollection and regret of the past.
There is one impression which he conveys
more entirely than all other poets, namely,
the sense of privation, the loss of all things,
of friends, of good name, of country—he is
even without God in the world. He converses
only with the spirits of the departed ; with
the motionless and silent clouds. The cold
moonlight sheds its faint lustre on his head ;
the fox peeps out of the ruined tower ; the
thistle waves its beard to the wandering gale ;
and the strings of his harp seem, as the hand
of age, as the tale of other times, passes over
them, to sigh and rustle like the dry reeds in
the winter's wind ! The feeling of cheerless
desolation, of the loss of the pith and sap of
existence, of the annihilation of the substance,
and the clinging to the shadow of all things
as in a mock embrace, is here perfect. In
this way, the lamentation of Selma for the
loss of Salgar is the finest of all. If it were
indeed possible to shew that this writer was
nothing, it would only be another instance of
mutability, another blank made, another void
left in the heart, another confirmation of that
feeling which makes him so often complain,
" Roll on, ye dark brown years, ye bring no
joy on your wing to Ossian !"

LECTURE II.

---◆---

ON CHAUCER AND SPENSER.

HAVING, in the former Lecture, given some account of the nature of poetry in general, I shall proceed, in the next place, to a more particular consideration of the genius and history of English poetry. I shall take, as the subject of the present lecture, Chaucer and Spenser, two out of four of the greatest names in poetry which this country has to boast. Both of them, however, were much indebted to the early poets of Italy, and may be considered as belonging, in a certain degree, to the same school. The freedom and copiousness with which our most original writers, in former periods, availed themselves of the productions of their predecessors, frequently transcribing whole passages, without scruple or acknowledgement, may appear contrary to the etiquette of modern literature, when the whole stock of poetical common-places has become public property, and no one is compelled to trade upon any particular author. But it is not so much a subject of wonder, at a time when to read and write was of itself an honorary distinction, when learning was almost as great a rarity as genius, and when, in fact, those who first transplanted the beauties of other languages into their own, might be considered as public benefactors, and the founders of a national literature.—There are poets older than Chaucer, and in the interval between him and Spenser ; but their genius was not such as to place them in any point of comparison with either of these celebrated men ; and an inquiry into their particular merits or defects might seem rather to belong to the province of the antiquary than be thought generally interesting to the lovers of poetry in the present day.

Chaucer (who has been very properly considered as the father of English poetry) preceded Spenser by two centuries. He issu pposed to have been born in London, in the year 1328, during the reign of Edward III., and to have died in 1400, at the age of seventy-two. He received a learned education at one, or at both, of the Universities, and travelled early into

Italy, where he became thoroughly imbued with the spirit and excellences of the great Italian poets and prose-writers, Dante, Petrarch, and Boccaccio ; and is said to have had a personal interview with one of these, Petrarch. He was connected, by marriage, with the famous John of Gaunt, through whose interest he was introduced into several public employments.   Chaucer was an active partisan, a religious reformer, and, from the share he took in some disturbances, on one occasion, he was obliged to fly the country. On his return, he was imprisoned, and made his peace with government, as it is said, by a discovery of his associates.   Fortitude does not appear, at any time, to have been the distinguishing virtue of poets.—There is, however, an obvious similarity between the practical turn of Chaucer's mind and restless impatience of his character, and the tone of his writings.   Yet it would be too much to attribute the one to the other as cause and effect : for Spenser, whose poetical temperament was as effeminate as Chaucer's was stern and masculine, was equally engaged in public affairs, and had mixed equally in the great world.   So much does native disposition predominate over accidental circumstances, moulding them to its previous bent and purposes !   For, while

Chaucer's intercourse with the busy world, and collision with the actual passions and conflicting interests of others, seemed to brace the sinews of his understanding, and gave to his writings the air of a man who describes persons and things that he had known and been intimately concerned in ; the same opportunities, operating on a differently constituted frame, only served to alienate Spenser's mind the more from the "close pent-up" scenes of ordinary life, and to make him "rive their concealing continents," to give himself up to the unrestrained indulgence of "flowery tenderness."

It is not possible for any two writers to be more opposite in this respect. Spenser delighted in luxurious enjoyment; Chaucer, in severe activity of mind. As Spenser was the most romantic and visionary, Chaucer was the most practical of all the great poets, the most a man of business and the world. His poetry reads like history. Every thing has a downright reality ; at least in the relator's mind. A simile, or a sentiment, is as if it were given in upon evidence. Thus he describes Cressid's first avowal of her love :

"And as the new abashed nightingale,
    That stinteth first when she beginneth sing,
    When that she hearetn any herde's tale,
    Or in the hedges any wight stirring,

> And after, sicker, doth her voice outring ;
> Right so Cresseide, when that her dread stent,
> Open'd her heart, and told him her intent."

This is so true and natural, and beautifully
simple, that the two things seem identified
with each other. Again, it is said in the
Knight's Tale—

> " Thus passeth yere by yere, and day by day,
> Till it felle ones in a morwe of May,
> That Emelie that fayrer was to sene
> Than is the lilie upon his stalke grene ;
> And fresher than the May with floures newe,
> For with the rose-colour strof hire hewe :
> I n'ot which was the finer of hem two."

This scrupulousness about the literal preference, as if some question of matter of fact
was at issue, is remarkable. I might mention
that other, where he compares the meeting
between Palamon and Arcite to a hunter waiting for a lion in a gap ;—

> " That stondeth at a gap with a spere,
> Whan hunted is the lion or the bere,
> And hereth him come rushing in the greves,
> And breking bothe the boughes and the leves :"—

or that still finer one of Constance, when she
is condemned to death :

> " Have ye not seen sometime a pale face
> (Among a prees) of him that hath been lad
> Toward his deth, whereas he geteth no grace,
> And swiche a colour in his face hath had,
> Men mighten know him that was so bestad,

> Amonges all the faces in that route.
> So stant Custance, and loketh hire aboute."

The beauty, the pathos here does not seem to
be of the poet's seeking, but a part of the
necessary texture of the fable. He speaks of
what he wishes to describe with the accuracy,
the discrimination of one who relates what
has happened to himself, or has had the best
information from those who have been eye-
witnesses of it. The strokes of his pencil
always tell. He dwells only on the essential,
on that which would be interesting to the persons really concerned : yet, as he never omits
any material circumstance, he is prolix from
the number of points on which he touches,
without being diffuse on any one ; and is sometimes tedious from the fidelity with which he
adheres to his subject, as other writers are
from the frequency of their digressions from
it. The chain of his story is composed of a
number of fine links, closely connected together, and rivetted by a single blow. There is
an instance of the minuteness which he intro-
duces into his most serious descriptions in his
account of Palamon when left alone in his cell :

> " Swiche sorrow he maketh that the grete tour
> Resouned of his yelling and clamour :
> The pure fetters on his shinnes grete
> Were of his bitter salte teres wete."

The mention of this last circumstance looks like a part of the instructions he had to follow, which he had no discretionary power to leave out or introduce at pleasure. He is contented to find grace and beauty in truth. He exhibits for the most part the naked object, with little drapery thrown over it. His metaphors, which are few, are not for ornament, but use, and as like as possible to the things themselves. He does not affect to shew his power over the reader's mind, but the power which his subject has over his own. The readers of Chaucer's poetry feel more nearly what the persons he describes must have felt than perhaps those of any other poet. His sentiments are not voluntary effusions of the poet's fancy, but founded on the natural impulses and habitual prejudices of the characters he has to represent. There is an inveteracy of purpose, a sincerity of feeling, which never relaxes or grows vapid, in whatever they do or say. There is no artificial, pompous display, but a strict parsimony of the poet's materials, like the rude simplicity of the age in which he lived. His poetry resembles the root just springing from the ground rather than the full-blown flower. His muse is no " babbling gossip of the air," fluent and redundant ; but, like a stammerer, or a dumb

person, that has just found the use of speech,
crowds many things together with eager haste,
with anxious pauses, and fond repetitions, to
prevent mistake. His words point as an
index to the objects, like the eye or finger.
There were none of the common-places of
poetic diction in our author's time, no reflected lights of fancy, no borrowed roseate tints ;
he was obliged to inspect things for himself,
to look narrowly, and almost to handle the
object, as in the obscurity of morning we
partly see and partly grope our way; so
that his descriptions have a sort of tangible
character belonging to them, and produce
the effect of sculpture on the mind. Chaucer
had an equal eye for truth of nature and discrimination of character; and his interest in
what he saw gave new distinctness and force
to his power of observation. The picturesque
and the dramatic are in him closely blended
together, and hardly distinguishable ; for he
principally describes external appearances as
indicating character, as symbols of internal
sentiment. There is a meaning in what he
sees ; and it is this which catches his eye by
sympathy. Thus the costume and dress of
the Canterbury Pilgrims—of the Knight—the
Squire—the Oxford Scholar—the Gap-toothed
Wife of Bath, and the rest, speak for them-

selves.   To take one or two of these at ran-
dom :

> " There was also a Nonne, a Prioresse,
>   That of hire smiling was ful simple and coy ;
>   Hire gretest othe n'as but by seint Eloy :
>   And she was cleped Madame Eglentine.
>   Ful wel she sange the service divine
>   Entuned in hire nose ful swetely ;
>   And Frenche she spake ful fayre and fetisly,
>   After the scole of Stratford atte Bowe,
>   For Frenche of Paris was to hire unknowe.
>   At mete was she wel ytaughte withalle ;
>   She lette no morsel from hire lippes falle,
>   Ne wette hire fingres in hire sauce depe.
>   *   *   *   *   *   *
>   And sikerly she was of great disport,
>   And ful pleasant, and amiable of port,
>   And peined hire to contrefeten chere
>   Of court, and ben estatelich of manere,
>   And to ben holden digne of reverence.
>   But for to speken of hire conscience,
>   She was so charitable and so pitous,
>   She wolde wepe if that she saw a mous
>   Caughte in a trappe, if it were ded or bledde,
>   Of smale houndes hadde she, that she fedde
>   With rosted flesh, and milk, and wastel brede,
>   But sore wept she if on of hem were dede,
>   Or if men smote it with a yerde smert :
>   And all was conscience and tendre herte.
>   Full semely hire wimple ypinched was ;
>   Hire nose tretis ; hire eyen grey as glas ;
>   Hire mouth ful smale : and therto soft and red ;
>   But sickerly she hadde a fayre forehed.
>   It was almost a spanne brode, I trowe."
>   *   *   *   *   *   *   *   *
> " A Monk there was, a fayre for the maistrie,
>   An out-rider, that loved venerie :

A manly man, to ben an Abbot able.
Ful many a deinte hors hadde he in stable :
And whan he rode, men mighte his bridel here,
Gingeling in a whistling wind as clere,
And eke as loude, as doth the chapell belle,
Ther as this lord was keper of the celle.
   The reule of Seint Maure and of Seint Beneit,
Because that it was olde and somdele streit,
This ilke monk lette olde thinges pace,
And held after the newe world the trace.
He yave not of the text a pulled hen,
That saith, that hunters ben not holy men ;—
Therefore he was a prickasoure a right :
Greihoundes he hadde as swift as foul of flight :
Of pricking and of hunting for the hare
Was all his lust, for no cost wolde he spare.
   I saw his sleves purfiled at the hond
With gris, and that the finest of the lond.
And for to fasten his hood under his chinne,
He had of gold ywrought a curious pinne :
A love-knotte in the greter end ther was.
His hed was balled, and shone as any glas,
And eke his face, as it hadde ben anoint.
He was a lord ful fat and in good point.
His eyen stepe, and rolling in his hed,
That stemed as a forneis of a led.
His botes souple, his hors in gret estat,
Now certainly he was a fayre prelat.
He was not pale as a forpined gost.
A fat swan loved he best of any rost.
His palfrey was as browne as is a berry."

The Serjeant at law is the same identical
individual as Lawyer Dowling in Tom Jones,
who wished to divide himself into a hundred
pieces, to be in a hundred places at once.

> " No wher so besy a man as he ther n'as,
>   And yet he semed besier than he was."

The Frankelein, in " whose hous it snewed of
mete and drinke ;" the Shipman, " who rode
upon a rouncie, as he couthe ;" the Doctour
of Phisike, " whose studie was but litel of the
Bible ;" the Wif of Bath, in

> " All whose parish ther was non,
>   That to the offring before hire shulde gon,
>   And if ther did, certain so wroth was she,
>   That she was out of alle charitee ;"

—the poure Persone of a toun, " whose parish was wide, and houses fer asonder ;" the
Miller, and the reve, "a slendre colerike man,"
are all of the same stamp. They are every
one samples of a kind ; abstract definitions of
a species. Chaucer, it has been said, num-
bered the classes of men, as Linnæus num-
bered the plants. Most of them remain to
this day : others, that are obsolete, and may
well be dispensed with, still live in his descriptions of them. Such is the Sompnoure :

> " A Sompnoure was ther with us in that place,
>   That hadde a fire-red cherubinnes face,
>   For sausefleme he was, with eyen narwe,
>   As hote he was, and likerous as a sparwe,
>   With scalled browes blake, and pilled berd
>   Of his visage children were sore aferd.
>   Ther n'as quicksilver, litarge, ne brimston,
>   Boras, ceruse, ne oile of tartre non,
>   Ne oinement that wolde clense or bite,

That him might helpen of his whelkes white,
Ne of the knobbes sitting on his chekes.
Wel loved he garlike, onions, and lekes,
And for to drinke strong win as rede as blood.
Than wolde he speke, and crie as he were wood.
And whan that he well dronken had the win,
Than wold he speken no word but Latin.
A fewe termes coude he, two or three,
That he had lerned out of som decree ;
No wonder is, he heard it all the day.—
   In danger hadde he at his owen gise
The yonge girles of the diocise,
And knew hir conseil, and was of hir rede.
A gerlond hadde he sette upon his hede
As gret as it were for an alestake :
A bokeler hadde he made him of a cake.
With him ther rode a gentil Pardonere—
That hadde a vois as smale as hath a gote.''

It would be a curious speculation (at least
for those who think that the characters of men
never change, though manners, opinions, and
institutions may,) to know what has become of
this character of the Sompnoure in the present day ; whether or not it has any technical
representative in existing professions; into
what channels and conduits it has withdrawn
itself, where it lurks unseen in cunning obscurity, or else shews its face booldly, pampered into all the insolence of office, in some
other shape, as it is deterred or encouraged by
circumstances. *Chaucer's characters mo-
dernized*, upon this principle of historic

E

derivation, would be an useful addition to our knowledge of human nature.   But who is there to undertake it?

The descriptions of the equipage and accoutrements of the two kings of Thrace and Inde, in the Knight's Tale, are as striking and grand as the others are lively and natural:

"Ther maist thou se coming with Palamon
Licurge himself, the grete king of Trace:
Blake was his berd, and manly was his face,
The cercles of his eyen in his hed
They gloweden betwixen yelwe and red,
And like a griffon loked he about,
With kemped heres on his browes stout;
His limmes gret, his braunes hard and stronge,
His shouldres brode, his armes round and longe.
And, as the guise was in his contree,
Ful highe upon a char of gold stood he,
With foure white bolles in the trais.
Instede of cote-armure on his harnais,
With nayles yelwe, and bright as any gold,
He hadde a beres skin, cole-blake for old.
His longe here was kempte behind his bak,
As any ravenes fether it shone for blake.
A wreth of gold arm-gret, of huge weight,
Upon his hed sate full of stones bright,
Of fine rubins and of diamants.
About his char ther wenten white alauns,
Twenty and mo, as gret as any stere,
To hunten at the leon or the dere,
And folwed him, with mosel fast ybound.—
    With Arcite, in stories as men find,
The grete Emetrius, the king of Inde,
Upon a stede bay, trapped in stele,

Covered with cloth of gold diapred wele,
Came riding like the god of armes, Mars.
His cote-armure was of a cloth of Tars,
Couched with perles, white, and round and grete.
His sadel was of brent gold new ybete ;
A mantelet upon his shouldres hanging
Bret-ful of rubies red, as fire sparkling.
His crispe here like ringes was yronne,
And that was yelwe, and glitered as the Sonne.
His nose was high, his eyen bright citrin,
His lippes round, his colour was sanguin,
A fewe fraknes in his face yspreint,
Betwixen yelwe and blake somdel ymeint,
And as a leon he his loking caste.
Of five-and-twenty yere his age I caste.
His berd was wel begonnen for to spring ;
His vois was as a trompe thundering.
Upon his hed he wered of laurer grene
A gerlond freshe and lusty for to sene.
Upon his hond he bare, for his deduit,
An egle tame, as any lily whit.—
About this king ther ran on every part
Ful many a tame leon and leopart."

What a deal of terrible beauty there is contained in this description ! The imagination
of a poet brings such objects before us as
when we look at wild beasts in a menagerie ;
their claws are pared, their eyes glitter like
harmless lightning ; but we gaze at them with
a pleasing awe, clothed in beauty, formidable
in the sense of abstract power.

Chaucer's descriptions of natural scenery
possess the same sort of characteristic excel-

lence, or what might be termed *gusto*. They
have a local truth and freshness, which gives
the very feeling of the air, the coolness or
moisture of the ground. Inanimate objects
are thus made to have a fellow-feeling in the
interest of the story, and render back the sentiment of the speaker's mind. One of the
finest parts of Chaucer is of this mixed kind.
It is the beginning of the Flower and the Leaf,
where he describes the delight of that young
beauty, shrouded in her bower, and listening
in the morning of the year to the singing of
the nightingale ; while her joy rises with the
rising song, and gushes out afresh at every
pause, and is borne along with the full tide of
pleasure, and still increases, and repeats, and
prolongs itself, and knows no ebb. The coolness of the arbour, its retirement, the early
time of the day, the sudden starting up of the
birds in the neighbouring bushes, the eager
delight with which they devour and rend the
opening buds and flowers, are expressed with
a truth and feeling which make the whole appear like the recollection of an actual scene :

> "Which as me thought was right a pleasing sight,
> And eke the briddes song for to here,
> Would haue rejoyced any earthly wight,
> And I that couth not yet in no manere
> Heare the nightingale of all the yeare,

Ful busily herkened with herte and with eare,
If I her voice perceiue coud any where.

And I that all this pleasaunt sight sie,
Thought sodainly I felt so sweet an aire
Of the eglentere, that certainely
There is no herte I deme in such dispaire,
Ne with thoughts froward and contraire,
So ouerlaid, but it should soone haue bote,
If it had ones felt this savour sote.

And as I stood and cast aside mine eie,
I was ware of the fairest medler tree
That ever yet in all my life I sie
As full of blossomes as it might be,
Therein a goldfinch leaping pretile
Fro bough to bough, and as him list he eet
Here and there of buds and floures sweet.

And to the herber side was joyning
This faire tree, of which I haue you told,
And at the last the brid began to sing,
Whan he had eaten what he eat wold,
So passing sweetly, that by manifold
It was more pleasaunt than I coud deuise
And whan his song was ended in this wise,

The nightingale with so merry a note
Answered him that all the wood rong
So sodainly, that as it were a sote,
I stood astonied, so was I with the song
Thorow rauished, that til late and long,
I ne wist in what place I was, ne where,
And ayen me thought she song euen by mine ere.

Wherefore I waited about busily
On euery side, if I her might see,
And at the last I gan full well aspie

Where she sat in a fresh grene laurer tree,
On the further side euen right by me,
That gaue so passing a delicious smell,
According to the eglentere full well,

Whereof I had so inly great pleasure,
That as me thought I surely rauished was
Into Paradice, where my desire
Was for to be, and no ferther passe
As for that day, and on the sote grasse
I sat me downe, for as for mine entent,
The birds' song was more conuenient,

And more pleasaunt to me, by manifold,
Than meat or drinke, or any other thing,
Thereto the herber was so fresh and cold,
The wholesome sauours eke so comforting,
That, as I demed, sith the beginning
Of the world was neuer seene or than
So pleasaunt a ground of none earthly man.

And as I sat the birds harkening thus,
Me thought that I heard voices sodainly
The most sweetest and most delicious
That euer any wight I trow truly
Heard in their life, for the armony
And sweet accorde was in so good musike,
That the uoice to angels was most like."

There is here no affected rapture, no flowery
sentiment: the whole is an ebullition of natural
delight " welling out of the heart," like water
from a crystal spring.   Nature is the soul of
art : there is a strength as well as a simplicity
in the imagination, that reposes entirely on
nature, that nothing else can supply.   It was

the same trust in nature, and reliance on his
subject, which enabled Chaucer to describe
the grief and patience of Griselda ; the faith
of Constance ; and the heroic perseverance of
the little child, who, going to school through
the streets of Jewry,

> " Oh *Alma Redemptoris mater*, loudly sung,"

and who after his death still triumphed in his
song. Chaucer has more of this deep, internal,
sustained sentiment, than any other writer,
except Boccaccio. In depth of simple pathos,
and intensity of conception, never swerving
from his subject, I think no other writer comes
near him, not even the Greek tragedians.   I
wish to be allowed to give one or two instances
of what I mean. I will take the following
from the Knight's Tale. The distress of Arcite,
in consequence of his banishment from his
love, is thus described :

> " Whan that Arcite to Thebes comen was,
>   Ful oft a day he swelt and said Alas,
>   For sene his lady shall he never mo.
>   And shortly to concluden all his wo,
>   So mochel sorwe hadde never creature,
>   That is or shall be, while the world may dure.
>   His slepe, his mete, his drinke is him byraft.
>   That lene he wex, and drie as is a shaft
>   His eyen holwe, and grisly to behold,
>   His hewe salwe, and pale as ashen cold,
>   And solitary he was, and ever alone,

> And wailing all the night, making his mone.
> And if he herde song or instrument,
> Than wold he wepe, he mighte not be stent.
> So feble were his spirites, and so low,
> And changed so that no man coude know
> His speche, ne his vois, though men it herd."

This picture of the sinking of the heart, of the wasting away of the body and mind, of the gradual failure of all the faculties under the contagion of a rankling sorrow, cannot be surpassed.   Of the same kind is his farewell to his mistress, after he has gained her hand and lost his life in the combat :

> " Alas the wo ! alas the peines stronge,
> That I for you have suffered, and so longe !
> Alas the deth ! alas min Emilie !
> Alas departing of our compagnie ;
> Alas min hertes quene ! alas my wif !
> Min hertes ladie, ender of my lif !
> What is this world ? what axen men to have?
> Now with his love, now in his colde grave
> Alone withouten any compagnie."

The death of Arcite is the more affecting as it comes after triumph and victory, after the pomp of sacrifice, the solemnities of prayer, the celebration of the gorgeous rites of chivalry.   The descriptions of the three temples of Mars, of Venus, and Diana, of the ornaments and ceremonies used in each, with the reception given to the offerings of the lovers, have a beauty and grandeur, much

of which is lost in Dryden's version.   For
instance, such lines as the following are not
rendered with their true feeling:

> " Why shulde I not as well eke tell you all
>   The purtreiture that was upon the wall
>   Within the temple of mighty Mars the rede—
>   That highte the gret temple of Mars in Trace
>   In thilke colde and frosty region,
>   Ther as Mars hath his sovereine mansion.
>   First on the wall was peinted a forest,
>   In which ther wonneth neyther man ne best,
>   With knotty knarry barrein trees old
>   Of stubbes sharpe and hidous to behold ;
>   In which ther ran a romble and a swough,
>   As though a storm shuld bresten every bough."

And again, among innumerable terrific images
of death and slaughter painted on the wall, is
this one :

> " The statue of Mars upon a carte stood
>   Armed, and looked grim as he were wood.
>   A wolf ther stood beforne him at his fete
>   With eyen red, and of a man he ete."

The story of Griselda is in Boccaccio; but
the Clerk of Oxenforde, who tells it, professes
to have learned it from Petrarch.   This story
has gone all over Europe, and has passed into
a proverb.   In spite of the barbarity of the
circumstances, which are abominable, the
sentiment remains unimpaired and unalterable.
It is of that kind " that heaves no sigh, that

sheds no tear ;" but it hangs upon the beatings
of the heart; it is a part of the very being ;
it is as inseparable from it as the breath we
draw.   It is still and calm as the face of death.
Nothing can touch it in its etherial purity :
tender as the yielding flower, it is fixed as the
marble firmament.   The only remonstrance
she makes, the only complaint she utters
against all the ill-treatment she receives, is
that single line where, when turned back
naked to her father's house, she says,

> " Let me not like a worm go by the way."

The first outline given of the character is
inimitable ;

> " Nought fer fro thilke paleis honourable,
> Wher as this markis shope his marriage,
> Ther stood a thorpe, of sighte delitable,
> In which that poure folk of that village
> Hadden hir bestes and her herbergage,
> And of hir labour toke hir sustenance,
> After that the erthe yave hem habundance.
>
> Among this poure folk ther dwelt a man,
> Which that was holden pourest of hem all :
> But highe God sometime senden can
> His grace unto a litel oxes stall :
> Janicola men of that thorpe him call.
> A doughter had he, faire ynough to sight,
> And Grisildis this yonge maiden hight.
>
> But for to speke of virtuous beautee,
> Than was she on the fairest under Sonne :

Ful pourely yfostred up was she :
No likerous lust was in hire herte yronne ;
Ful ofter of the well than of the tonne
She dranke, and for she wolde vertue plese,
She knew wel labour, but non idel ese.

But though this mayden tendre were of age,
Yet in the brest of hire virginitee
Ther was enclosed sad and ripe corage :
And in gret reverence and charitee
Hire olde poure fader fostred she :
A few sheep spinning on the feld she kept,
She wolde not ben idel til she slept.

And whan she homward came she wolde bring
Wortes and other herbes times oft,
The which she shred and sethe for hire Lving,
And made hire bed ful hard, and nothing soft :
And ay she kept hire fadres lif on loft
With every obeisance and diligence,
That child may don to fadres reverence.

Upon Grisilde, this poure creature,
Ful often sithe this markis sette his eye,
As he on hunting rode peraventure :
And whan it fell that he might hire espie,
He not with wonton loking of folie
His eyen cast on hire, but in sad wise
Upon hire chere he wold him oft avise.

Commending in his herte hire womanhede,
And eke hire vertue, passing any wight
Of so yong age, as wel in chere as dede.
For though the people have no gret insight
In vertue, he considered ful right
Hire bountee, and disposed that he wold
Wedde hire only, if ever he wedden shold.

> Grisilde of this (God wot,) ful innocent,
> That for hire shapen was all this array,
> To fetchen water at a welle is went,
> And cometh home as sone as ever she may.
> For wel she had heard say that thilke day
> The markis shulde wedde, and, if she might,
> She wolde fayn han seen som of that sight.
>
> She thought, "I wol with other maidens stond,
> That ben my felawes, in our dore, and see
> The markisesse, and thereto wol I fond
> To don at home, as sone as it may be,
> The labour which longeth unto me,
> And than I may at leiser hire behold,
> If she this way unto the castel hold."
>
> And she wolde over the threswold gon
> The markis came and gan hire for to call,
> And she set doun her water-pot anon
> Beside the threswold in an oxes stall,
> And doun upon hire knees she gan to fall.
> And with sad countenance kneleth still,
> Till she had heard what was the lordes will."

The story of the little child slain in Jewry, (which is told by the Prioress, and worthy to be told by her who was "all conscience and tender heart,") is not less touching than that of Griselda. It is simple and heroic to the last degree. The poetry of Chaucer has a religious sanctity about it, connected with the manners and superstitions of the age. It has all the spirit of martyrdom.

It has also all the extravagance and the utmost licentiousness of comic humour, equally arising

out of the manners of the time.   In this too
Chaucer resembled Boccaccio, that he excelled
in both styles, and could pass at will, " from
grave to gay, from lively to severe ;" but he
never confounded the two styles together (except from that involuntary and unconscious
mixture of the pathetic and humorous which
is almost always to be found in nature,) and
was exclusively taken up with what he set
about, whether it was jest or earnest.   The
Wife of Bath's Prologue (which Pope has
very admirably modernised) is, perhaps, une-
qualled as a comic story.   The Cock and the
Fox is also excellent for lively strokes of character and satire.   January and May is not so
good as some of the others.   Chaucer's versification, considering the time at which he wrote,
and that versification is a thing in a great degree mechanical, is not one of his least merits.
It has considerable strength and harmony, and
its apparent deficiency in the latter respect
arises chiefly from the alterations which have
since taken place in the pronunciation or mode
of accenting the words of the language.   The
best general rule for reading him is to pronounce the final *e*, as in reading Italian.

It was observed in the last Lecture that
painting describes what the object is in itself,
poetry what it implies or suggests.   Chaucer's

poetry is not, in general, the best confirmation
of the truth of this distinction, for his poetry
is more picturesque and historical than almost
any other.   But there is one instance in point
which I cannot help giving in this place.   It
is the story of the three thieves who go in
search of Death to kill him, and who, meeting
with him, are entangled in their fate by his
words, without knowing him.   In the printed
catalogue to Mr. West's (in some respects very
admirable) picture of Death on the Pale Horse,
it is observed that, " In poetry the same effect
is produced by a few abrupt and rapid gleams
of description, touching, as it were with fire,
the features and edges of a general mass of
awful obscurity ; but in painting, such indis-
tinctness would be a defect, and imply that the
artist wanted the power to pourtray the conceptions of his fancy.   Mr. West was of opinion that to delineate a physical form, which
in its moral impression would approximate to
that of the visionary Death of Milton, it was
necessary to endow it, if possible, with the appearance of super-human strength and energy.
He has therefore exerted the utmost force and
perspicuity of his pencil on the central figure."
—One might suppose from this, that the way
to represent a shadow was to make it as sub-
stantial as possible. Oh, no ! Painting has its

prerogatives (and high ones they are), but they lie in representing the visible, not the invisible. The moral attributes of Death are powers and effects of an infinitely wide and general description, which no individual or physical form can possibly represent but by a courtesy of speech, or by a distant analogy. The moral impression of Death is essentially visionary; its reality is in the mind's eye. Words are here the only *things;* and things, physical forms, the mere mockeries of the understanding. The less definite, the less bodily the conception, the more vast, unformed, and unsubstantial, the nearer does it approach to some resemblance of that omnipresent, lasting, universal, irresistible principle, which every where, and at some time or other, exerts its power over all things. Death is a mighty abstraction, like Night, or Space, or Time. He is an ugly customer, who will not be invited to supper, or to sit for his picture. He is with us and about us, but we do not see him. He stalks on before us, and we do not mind him: he follows us close behind, and we do not turn to look back at him. We do not see him making faces at us in our life-time, nor perceive him afterwards sitting in mock-majesty, a twin-skeleton, beside us, tickling our bare ribs, and staring into our hollow eye-balls ! Chaucer knew this.

He makes three riotous companions go in
search of Death to kill him, they meet with an
old man whom they reproach with his age,
and ask why he does not die, to which he answers thus :

> " Ne Deth, alas ! ne will not han my lif.
>   Thus walke I like a restless caitiff,
>   And on the ground, which is my modres gate,
>   I knocke with my staf, erlich and late,
>   And say to hire, ' Leve mother, let me in.
>   Lo, how I vanish, flesh and blood and skin,
>   Alas ! when shall my bones ben at reste ?
>   Mother, with you wolde I changen my cheste,
>   That in my chambre longe time hath be,
>   Ye, for an heren cloute to wrap in me.'
>   But yet to me she will not don that grace,
>   For which ful pale and welked is my face."

They then ask the old man where they shall
find out death to kill him, and he sends them
on an errand which ends in the death of all
three.   We hear no more of him, but it is
Death that they have encountered.

The interval between Chaucer and Spenser
is long and dreary.   There is nothing to fill
up the chasm but the names of Occleve, "ancient Gower," Lydgate, Wyatt, Surry, and
Sackville.   Spenser flourished in the reign of
Queen Elizabeth, and was sent with Sir John
Davies into Ireland, of which he has left behind
him some tender recollections in his description of the bog of Allan, and a record in an

ably written paper, containing observations on the state of that country and the means of improving it, which remain in full force to the present day. Spenser died at an obscure inn in London, it is supposed in distressed circumstances. The treatment he received from Burleigh is well known. Spenser, as well as Chaucer, was engaged in active life; but the genius of his poetry was not active: it is inspired by the love of ease, and relaxation from all the cares and business of life. Of all the poets, he is the most poetical. Though much later than Chaucer, his obligations to preceding writers were less. He has in some measure borrowed the plan of his poem (as a number of distinct narratives) from Ariosto; but he has engrafted upon it an exuberance of fancy, and an endless voluptuousness of sentiment, which are not to be found in the Italian writer. Farther, Spenser is even more of an inventor in the subject-matter. There is an originality, richness, and variety in his allegorical personages and fictions, which almost vies with the splendour of the ancient mythology. If Ariosto transports us into the regions of romance, Spenser's poetry is all fairy-land. In Ariosto, we walk upon the ground, in company, gay, fantastic, and adventurous enough. In Spenser, we wander in another world,

among ideal beings.   The poet takes and lays
us in the lap of a lovelier nature, by the sound
of softer streams, among greener hills and
fairer valleys.   He paints nature, not as we
find it, but as we expected to find it; and ful-
fils the delightful promise of our youth.   He
waves his wand of enchantment—and at once
embodies airy beings, and throws a delicious
veil over all actual objects.   The two worlds of
reality and of fiction are poised on the wings
of his imagination.   His ideas, indeed, seem
more distinct than his perceptions.   He is the
painter of abstractions, and describes them
with dazzling minuteness.   In the mask of
Cupid he makes the god of love " clap on
high his coloured winges *twain:*" and it is
said of Gluttony, in the Procession of the
Passions,

> " In green vine leaves he was right fitly clad."

At times he becomes picturesque from his
intense love of beauty; as where he compares
Prince Arthur's crest to the appearance of
the almond tree :

> " Upon the top of all his lofty crest,
>   A bunch of hairs discolour'd diversely
> With sprinkled pearl and gold full richly drest,
>   Did shake and seem'd to daunce for jollity ;
> Like to an almond tree ymounted high

On top of green Selenis all alone,
With blossoms brave bedecked daintily ;
    Her tender locks do tremble every one
At every little breath that under heav'n is blown."

The love of beauty, however, and not of truth, is the moving principle of his mind; and he is guided in his fantastic delineations by no rule but the impulse of an inexhaustible imagination. He luxuriates equally in scenes of Eastern magnificence, or the still solitude of a hermit's cell—in the extremes of sensuality, or refinement.

In reading the Faery Queen, you see a little withered old man by a wood-side opening a wicket, a giant, and a dwarf lagging far behind, a damsel in a boat upon an enchanted lake, wood-nymphs, and satyrs; and all of a sudden you are transported into a lofty palace, with tapers burning, amidst knights and ladies, with dance and revelry, and song, " and mask, and antique pageantry." What can be more solitary, more shut up in itself, than his description of the house of Sleep, to which Archimago sends for a dream :

" And, more to lull him in his slumber soft,
    A trickling stream from high rock tumbling down,
And ever-drizzling rain upon the loft,
    Mix'd with a murmuring wind, much like the sound
Of swarming bees, did cast him in a swound,

> No other noise, nor people's troublous cries,
>   That still are wont t' annoy the walled town,
>   Might there be heard ; but careless quiet lies
> Wrapt in eternal silence, far from enemies."

It is as if " the honey-heavy dew of slumber"
had settled on his pen in writing these lines.
How different in the subject (and yet how
like in beauty) is the following description of
the Bower of Bliss :

> " Eftsoones they heard a most melodious sound
>   Of all that mote delight a dainty ear ;
> Such as at once might not on living ground,
>   Save in this Paradise, be heard elsewhere :
> Right hard it was for wight which did it hear
>   To tell what manner musicke that mote be ;
> For all that pleasing is to living eare
>   Was there consorted in one harmonie ;
> Birds, voices, instruments, windes, waters, all agree.
>
> The joyous birdes shrouded in chearefull shade
>   Their notes unto the voice attempred sweet :
> The angelical soft trembling voices made
>   To th' instruments divine respondence meet.
> The silver sounding instruments did meet
>   With the base murmur of the water's fall ;
> The water's fall with difference discreet,
>   Now soft, now loud, unto the wind did call ;
> The gentle warbling wind low answered to all."

The remainder of the passage has all that
voluptuous pathos, and languid brilliancy of
fancy, in which this writer excelled :

> " The whiles some one did chaunt this lovely lay ;
>   Ah ! see, whoso fayre thing dost fain 'o see,

In springing flower the image of thy day !
 Ah! see the virgin rose, how sweetly she
Doth first peep forth with bashful modesty,
 That fairer seems the less ye see her may !
Lo ! see soon after how more bold and free
 Her bared bosom she doth broad display ;
Lo ! see soon after, how she fades and falls away !

So passeth in the passing of a day
 Of mortal life the leaf, the bud, the flower ;
Ne more doth flourish after first decay,
 That erst was sought, to deck both bed and bower
Of many a lady and many a paramour !
 Gather therefore the rose whilst yet is prime,
For soon comes age that will her pride deflower ;
 Gather the rose of love whilst yet is time,
Whilst loving thou mayest loved be with equal crime.*

He ceased ; and then gan all the quire of birds
 Their divers notes to attune unto his lay,
As in approvance of his pleasing wordes.
 The constant pair heard all that he did say,
Yet swerved not, but kept their forward way
 Through many covert groves and thickets close,
In which they creeping did at last display †
 That wanton lady with her lover loose,
Whose sleepy head she in her lap did soft dispose.

Upon a bed of roses she was laid,
 As faint through heat, or dight to pleasant sin ;
And was arrayed or rather disarrayed,
 All in a veil of silk and silver thin,
That hid no whit her alabaster skin,
 But rather shewed more white, if more might be :
More subtle web Arachne cannot spin ;

---

* Taken from Tasso.

† This word is an instance of those unwarrantable free-
doms which Spenser sometimes took with language.

Nor the fine nets, which oft we woven see
Of scorched dew, do not in the air more lightly flee.

Her snowy breast was bare to greedy spoil
   Of hungry eyes which n' ote therewith be fill'd,
And yet through languor of her late sweet toil
   Few drops more clear than nectar forth distill'd,
That like pure Orient perles adown it trill'd;
   And her fair eyes sweet smiling in delight
Moisten'd their fiery beams, with which she thrill'd
   Frail hearts, yet quenched not; like starry light,
Which, sparkling on the silent waves, does seem more
      bright."

The finest things in Spenser are, the character of Una, in the first book; the House of Pride; the Cave of Mammon, and the Cave of Despair; the account of Memory, of whom it is said, among other things,

" The wars he well remember'd of King Nine,
   Of old Assaracus and Inachus divine;"

the description of Belphœbe; the story of Florimel and the Witch's son; the Gardens of Adonis, and the Bower of Bliss; the Mask of Cupid; and Colin Clout's vision, in the last book. But some people will say that all this may be very fine, but that they cannot understand it on account of the allegory. They are afraid of the allegory as if they thought it would bite them: they look at it as a child looks at a painted dragon, and think it will strangle them in its shining folds. This is very idle. If they do not meddle with the allegory, the allegory will not meddle with them. Without minding it at all, the whole is as plain as a pike-staff. It might as well be pretended that we cannot see Poussin's pictures for the allegory, as that the allegory prevents us from understanding Spenser. For instance, when Britomart, seated amidst the young warriors, lets fall her hair and discovers her sex, is it necessary to know the part she plays in the allegory, to understand the beauty of the following stanza ?

> " And eke that stranger knight amongst the rest
>   Was for like need enforc'd to disarray,
> Tho' when as vailed was her lofty crest,
>   Her golden locks that were in trammels gay
> Upbounden, did themselves adown display,
>   And raught unto her heels like sunny beams
> That in a cloud their light did long time stay ;
>   Their vapour faded, shew their golden gleams,
> And through the persant air shoot forth their azure
>   streams."

Or is there any mystery in what is said of Belphœbe, that her hair was sprinkled with flowers and blossoms which had been entangled in it as she fled through the woods ? Or is it necessary to have a more distinct idea of Proteus than that which is given of him in his boat, with the frighted Florimel at his feet, while

> "———the cold icicles from his rough beard
>   Dropped adown upon her snowy breast!"

Or is it not a sufficient account of one of the sea-gods, that pass by them, to say—

> " That was Arion crowned :—
>   So went he playing on the watery plain."

Or to take the Procession of the Passions that draw the coach of Pride, in which the figures of Idleness, of Gluttony, of Lechery, of Avarice, of Envy, and of Wrath speak, one should think, plain enough for themselves; such as this of Gluttony :

> " And by his side rode loathsome Gluttony,
>   Deformed creature, on a filthy swine ;
>   His belly was up blown with luxury ;
>   And eke with fatness swollen were his eyne;
>   And like a crane his neck was long and fine,
>   With which he swallowed up excessive feast,
> For want whereof poor people oft did pine.
>
>   In green vine leaves he was right fitly clad :
>   For other clothes he could not wear for heat ;
>   And on his head an ivy garland had,
>   From under which fast trickled down the sweat :
>   Still, as he rode, he somewhat still did eat.
>   And in his hand did bear a bouzing can,
>   Of which he supt so oft that on his seat
>   His drunken corse he scarce upholden can ;
> In shape and size more like a monster than a man."

Or this of Lechery :

> " And next to him rode lustfull Lechery
>   Upon a bearded goat, whose rugged hair

And whaly eyes (the sign of jealousy)
    Was like the person's self whom he did bear :
Who rough and black and filthy did appear.
    Unseemly man to please fair lady's eye :
Yet he of ladies oft was loved dear,
    When fairer faces were bid standen by :
O ! who does know the bent of woman's fantasy ?

In a green gown he clothed was full fair,
    Which underneath did hide his filthiness ;
And in his hand a burning heart he bare,
    Full of vain follies and new fangleness ;
For he was false and fraught with fickleness ;
    And learned had to love with secret looks ;
And well could dance ; and sing with ruefulness ;
    And fortunes tell; and read in loving books ;
And thousand other ways to bait his fleshly hooks.

Inconstant man that loved all he saw,
    And lusted after all that he did love ;
Ne would his looser life be tied to law ;
    But joyed weak women's hearts to tempt and prove,
If from their loyal loves he might them move."

This is pretty plain - spoken.   Mr. Southey
says, of Spenser,

        ————" Yet not more sweet
   Than pure was he, and not more pure than wise ;
   High priest of all the Muses' mysteries !"

On the contrary, no one was more apt to pry
into mysteries which do not strictly belong to
the Muses.

    Of the same kind with the Procession of
the Passions, as little obscure, and still more

beautiful, is the Mask of Cupid, with his train
of votaries :

" The first was Fancy, like a lovely boy
        Of rare aspéct, and beauty without peer ;

    His garment neither was of silk nor say,
        But painted plumes in goodly order dight,
    Like as the sun-burnt Indians do array
        Their tawny bodies in their proudest plight :
    As those same plumes so seem'd he vain and light,
        That by his gait might easily appear ;
    For still he far'd as dancing in delight,
        And in his hand a windy fan did bear
That in the idle air he mov'd still here and there.

    And him beside march'd amorous Desire,
        Who seem'd of riper years than the other swain,
    Yet was that other swain this elder's sire,
        And gave him being, common to them twain :
    His garment was disguised very vain,
        And his embroidered bonnet sat awry ;
    'Twixt both his hands few sparks he close did strain,
        Which still he blew, and kindled busily,
That soon they life conceiv'd and forth in flames did fly.

    Next after him went Doubt, who was yclad
        In a discolour'd coat of strange disguise,
    That at his back a broad capuccio had,
        And sleeves dependant *Albanese-wise ;*
    He lookt askew with his mistrustful eyes,
        And nicely trod, as thorns lay in his way,
    Or that the floor to shrink he did avise ;
        And on a broken reed he still did stay
His feeble steps, which shrunk when hard thereon he lay.

    With him went Daunger, cloth'd in ragged weed,
        Made of bear's skin, that him more dreadful made ;

Yet his own face was dreadfull, ne did need
　　Strange horror to deform his grisly shade ;
A net in th' one hand, and a rusty blade
　　In th' other was ; this Mischiefe, that Mishap ;
With th' one his foes he threat'ned to invade,
　　With th' other he his |friends meant to enwrap ;
For whom he could not kill he practiz'd to entrap.

Next him was Fear, all arm'd from top to toe,
　　Yet thought himselfe not safe enough thereby,
But fear'd each shadow moving to and fro ;
　　And his own arms when glittering he did spy
Or clashing heard, he fast away did fly,
　　As ashes pale of hue, and winged-heel'd ;
And evermore on Daunger fixt his eye,
　　'Gainst whom he always bent a brazen shield,
Which his right hand unarmed fearfully did wield.

With him went Hope in rank, a handsome maid,
　　Of chearfull look and lovely to behold ;
In silken samite she was light array'd,
　　And her fair locks were woven up in gold ;
She always smil'd, and in her hand did hold
　　An holy-water sprinkled dipt in dew,
With which she sprinkled favours manifold
　　On whom she list, and did great liking shew,
Great liking unto many, but true love to few.

Next after them, the winged God himself
　　Came riding on a lion ravenous,
Taught to obey the menage of that elfe
　　That man and beast with power imperious
Subdueth to his kingdom tyrannous :
　　His blindfold eyes he bade awhile unbind;
That his proud spoil of that same dolorous
　　Fair dame he might behold in perfect kind ;
Which seen, he much rejoiced in his cruel mind.

Of which full proud, himself uprearing high,
  He looked round about with stern disdain,
And did survey his goodly company :
  And, marshalling the evil-ordered train,
With that the darts which his right hand did strain,
  Full dreadfully he shook, that all did quake,
And clapt on high his colour'd winges twain,
  That all his many it afraid did make :
Tho' blinding him again, his way he forth did take."

The description of Hope, in this series of
historical portraits, is one of the most beautiful
in Spenser : and the triumph of Cupid, at
the mischief he has made, is worthy of the
malicious urchin deity.   In reading these
descriptions, one can hardly avoid being reminded of Rubens's allegorical pictures ; but
the account of Satyrane's taming the lion's
whelps and lugging the bear's cubs along in
his arms while yet an infant, whom his
mother so naturally advises to " go seek some
other play-fellows," has even more of this high
picturesque character.   Nobody but Rubens
could have painted the fancy of Spenser ; and
he could not have given the sentiment, the
airy dream that hovers over it !

With all this, Spenser neither makes us
laugh nor weep.   The only jest in his poem
is an allegorical play upon words, where he
describes Malbecco as escaping in the herd of
goats, " by the help of his fayre horns on
hight."   But he has been unjustly charged

with a want of passion and of strength. He
has both in an immense degree. He has not
indeed the pathos of immediate action or suffering, which is more properly the dramatic;
but he has all the pathos of sentiment and romance—all that belongs to distant objects of
terror, and uncertain, imaginary distress. His
strength, in like manner, is not strength
of will or action, of bone and muscle, nor
is it coarse and palpable—but it assumes
a character of vastness and sublimity seen
through the same visionary medium, and
blended with the appalling associations of
preternatural agency. We need only turn, in
proof of this, to the Cave of Despair, or the
Cave of Mammon, or to the account of the
change of Malbecco into Jealousy. The
following stanzas, in the description of the
Cave of Mammon, the grisly house of Plutus,
are unrivalled for the portentous massiness of
the forms, the splendid chiaro-scuro, and
shadowy horror.

" That house's form within was rude and strong,
    Like an huge cave hewn out of rocky clift,
  From whose rough vault the ragged breaches hung,
    Embossed with massy gold of glorious gift,
  And with rich metal loaded every rift,
    That heavy ruin they did seem to threat :
  And over them Arachne high did lift
    Her cunning web, and spread her subtle net,
Enwrapped in foul smoke, and clouds more black than jet.

Both roof and floor, and walls were all of gold,
    But overgrown with dust and old decay,*
And hid in darkness that none could behold
    The hue thereof : for view of cheerful day
Did never in that house itself display,
    But a faint shadow of uncertain light ;
Such as a lamp whose life doth fade away ;
    Or as the moon clothed with cloudy night
Does show to him that walks in fear and sad affright.

        *   *   *   *   *   *   *

And over all sad Horror with grim hue
    Did always soar, beating his iron wings ;
And after him owls and night-ravens flew,
    The hateful messengers of heavy things,
Of death and dolour telling sad tidings ;
    Whiles sad Celleno, sitting on a clift,
A song of bitter bale and sorrow sings,
    That heart of flint asunder could have rift ;
Which having ended, after him she flieth swift."

The Cave of Despair is described with equal
gloominess and power of fancy ; and the fine
moral declamation of the owner of it, on the
evils of life, almost makes one in love with
death. In the story of Malbecco, who is
hunted by jealousy, and in vain strives to run
away from his own thoughts—

---

* " That all with one consent praise new-born gauds,
    Tho' they are made and moulded of things past,
    And give to Dust that is a little gilt,
    More laud than gold o'er-dusted."

                    Troilus and Cressida.

" High over hill and over dale he flies "—

the truth of human passion and the preternatural ending are equally striking. — It is not fair to compare Spenser with Shakspeare, in point of interest. A fairer comparison would be with Comus; and the result would not be unfavourable to Spenser. There is only one work of the same allegorical kind, which has more interest than Spenser (with scarcely less imagination) : and that is the Pilgrims's Progress. The three first books of the Faery Queen are very superior to the three last. One would think that Pope, who used to ask if any one had ever read the Faery Queen through, had only dipped into these last. The only things in them equal to the former are the account of Talus, the Iron Man, and the delightful episode of Pastorella.

The language of Spenser is full, and copious, to overflowing : it is less pure and idiomatic than Chaucer's, and is enriched and adorned with phrases borrowed from the different languages of Europe, both ancient and modern. He was, probably, seduced into a certain license of expression by the difficulty of filling up the moulds of his complicated rhymed stanza from the limited resources of his native language. This stanza, with alternate and repeatedly recurring rhymes, is

borrowed from the Italians. It was peculiarly
fitted to their language, which abounds in
similar vowel terminations, and is as little
adapted to ours, from the stubborn, unaccommodating resistance which the consonant endings of the northern languages make to this
sort of endless sing-song.—Not that I would
on that account part with the stanza of Spenser. We are, perhaps, indebted to this very
necessity of finding out new forms of expression, and to the occasional faults to which it
led, for a poetical language, rich and varied
and magnificent beyond all former, and almost
all later, example. His versification is, at once,
the most smooth and the most sounding in
the language. It is a labyrinth of sweet sounds,
" in many a winding bout of linked sweetness
long drawn out,"— that would cloy by their
very sweetness, but that the ear is constantly
relieved and enchanted by their continued variety of modulation—dwelling on the pauses of
the action, or flowing on in a fuller tide of harmony with the movement of the sentiment.
It has not the bold dramatic transitions of
Shakspeare's blank verse, nor the high-raised
tone of Milton's ; but it is the perfection of
melting harmony, dissolving the soul in pleasure, or holding it captive in the chains of
suspense. Spenser was the poet of our waking

dreams; and he has invented not only a language, but a music of his own for them.
The undulations are infinite, like those of
the waves of the sea: but the effect is still
the same, lulling the senses into a deep oblivion of the jarring noises of the world,
from which we have no wish to be ever
recalled.

LECTURE III.

———◆———

ON SHAKSPEARE AND MILTON.

In looking back to the great works of genius in former times, we are sometimes disposed to wonder at the little progress which has since been made in poetry, and in the arts of imitation in general. But this is perhaps a foolish wonder. Nothing can be more contrary to the fact, than the supposition that in what we understand by the *fine arts*, as painting, and poetry, relative perfection is only the result of repeated efforts in successive periods, and that what has been once well done, constantly leads to something better. What is mechanical, reducible to rule, or capable of demonstration, is progressive, and admits of gradual improvement : what is not mechanical, or definite, but depends on feeling, taste, and genius, very soon becomes stationary, or retrograde, and loses more than it gains by transfusion. The contrary opinion is a vulgar error, which has grown up, like many others, from transferring an analogy of one kind to something quite distinct, without taking into the account the difference in the nature of the things, or attending to the difference of the results. For most persons, finding what wonderful advances have been made in biblical criticism, in chemistry, in mechanics, in geometry, astronomy, &c., *i.e.* in things depending on mere inquiry and experiment, or on absolute demonstration, have been led hastily to conclude that there was a general tendency in the efforts of the human intellect to improve by repetition, and, in all other arts and institutions, to grow perfect and mature by time. We look back upon the theological creed of our ancestors, and their discoveries in natural philosophy, with a smile of pity : science, and the arts connected with it, have all had their infancy, their youth, and manhood, and seem to contain in them no principle of limitation or decay : and, enquiring no farther about the matter, we infer, in the intoxication of our pride, and the height of our self-congratulation, that the same progress has been made, and will continue to be made, in all other things which are the work of man.

The fact, however, stares us so plainly in the face that one would think the smallest reflection must suggest the truth, and overturn our sanguine theories. The greatest poets, the ablest orators, the best painters, and the finest sculptors that the world ever saw, appeared soon after the birth of these arts, and lived in a state of society which was, in other respects, comparatively barbarous. Those arts, which depend on individual genius and incommunicable power, have always leaped at once from infancy to manhood, from the first rude dawn of invention to their meridian height and dazzling lustre, and have in general declined ever after. This is the peculiar distinction and privilege of each, of science and of art : — of the one, never to attain its utmost limit of perfection ; and of the other, to arrive at it almost at once. Homer, Chaucer, Spenser, Shakspeare, Dante, and Ariosto, (Milton alone was of a later age, and not the worse for it) —Raphael, Titian, Michael Angelo, Correggio, Cervantes, and Boccaccio, the Greek sculptors and tragedians, — all lived near the beginning of their arts — perfected, and all but created, them. These giant-sons of genius stand indeed upon the earth, but they tower above their fellows ; and the long line of their successors, in different ages, does not interpose any object to obstruct their view, or lessen their brightness. In strength and stature they are unrivalled; in grace and beauty they have not been surpassed. In after ages and more refined periods (as they are called), great men have arisen one by one, as it were by throes and at intervals; though, in general, the best of these cultivated and artificial minds were of an inferior order; as Tasso and Pope, among poets; Guido and Vandyke, among painters. But in the earlier stages of the arts, as soon as the first mechanical difficulties had been got over, and the language was sufficiently acquired, they rose by clusters, and in constellations, never so to rise again!

The arts of painting and poetry are conversant with the world of thought within us, and with the world of sense around us—with what we know, and see, and feel intimately. They flow from the sacred shrine of our own breasts, and are kindled at the living lamp of nature. But the pulse of the passions assuredly beat as high, the depths and soundings of the human heart were as well understood, three thousand or three hundred years ago as they are at present: the face of nature and "the human face divine" shone as bright then as they have ever done. But it is *their* light, reflected by true genius on art, that marks out its path before it, and sheds a glory round the Muses' feet like that which

> " Circled Una's angel face,
> And made a sunshine in the shady place."

The four greatest names in English poetry, are almost the four first we come to—Chaucer, Spenser, Shakspeare, and Milton. There are no others that can really be put in competition with these. The two last have had justice done them by the voice of common fame. Their names are blazoned in the very firmament of reputation; while the two first, (though " the fault has been more in their stars than in themselves, that they are underlings ") either never emerged far above the horizon, or were too soon involved in the obscurity of time. The three first of these are excluded from Dr. Johnson's Lives of the Poets (Shakspeare indeed is so from the dramatic form of his compositions) : and the fourth, Milton, is admitted with a reluctant and churlish welcome.

In comparing these four writers together, it might be said that Chaucer excels as the poet of manners, or of real life; Spenser, as the poet of romance; Shakspeare, as the poet of nature (in the largest use of the term) ; and Milton, as the poet of morality. Chaucer most frequently describes things as they are ; Spenser, as we wish them to be ; Shakspeare, as they

would be ; and Milton, as they ought to be.
As poets, and as great poets, imagination,
that is, the power of feigning things according
to nature, was common to them all : but the
principle or moving power, to which this
faculty was most subservient in Chaucer, was
habit, or inveterate prejudice ; in Spenser,
novelty, and the love of the marvellous ; in
Shakspeare, it was the force of passion, combined with every variety of possible circumstances ; and in Milton, only with the highest.
The characteristic of Chaucer is intensity ; of
Spenser, remoteness ; of Milton, elevation ;
of Shakspeare, every thing. It has been said,
by some critic, that Shakspeare was distinguished from the other dramatic writers of his
day only by his wit; that they had all his
other qualities but that ; that one writer had
as much sense, another as much fancy, another
as much knowledge of character, another the
same depth of passion, and another as great a
power of language. This statement is not
true; nor is the inference from it well-founded,
even if it were. This person does not seem
to have been aware that, upon his own show-
ing, the great distinction of Shakspeare's
genius was its virtually including the genius
of all the great men of his age, and not his
differing from them in one accidental parti-

cular. But to have done with such minute
and literal trifling.

The striking peculiarity of Shakspeare's
mind was its generic quality, its power of
communication with all other minds—so that
it contained a universe of thought and feeling
within itself, and had no one peculiar bias, or
exclusive excellence more than another. He
was just like any other man, but that he was
like all other men. He was the least of an
egotist that it was possible to be. He was
nothing in himself ; but he was all that others
were, or that they could become. He not
only had in himself the germs of every faculty
and feeling, but he could follow them by
anticipation, intuitively, into all their conceivable ramifications, through every change of
fortune or conflict of passion, or turn of
thought. He " had a mind reflecting ages
past," and present :—all the people that ever
lived are there. There was no respect of
persons with him. His genius shone equally
on the evil and on the good, on the wise and
on the foolish, the monarch and the beggar :
" All corners of the earth, kings, queens,
and states, maids, matrons, nay, the secrets of
the grave," are hardly hid from his searching
glance. He was like the genius of humanity,
changing places with all of us at pleasure, and

playing with our purposes as with his own.
He turned the globe round for his amusement,
and surveyed the generations of men, and the
individuals as they passed, with their different
concerns, passions, follies, vices, virtues,
actions, and motives—as well those that they
knew, as those which they did not know or
acknowledge to themselves. The dreams of
childhood, the ravings of despair, were the
toys of his fancy. Airy beings waited at his
call, and came at his bidding. Harmless
fairies "nodded to him, and did him curtesies:"
and the night-hag bestrode the blast at the
command of "his so potent art." The world
of spirits lay open to him, like the world of
real men and women : and there is the same
truth in his delineations of the one as of the
other ; for if the preternatural characters he
describes could be supposed to exist, they
would speak, and feel and act, as he makes
them. He had only to think of any thing in
order to become that thing, with all the
circumstances belonging to it. When he
conceived of a character, whether real or
imaginary, he not only entered into all its
thoughts and feelings, but seemed instantly,
and as if by touching a secret spring, to be
surrounded with all the same objects, " subject
to the same skyey influences," the same local,

outward, and unforeseen accidents which
would occur in reality. Thus the character
of Caliban not only stands before us with a
language and manners of its own, but the
scenery and situation of the enchanted island
he inhabits, the traditions of the place, its
strange noises, its hidden recesses, " his frequent haunts and ancient neighbourhood,"
are given with a miraculous truth of nature,
and with all the familiarity of an old recollection. The whole " coheres semblably
together" in time, place, and circumstance.
In reading this author, you do not merely
learn what his characters say,—you see their
persons. By something expressed or understood, you are at no loss to decypher their
peculiar physiognomy, the meaning of a look,
the grouping, the bye-play, as we might see
it on the stage. A word, an epithet paints a
whole scene, or throws us back whole years in
the history of the person represented. So (as
it has been ingeniously remarked) when Pros-
pero describes himself as left alone in the boat
with his daughter, the epithet which he applies to her, " Me and thy *crying* self," flings
the imagination instantly back from the grown
woman to the helpless condition of infancy,
and places the first and most trying scene of
his misfortunes before us, with all that he

must have suffered in the interval. How
well the silent anguish of Macduff is conveyed to the reader, by the friendly expostulation of Malcolm—"What! man, ne'er pull
your hat upon your brows!" Again, Hamlet,
in the scene with Rosencrantz and Guilden-
stern, somewhat abruptly concludes his fine
soliloquy on life by saying, "Man delights
not me, nor woman neither,—though by your
smiles you seem to say so." Which is explained by their answer—"My lord, we had
no such stuff in our thoughts. But we smiled
to think, if you delight not in man, what len-
ten entertainment the players shall receive
from you whom we met on the way :"—as if
while Hamlet was making this speech, his two
old schoolfellows from Wittenburg had been
really standing by, and he had seen them
smiling by stealth, at the idea of the players
crossing their minds. It is not "a combina-
tion and a form" of words, a set speech or
two, a preconcerted theory of a character,
that will do this: but all the persons concerned
must have been present in the poet's imagination, as at a kind of rehearsal ; and whatever
would have passed through their minds on
the occasion, and have been observed by
others, passed through his, and is made
known to the reader.—I may add in passing,

that Shakspeare always gives the best directions for the costume and carriage of his heroes. Thus, to take one example, Ophelia gives the following account of Hamlet; and as Ophelia had seen Hamlet, I should think her word ought to be taken against that of any modern authority.

> "*Ophelia.* My lord, as I was reading in my closet,
> Prince Hamlet, with his doublet all unbrac'd,
> No hat upon his head, his stockings loose,
> Ungartered, and down-gyved to his ancle,
> Pale as his shirt, his knees knocking each other,
> And with a look so piteous,
> As if he had been sent from hell
> To speak of horrors, thus he comes before me.
>   *Polonius.* Mad for thy love!
>   *Oph.* My lord, I do not know,
> But truly I do fear it.
>   *Pol.*   What said he?
>   *Oph.* He took me by the wrist, and held me hard.
> Then goes he to the length of all his arm;
> And with his other hand thus o'er his brow,
> He falls to such perusal of my face,
> As he would draw it : long staid he so ;
> At last a little shaking of my arm,
> And thrice his head thus waving up and down,
> He rais'd a sigh so piteous and profound,
> As it did seem to shatter all his bulk,
> And end his being. That done, he lets me go,
> And, with his head over his shoulder turn'd,
> He seem'd to find his way without his eyes ;
> For out of doors he went without their help,
> And to the last bended their light on me."
>
>   *Act. II. Scene* 1.

How, after this airy, fantastic idea of irregular
grace and bewildered melancholy, any one can
play Hamlet, as we have seen it played, with
strut, and stare and antic right-angled sharp-
pointed gestures, it is difficult to say, unless it
be that Hamlet is not bound, by the prompt-
er's cue, to study the part of Ophelia.   The
account of Ophelia's death begins thus :

" There is a willow hanging o'er a brook,
   That shows its hoary leaves in the glassy stream."—

Now this is an instance of the same unconscious power of mind which is as true to
nature as itself.   The leaves of the willow
are, in fact, white underneath, and it is this
part of them which would appear " hoary" in
the reflection in the brook.   The same sort
of intuitive power, the same faculty of bringing every object in nature, whether present or
absent, before the mind's eye, is observable
in the speech of Cleopatra, when conjectur-
ing what were the employments of Antony in
his absence :—" He's speaking now, or murmuring, Where's my serpent of old Nile ?"
How fine to make Cleopatra have this consciousness of her own character, and to make
her feel that it is this for which Antony is in
love with her !   She says, after the battle of
Actium, when Antony has resolved to risk

another fight, " It is my birth-day ; I had
thought to have held it poor : but since my
lord is Antony again, I will be Cleopatra."
What other poet would have thought of such
a casual resource of the imagination, or
would have dared to avail himself of it? The
thing happens in the play as it might have
happened in fact.   That which, perhaps,
more than any thing else distinguishes the
dramatic productions of Shakspeare from all
others, is this wonderful truth and individu-
ality of conception.   Each of his characters is
as much itself, and as absolutely independent
of the rest, as well as of the author, as if they
were living persons, not fictions of the mind.
The poet may be said, for the time, to iden-
tify himself with the character he wishes to
represent, and to pass from one to another,
like the same soul successively animating different bodies.   By an art like that of the
ventriloquist, he throws his imagination out of
himself, and makes every word appear to proceed from the mouth of the person in whose
name it is given. His plays alone are properly
expressions of the passions, not descriptions
of them.   His characters are real beings of
flesh and blood ; they speak like men, not
like authors.   One might suppose that he
had stood by at the time, and overheard what

passed.   As in our dreams we hold con-
versations with ourselves, make remarks, or
communicate intelligence, and have no idea of
the answer which we shall receive, and which
we ourselves make, till we hear it—so the
dialogues in Shakspeare are carried on without
any consciousness of what is to follow, without
any appearance of preparation or premedita-
tion.   The gusts of passion come and go like
sounds of music borne on the wind. Nothing is
made out by formal inference and analogy, by
climax and antithesis : all comes, or seems to
come, immediately from nature. Each object
and circumstance exists in his mind, as it
would have existed in reality : each several
train of thought and feeling goes on of itself,
without confusion or effort.   In the world of
his imagination, every thing has a life, a place,
and being of its own !

Chaucer's characters are sufficiently distinct
from one another, but they are too little varied
in themselves, too much like identical propo-
sitions. They are consistent, but uniform; we
get no new idea of them from first to last ;
they are not placed in different lights, nor are
their subordinate *traits* brought out in new
situations ; they are like portraits or physiog-
nomical studies, with the distinguishing features marked with inconceivable truth and

precision, but that preserve the same unaltered air and attitude. Shakspeare's are historical figures, equally true and correct, but put into action, where every nerve and muscle is displayed in the struggle with others, with all the effect of collision and contrast, with every variety of light and shade. Chaucer's characters are narrative, Shakspeare's dramatic, Milton's epic. That is, Chaucer told only as much of his story as he pleased, as was required for a particular purpose. He answered for his characters himself. In Shakspeare they are introduced upon the stage, are liable to be asked all sorts of questions, and are forced to answer for themselves. In Chaucer we perceive a fixed essence of character. In Shakspeare there is a continual composition and decomposition of its elements, a fermentation of every particle in the whole mass, by its alternate affinity or antipathy to other principles which are brought in contact with it. Till the experiment is tried, we do not know the result, the turn which the character will take in its new circumstances. Milton took only a few simple principles of character, and raised them to the utmost conceivable grandeur, and refined them from every base alloy. His imagination, " nigh sphered in Heaven," claimed kindred only with what he saw from

that height, and could raise to the same elevation with itself. He sat retired and kept his
state alone, " playing with wisdom ;" while
Shakspeare mingled with the crowd, and
played the host, " to make society the sweeter
welcome."

The passion in Shakspeare is of the same
nature as his delineation of character. It is
not some one habitual feeling, or sentiment,
preying upon itself, growing out of itself, and
moulding every thing to itself; it is passion
modified by passion, by all the other feelings
to which the individual is liable, and to which
others are liable with him ; subject to all the
fluctuations of caprice and accident ; calling
into play all the resources of the understanding
and all the energies of the will; irritated by
obstacles, or yielding to them ; rising from
small beginnings to its utmost height ; now
drunk with hope, now stung to madness, now
sunk in despair, now blown to air with a
breath, now raging like a torrent. The human
soul is made the sport of fortune, the prey
of adversity : it is stretched on the wheel of
destiny, in restless ecstacy. The passions are
in a state of projection. Years are melted
down to moments, and every instant teems
with fate. We know the results, we see the
process. Thus, after Iago has been boasting

to himself of the effect of his poisonous suggestions on the mind of Othello, " which,
with a little act upon the blood, will work like
mines of sulphur," he adds—

> " Look where he comes ! not poppy, nor mandragora,
>   Nor all the drowsy syrups of the East,
>   Shall ever medicine thee to that sweet sleep
>   Which thou ow'dst yesterday."—

And he enters at this moment, like the crested
serpent, crowned with his wrongs and raging
for revenge ! The whole depends upon the
turn of a thought. A word, a look, blows the
spark of jealousy into a flame ; and the explo-
sion is immediate and terrible as a volcano.
The dialogues in Lear, in Macbeth, that
between Brutus and Cassius, and nearly all
those in Shakspeare, where the interest is
wrought up to its highest pitch, afford examples
of this dramatic fluctuation of passion. The
interest in Chaucer is quite different ; it is like
the course of a river, strong, and full, and
increasing. In Shakspeare, on the contrary,
it is like the sea, agitated this way and that,
and loud-lashed by furious storms ; while, in
the still pauses of the blast, we distinguish
only the cries of despair, or the silence of
death ! Milton, on the other hand, takes the
imaginative part of passion — that which remains after the event, which the mind reposes

on when all is over, which looks upon circumstances from the remotest elevation of thought and fancy, and abstracts them from the world of action to that of contemplation. The objects of dramatic poetry affect us by sympathy, by their nearness to ourselves, as they take us by surprise, or force us upon action, " while rage with rage doth sympathise :" the objects of epic poetry affect us through the medium of the imagination, by magnitude and distance, by their permanence and universality. The one fill us with terror and pity, the other with admiration and delight. There are certain objects that strike the imagination, and inspire awe in the very idea of them, independently of any dramatic interest, that is, of any connection with the vicissitudes of human life. For instance, we cannot think of the pyramids of Egypt, of a Gothic ruin, or an old Roman encampment, without a certain emotion, a sense of power and sublimity coming over the mind. The heavenly bodies that hang over our heads wherever we go, and " in their untroubled element shall shine when we are laid in dust, and all our cares forgotten," affect us in the same way. Thus Satan's address to the Sun has an epic, not a dramatic interest ; for though the second person in the dialogue makes no answer and feels no concern, yet the

eye of that vast luminary is upon him, like the
eye of Heaven, and seems conscious of what
he says, like an universal presence. Dramatic
poetry and epic, in their perfection, indeed,
approximate to and strengthen one another.
Dramatic poetry borrows aid from the dignity
of persons and things, as the heroic does from
human passion, but in theory they are distinct.
When Richard II. calls for the looking-glass
to contemplate his faded majesty in it, and
bursts into that affecting exclamation : " Oh,
that I were a mockery-king of snow, to melt
away before the sun of Bolingbroke," we have
here the utmost force of human passion, combined with the ideas of regal splendour and
fallen power.   When Milton says of Satan :

> " ———— His form had not yet lost
> All her original brightness, nor appear'd
> Less than archangel ruin'd, and th' excess
> Of glory obscur'd ;"—

the mixture of beauty, of grandeur, and pathos,
from the sense of irreparable loss, of never-
ending, unavailing regret, is perfect.

The great fault of a modern school of
poetry is that it is an experiment to reduce
poetry to a mere effusion of natural sensibility;
or, what is worse, to divest it both of imaginary splendour and human passion, to surround
the meanest objects with the morbid feelings

and devouring egotism of the writers' own minds. Milton and Shakspeare did not so understand poetry. They gave a more liberal interpretation both to nature and art. They did not do all they could to get rid of the one and the other, to fill up the dreary void with the Moods of their own Minds. They owe their power over the human mind to their having had a deeper sense than others of what was grand in the objects of nature, or affecting in the events of human life. But to the men I speak of there is nothing interesting, nothing heroical, but themselves. To them the fall of gods or of great men is the same. They do not enter into the feeling. They cannot understand the terms. They are even debarred from the last poor, paltry consolation of an unmanly triumph over fallen greatness; for their minds reject, with a convulsive effort and intolerable loathing, the very idea that there ever was, or was thought to be, any thing superior to themselves. All that has ever excited the attention or admiration of the world they look upon with the most perfect indifference; and they are surprised to find that the world repays their indifference with scorn. "With what measure they mete, it has been meted to them again."—

Shakspeare's imagination is of the same

plastic kind as his conception of character or passion. " It glances from heaven to earth, from earth to heaven." Its movement is rapid and devious. It unites the most opposite extremes ; or, as Puck says, in boasting of his own feats, " puts a girdle round about the earth in forty minutes." He seems always hurrying from his subject, even while describing it ; but the stroke, like the lightning's, is sure as it is sudden. He takes the widest possible range, but from that very range he has his choice of the greatest variety and aptitude of materials. He brings together images the most alike, but placed at the greatest distance from each other ; that is, found in circumstances of the greatest dissimilitude. From the remoteness of his combinations, and the celerity with which they are effected, they coalesce the more indissolubly together. The more the thoughts are strangers to each other, and the longer they have been kept asunder, the more intimate does their union seem to become. Their felicity is equal to their force. Their likeness is made more dazzling by their novelty. They startle, and take the fancy prisoner in the same instant. I will mention one or two which are very striking, and not much known, out of Troilus and Cressida. Æneas says to Agamemnon.

" I ask that I may waken reverence,
    And on the cheek be ready with a blush,
    Modest as morning, when she coldly eyes
    The youthful Phœbus."

Ulysses, urging Achilles to show himself in
the field, says—

" No man is the lord of any thing,
    Till he communicate his parts to others :
    Nor doth he of himself know them for aught,
    Till he behold them formed in the applause,
    Where they're extended ! which like an arch reverberates
    The voice again, or like a gate of steel,
    Fronting the sun, receives and renders back
    Its figure and its heat."

Patroclus gives the indolent warrior the same
advice.

    " Rouse yourself; and the weak wanton Cupid
        Shall from your neck unloose his amorous fold,
        And like a dew-drop from the lion's mane
        Be shook to air."

Shakspeare's language and versification are
like the rest of him. He has a magic power
over words: they come winged at his bidding;
and seem to know their places. They are
struck out at a heat, on the spur of the occasion, and have all the truth and vividness
which arise from an actual impression of the
objects. His epithets and single phrases are
like sparkles, thrown off from an imagination
fired by the whirling rapidity of its own mo-

tion. His language is hieroglyphical. It translates thoughts into visible images. It abounds in sudden transitions and elliptical expressions. This is the source of his mixed metaphors, which are only abbreviated forms of speech. These, however, give no pain from long custom. They have, in fact, become idioms in the language. They are the building, and not the scaffolding to thought. We take the meaning and effect of a well-known passage entire, and no more stop to scan and spell out the particular words and phrases, than the syllables of which they are composed. In trying to recollect any other author, one sometimes stumbles, in case of failure, on a word as good. In Shakspeare, any other word but the true one, is sure to be wrong. If any body, for instance, could not recollect the words of the following description,

" ———— Light thickens,
And the crow makes wing to the rooky wood,"

he would be greatly at a loss to substitute others for them equally expressive of the feeling. These remarks, however, are strictly applicable only to the impassioned parts of Shakspeare's language, which flowed from the warmth and originality of his imagination, and were his own. The language used for prose conversation and ordinary business

is sometimes technical, and involved in the
affectation of the time. Compare, for example,
Othello's apology to the senate, relating " his
whole course of love," with some of the preceding parts relating to his appointment, and
the official dispatches from Cyprus.   In this
respect, " the business of the state does him
offence."   His versification is no less powerful, sweet, and varied. It has every occasional
excellence, of sullen intricacy, crabbed and
perplexed, or of the smoothest and loftiest
expansion — from the ease and familiarity of
measured conversation to the lyrical sounds

> " ———— Of ditties highly penned,
> Sung by a fair queen in a summer's bower,
> With ravishing division to her lute."

It is the only blank verse in the language,
except Milton's, that for itself is readable.
It is not stately and uniformly swelling like
his, but varied and broken by the inequalities
of the ground it has to pass over in its uncertain course,

> " And so by many winding nooks it strays,
> With willing sport to the wild ocean."

It remains to speak of the faults of Shakspeare.   They are not so many or so great as
they have been represented; what there are
are chiefly owing to the following causes : —

The universality of his genius was, perhaps, a disadvantage to his single works; the variety of his resources, sometimes diverting him from applying them to the most effectual purposes. He might be said to combine the powers of Æschylus and Aristophanes, of Dante and Rabelais, in his own mind. If he had been only half what he was, he would perhaps have appeared greater. The natural ease and indifference of his temper made him sometimes less scrupulous than he might have been. He is relaxed and careless in critical places; he is in earnest throughout only in Timon, Macbeth, and Lear. Again, he had no models of acknowledged excellence constantly in view to stimulate his efforts, and, by all that appears, no love of fame. He wrote for the "great vulgar and the small," in his time, not for posterity. If Queen Elizabeth and the maids of honour laughed heartily at his worst jokes, and the catcalls in the gallery were silent at his best passages, he went home satisfied, and slept the next night well. He did not trouble himself about Voltaire's criticisms. He was willing to take advantage of the ignorance of the age in many things; and if his plays pleased others, not to quarrel with them himself. His very facility of production would make him set less value on his own

excellences, and not care to distinguish nicely
between what he did well or ill. His blunders
in chronology and geography do not amount
to above half a dozen, and they are offences
against chronology and geography, not against
poetry. As to the unities, he was right in
setting them at defiance. He was fonder of
puns than became so great a man. His bar-
barisms were those of his age. His genius
was his own. He had no objection to float
down with the stream of common taste and
opinion : he rose above it by his own buoy-
ancy, and an impulse which he could not keep
under, in spite of himself or others, and " his
delights did show most dolphin-like."

He had an equal genius for comedy and
tragedy ; and his tragedies are better than his
comedies, because tragedy is better than
comedy. His female characters, which have
been found fault with as insipid, are the finest
in the world. Lastly, Shakspeare was the
least of a coxcomb of any one that ever lived,
and much of a gentleman.

Shakspeare discovers in his writings little
religious enthusiasm, and an indifference to
personal reputation ; he had none of the bigo-
try of his age, and his political prejudices were
not very strong. In these respects, as well as
in every other, he formed a direct contrast to

Milton. Milton's works are a perpetual invocation to the Muses; a hymn to Fame. He had his thoughts constantly fixed on the contemplation of the Hebrew theocracy, and of a perfect commonwealth ; and he seized the pen with a hand just warm from the touch of the ark of faith. His religious zeal infused its character into his imagination ; so that he devotes himself with the same sense of duty to the cultivation of his genius, as he did to the exercise of virtue, or the good of his country. The spirit of the poet, the patriot, and the prophet, vied with each other in his breast. His mind appears to have held equal communion with the inspired writers, and with the bards and sages of ancient Greece and Rome ;—

> " Blind Thamyris, and blind Mœonides,
>   And Tiresias, and Phineus, prophets old."

He had a high standard, with which he was always comparing himself, nothing short of which could satisfy his jealous ambition.

> " ———— Sad task, yet argument
> Not less, but more heroic, than the wrath
> Of stern Achilles on his foe pursued,
> If answerable still, I can obtain.
>   ———— Unless an age too late, or cold
> Climate, or years, damp my extended wing."

He thought of nobler forms and nobler things

than those he found about him. He lived
apart, in the solitude of his own thoughts,
carefully excluding from his mind whatever
might distract its purposes or alloy its purity,
or damp its zeal. " With darkness and with
dangers compassed round," he had the mighty
models of antiquity always present to his
thoughts, and determined to raise a monument of equal height and glory, " piling up
every stone of lustre from the brook," for the
delight and wonder of posterity. He had
girded himself up, and, as it were, sanctified
his genius to this service from his youth.
" For after," he says, " I had from my first
years, by the ceaseless diligence and care of
my father, been exercised to the tongues, and
some sciences, as my age could suffer, by
sundry masters and teachers, it was found that
whether aught was imposed upon me by them,
or betaken to of my own choice, the style, by
certain vital signs it had, was likely to live ;
but much latelier, in the private academies of
Italy, perceiving that some trifles which I had
in memory, composed at under twenty or
thereabout, met with acceptance above what
was looked for ; I began thus far to assent
both to them and divers of my friends here at
home, and not less to an inward prompting
which now grew daily upon me, that by

labour and intense study (which I take to be my portion in this life), joined with the strong propensity of nature, I might perhaps leave something so written to after-times as they should not willingly let it die. The accomplishment of these intentions, which have lived within me ever since I could conceive myself any thing worth to my country, lies not but in a power above man's to promise; but that none hath by more studious ways endeavoured, and with more unwearied spirit that none shall, that I dare almost aver of myself, as far as life and free leisure will extend. Neither do I think it shame to covenant with any knowing reader, that for some few years yet, I may go on trust with him toward the payment of what I am now indebted, as being a work not to be raised from the heat of youth or the vapours of wine; like that which flows at waste from the pen of some vulgar amourist, or the trencher fury of a rhyming parasite, nor to be obtained by the invocation of Dame Memory and her Siren daughters, but by devout prayer to that eternal Spirit who can enrich with all utterance and knowledge, and sends out his Seraphim with the hallowed fire of his altar, to touch and purify the lips of whom he pleases: to this must be added industrious and select reading, steady observation, and insight into all seemly and generous arts and affairs.   Although it nothing content me to have disclosed thus much beforehand ; but that I trust hereby to make it manifest with what small willingness I endured to interrupt the pursuit of no less hopes than these, and leave a calm and pleasing solitariness, fed with cheerful and confident thoughts, to embark in a troubled sea of noises and hoarse disputes, from beholding the bright countenance of truth in the quiet and still air of delightful studies."

So that of Spenser :

> " The noble heart that harbours virtuous thought,
>   And is with child of glorious great intent,
> Can never rest until it forth have brought
>   The eternal brood of glory excellent."

Milton, therefore, did not write from casual impulse, but after a severe examination of his own strength, and with a resolution to leave nothing undone which it was in his power to do.   He always labours, and almost always succeeds.   He strives hard to say the finest things in the world, and he does say them. He adorns and dignifies his subject to the utmost : he surrounds it with every possible association of beauty or grandeur, whether moral, intellectual, or physical.   He refines on his descriptions of beauty ; loading sweets on sweets, till the sense aches at them; and raises his images of terror to a gigantic elevation, that " makes Ossa like a wart." In Milton, there is always an appearance of effort : in Shakspeare, scarcely any.

Milton has borrowed more than any other writer, and exhausted every source of imitation, sacred or prophane ; yet he is perfectly distinct from every other writer. He is a writer of centos, and yet in originality scarcely inferior to Homer. The power of his mind is stamped on every line. The fervour of his imagination melts down and renders malleable. as in a furnace, the most contradictory materials. In reading his works, we feel ourselves under the influence of a mighty intellect, that the nearer it approaches to others, becomes more distinct from them. The quantity of art in him shows the strength of his genius : the weight of his intellectual obligations would have oppressed any other writer. Milton's learning has all the effect of intuition. He describes objects, of which he could only have read in books, with the vividness of actual observation. His imagination has the force of nature. He makes words tell as pictures.

" Him followed Rimmon, whose delightful seat
    Was fair Damascus, on the fertile banks
    Of Abbana and Pharphar, lucid streams."

The word *lucid* here gives to the idea all the sparkling effect of the most perfect landscape.

And again :

> " As when a vulture on Imaus bred,
>   Whose snowy ridge the roving Tartar bounds,
>   Dislodging from a region scarce of prey,
>   To gorge the flesh of lambs and yeanling kids
>   On hills where flocks are fed, *flies towards the springs*
>   *Of Ganges or Hydaspes, Indian streams ;*
>   *But in his way lights on the barren plains*
>   *Of Sericana, where Chineses drive*
>   *With sails and wind their cany waggons light.*"

If Milton had taken a journey for the express purpose, he could not have described this scenery and mode of life better. Such passages are like demonstrations of natural history. Instances might be multiplied without end.

There is also a decided tone in his descriptions, an eloquent dogmatism, as if the poet spoke from thorough conviction, which Milton probably derived from his spirit of partisanship, or else his spirit of partisanship from the natural firmness and vehemence of his mind. In this Milton resembles Dante (the only one of the moderns with whom he has any thing in common), and it is remarkable that Dante, as well as Milton, was a political partisan. That approximation to the severity of impassioned prose, which has been made an objection to Milton's poetry, is one of its chief excellences.

We might be tempted to suppose that the vividness with which he describes visible objects was owing to their having acquired an unusual degree of strength in his mind, after the privation of his sight; but we find the same palpableness and truth in the descriptions which occur in his early poems. In Lycidas he speaks of " the great vision of the guarded mount," with that preternatural weight of impression with which it would present itself suddenly to " the pilot of some small night - foundered skiff:" and the lines in the Penseroso, describing " the wandering moon,

> " Riding near her highest noon,
>   Like one that had been led astray
>   Through the heaven's wide pathless way,"

are as if he had gazed himself blind in looking at her.   There is also the same depth of impression in his descriptions of the objects of all the different senses, whether colours, or sounds, or smells—the same absorption of his mind in whatever engaged his attention at the time.   Milton had as much of what is meant by *gusto* as any poet.*   He forms the most

---

* The infinite quantity of dramatic invention in Shakspeare takes from his *gusto*. The power he delights to show is not intense, but discursive. He never insists on any thing as much as he might, except a quibble.

intense conception of things, and then embodies them by a single stroke of his pen. He has an inveterate attachment to the objects he describes and to the words describing them :

" Wild above rule or art, *enormous* bliss."

It has been indeed objected to Milton, by a common perversity of criticism, that his ideas were musical rather than picturesque, as if, because they were in the highest degree musical, they must be (to keep the sage critical balance even, and to allow no one man to possess two qualities at the same time) proportionably deficient in other respects.— But Milton's poetry is not cast in any such narrow, common-place mould; it is not so barren of resources. His worship of the Muse was not so simple or confined. A sound arises " like a steam of rich distilled perfumes ;" we hear the pealing organ, but the incense on the altars is also there, and the statues of the gods are ranged around ! The ear indeed predominates over the eye, because it is more immediately affected, and because the language of music blends more immediately with, and forms a more natural accompaniment to, the variable and indefinite associations of ideas conveyed by words. But where the associations of the imagination are not the principal thing, the individual object is given by Milton with equal force and beauty. The strongest and best proof of this, as a characteristic power of his mind, is, that the persons of Adam and Eve, of Satan, &c., are always accompanied, in our imagination, with the grandeur of the naked figure; they convey to us the idea of sculpture. As an instance, take the following :

> " ———— He soon
> Saw within ken a glorious Angel stand,
> The same whom John saw also in the sun :
> His back was turned, but not his brightness hid ;
> Of beaming sunny rays a golden tiar
> Circled his head, nor less his locks behind
> Illustrious on his shoulders fledge with wings
> Lay waving round; on some great charge employ'd
> He seem'd, or fix'd in cogitation deep.
> Glad was the spirit impure, as now in hope
> To find who might direct his wand'ring flight
> To Paradise, the happy seat of man
> His journey's end, and our beginning woe.
> But first he casts to change his proper shape,
> Which else might work him danger or delay :
> And now a stripling cherub he appears,
> Not of the prime, yet such as in his face
> Youth smiled celestial, and to every limb
> Suitable grace diffus'd, so well he feign'd:
> Under a coronet his flowing hair
> In curls on either cheek play'd; wings he wore
> Of many a colour'd plume sprinkled with gold,
> His habit fit for speed succinct, and held
> Before his decent steps a silver wand."

The figures introduced here have all the elegance and precision of a Greek statue;

glossy and impurpled, tinged with golden light, and musical as the strings of Memnon's harp !

Again, nothing can be more magnificent than the portrait of Beelzebub :

> " With Atlantean shoulders fit to bear
> The weight of mightiest monarchies:"

Or the comparison of Satan, as he " lay floating many a rood," to " that sea beast,"

> " Leviathan, which God of all his works
> Created hugest that swim the ocean-stream ! "

What a force of imagination is there in this last expression ! What an idea it conveys of the size of that hugest of created beings, as if it shrunk up the ocean to a stream, and took up the sea in its nostrils as a very little thing! Force of style is one of Milton's greatest excellences. Hence, perhaps, he stimulates us more in the reading, and less afterwards. The way to defend Milton against all impugners is to take down the book and read it.

Milton's blank verse is the only blank verse in the language (except Shakspeare's) that deserves the name of verse. Dr. Johnson, who had modelled his ideas of versification on the regular sing-song of Pope, condemns the

Paradise Lost as harsh and unequal. I shall
not pretend to say that this is not sometimes
the case; for where a degree of excellence
beyond the mechanical rules of art is attempted, the poet must sometimes fail.   But
I imagine that there are more perfect examples
in Milton of musical expression, or of an
adaptation of the sound and movement of the
verse to the meaning of the passage, than in
all our other writers, whether of rhyme or
blank verse, put together (with the exception
already mentioned). Spenser is the most harmonious of our stanza writers, as Dryden is
the most sounding and varied of our rhymists.
But in neither is there any thing like the same
ear for music, the same power of approxi-
mating the varieties of poetical, to those of
musical, rhythm, as there is in our great epic
poet. The sound of his lines is moulded into
the expression of the sentiment, almost of the
very image. They rise or fall, pause or hurry
rapidly on, with exquisite art, but without the
least trick or affectation, as the occasion seems
to require.

The following are some of the finest instances :

" ———————— His hand was known
In heaven by many a tower'd structure high ;—
Nor was his name unheard or unador'd
In ancient Greece : and in the Ausonian land

Men called him Mulciber : and how he fell
From Heaven, they fabled, thrown by angry Jove
Sheer o'er the crystal battlements ; from morn
To noon he fell, from noon to dewy eve,
A summer's day ; and with the setting sun
Dropt from the zenith like a falling star
On Lemnos, the Ægean isle : thus they relate,
Erring."—

 " ——— But chief the spacious hall
Thick swarm'd, both on the ground and in the air,
Brush'd with the hiss of rustling wings.   As bees
In spring time, when the sun with Taurus rides,
Pour forth their populous youth about the hive
In clusters ; they among fresh dews and flow'rs
Fly to and fro : or on the smoothed plank,
The suburb of their straw-built citadel,
New rubb'd with balm, expatiate and confer
Their state affairs.   So thick the airy crowd
Swarm'd and were straiten'd ; till the signal giv'n,
Behold a wonder !   They but now who seem'd
In bigness to surpass earth's giant sons,
Now less than smallest dwarfs, in narrow room
Throng numberless, like that Pygmean race
Beyond the Indian mount, or fairy elves,
Whose midnight revels by a forest side
Or fountain, some belated peasant sees,
Or dreams he sees, while over-head the moon
Sits arbitress, and nearer to the earth
Wheels her pale course : they on their mirth and dance
Intent, with jocund music charm his ear ;
At once with joy and fear his heart rebounds."

I can only give another instance, though I
have some difficulty in leaving off.

" Round he surveys (and well might, where he stood
 So high above the circling canopy
 Of night's extended shade) from th' eastern point

> Of Libra to the fleecy star that bears
> Andromeda far off Atlantic seas
> Beyond the horizon: then from pole to pole
> He views in breadth, and without longer pause
> Down right into the world's first region throws
> His flight precipitant, and winds with ease
> Through the pure marble air his oblique way
> Amongst innumerable stars that shone
> Stars distant, but nigh hand seem'd other worlds;
> Or other worlds they seem'd or happy isles," &c.

The verse, in this exquisitely modulated passage, floats up and down as if it had itself wings. Milton has himself given us the theory of his versification—

> " Such as the meeting soul may pierce
> In notes with many a winding bout
> Of linked sweetness long drawn out."

Dr. Johnson and Pope would have converted his vaulting Pegasus into a rocking-horse. Read any other blank verse but Milton's,—Thomson's, Young's, Cowper's, Wordsworth's,—and it will be found, from the want of the same insight into "the hidden soul of harmony," to be mere lumbering prose.

To proceed to a consideration of the merits of Paradise Lost, in the most essential point of view, I mean as to the poetry of character and passion. I shall say nothing of the fable, or of other technical objections or excellences; but I shall try to explain at once the foundation of the interest belonging to the poem. I am ready to give up the dialogues in Heaven, where, as Pope justly observes, " God the Father turns a school-divine ;" nor do I consider the battle of the angels as the climax of sublimity, or the most successful effort of Milton's pen. In a word, the interest of the poem arises from the daring ambition and fierce passions of Satan, and from the account of the paradisaical happiness, and the loss of it by our first parents. Three-fourths of the work are taken up with these characters, and nearly all that relates to them is unmixed sublimity and beauty. The two first books alone are like two massy pillars of solid gold.

Satan is the most heroic subject that ever was chosen for a poem ; and the execution is as perfect as the design is lofty. He was the first of created beings, who, for endeavouring to be equal with the highest, and to divide the empire of heaven with the Almighty, was hurled down to hell. His aim was no less than the throne of the universe ; his means, myriads of angelic armies bright, the third part of the heavens, whom he lured after him with his countenance, and who durst defy the Omnipotent in arms. His ambition was the greatest, and his punishment was the greatest; but not so his despair, for his fortitude was as

great as his sufferings. His strength of mind
was matchless as his strength of body; the
vastness of his designs did not surpass the
firm, inflexible determination with which he
submitted to his irreversible doom, and final
loss of all good. His power of action and of
suffering was equal. He was the greatest
power that was ever overthrown, with the
strongest will left to resist or to endure. He
was baffled, not confounded. He stood like
a tower; or

> " ———— As when Heaven's fire
> Hath scathed the forest oaks or mountain pines."

He is still surrounded with hosts of rebel
angels, armed warriors, who own him as their
sovereign leader, and with whose fate he sympathises as he views them round, far as the
eye can reach; though he keeps aloof from
them in his own mind, and holds supreme
counsel only with his own breast. An outcast
from Heaven, Hell trembles beneath his feet,
Sin and Death are at his heels, and mankind
are his easy prey.

> " All is not lost; th' unconquerable will,
>   And study of revenge, immortal hate,
>   And courage never to submit or yield,
>   And what else is not to be overcome,"

are still his. The sense of his punishment
seems lost in the magnitude of it; the fierce-

ness of tormenting flames is qualified and made
innoxious by the greater fierceness of his pride;
the loss of infinite happiness to himself is com-
pensated in thought by the power of inflicting
infinite misery on others. Yet Satan is not the
principle of malignity, or of the abstract love of
evil, but of the abstract love of power, of pride,
of self-will personified, to which last principle
all other good and evil, and even his own, are
subordinate. From this principle he never
once flinches. His love of power and contempt for suffering are never once relaxed
from the highest pitch of intensity. His
thoughts burn like a hell within him ; but the
power of thought holds dominion in his mind
over every other consideration. The consciousness of a determined purpose, of " that
intellectual being, those thoughts that wander through eternity," though accompanied
with endless pain, he prefers to nonentity, to
" being swallowed up and lost in the wide
womb of uncreated night." He expresses the
sum and substance of all ambition in one line.
" Fallen cherub, to be weak is miserable,
doing or suffering ! " After such a conflict as
his, and such a defeat, to retreat in order, to
rally, to make terms, to exist at all, is something ; but he does more than this—he founds
a new empire in hell, and from it conquers

this new world, whither he bends his undaunted
flight, forcing his way through nether and
surrounding fires. The poet has not in all
this given us a mere shadowy outline; the
strength is equal to the magnitude of the conception. The Achilles of Homer is not more
distinct; the Titans were not more vast;
Prometheus, chained to his rock, was not a
more terrific example of suffering and of
crime. Wherever the figure of Satan is introduced, whether he walks or flies, "rising aloft
incumbent on the dusky air," it is illustrated
with the most striking and appropriate images:
so that we see it always before us, gigantic,
irregular, portentous, uneasy, and disturbed—
but dazzling in its faded splendour, the clouded
ruins of a god. The deformity of Satan is
only in the depravity of his will; he has no
bodily deformity to excite our loathing or disgust. The horns and tail are not there, poor
emblems of the unbending, unconquered spirit,
of the writhing agonies within. Milton was
too magnanimous and open an antagonist to
support his argument by the bye-tricks of a
hump and cloven foot; to bring into the fair
field of controversy the good old catholic prejudices of which Tasso and Dante have availed
themselves, and which the mystic German
critics would restore. He relied on the justice

of his cause, and did not scruple to give the
devil his due.   Some persons may think that
he has carried his liberality too far, and injured
the cause he professed to espouse by making
him the chief person in his poem.   Considering the nature of his subject, he would be
equally in danger of running into this fault,
from his faith in religion, and his love of re-
bellion ; and perhaps each of these motives
had its full share in determining the choice of
his subject.

Not only the figure of Satan, but his
speeches in council, his soliloquies, his address
to Eve, his share in the war in heaven, or in
the fall of man, show the same decided superiority of character.   To give only one instance,
almost the first speech he makes :

    " Is this the region, this the soil, the clime,
      Said then the lost archangel, this the seat
      That we must change for Heaven; this mournful gloom
      For that celestial light ?   Be it so, since he
      Who now is sov'rain can dispose and bid
      What shall be right: farthest from him is best
      Whom reason hath equal'd, force hath made supreme
      Above his equals.   Farewel happy fields,
      Where joy for ever dwells ! Hail horrors, hail
      Infernal world ! and thou, profoundest Hell,
      Receive thy new possessor ; one who brings
      A mind not to be chang'd by place or time.
      The mind is its own place, and in itself
      Can make a Heav'n of Hell, a Hell of Heav'n.
      What matter where, if I be still the same,

> And what I should be, all but less than he
> Whom thunder hath made greater ?   Here at least
> We shall be free ; th' Almighty hath not built
> Here for his envy, will not drive us hence :
> Here we may reign secure, and in my choice
> To reign is worth ambition, though in Hell :
> Better to reign in Hell than serve in Heaven."

The whole of the speeches and debates in Pandemonium are well worthy of the place and the occasion — with gods for speakers, and angels and archangels for hearers. There is a decided manly tone in the arguments and sentiments, an eloquent dogmatism, as if each person spoke from thorough conviction. The author might here turn his philippics against Salmasius to good account. The rout in Heaven is like the fall of some mighty structure, nodding to its base, " with hideous ruin and combustion down." But, perhaps, of all the passages in Paradise Lost, the description of the employments of the angels during the absence of Satan, some of whom " retreated in a silent valley, sing with notes angelical to many a harp their own heroic deeds and hapless fall by doom of battle," is the most perfect example of mingled pathos and sublimity.— What proves the truth of this noble picture in every part, and that the frequent complaint of want of interest in it is the fault of the reader, not of the poet, is that when any interest of a

practical kind takes a shape that can be at all
turned into this (and there is little doubt that
Milton had some such in his eye in writing it),
each party converts it to its own purposes,
feels the absolute identity of these abstracted
and high speculations; and that, in fact, a
noted political writer of the present day has
exhausted nearly the whole account of Satan
in the Paradise Lost, by applying it to a character whom he considered as, after the devil,
(though I do not know whether he would
make even that exception) the greatest enemy
of the human race.   This may serve to show
that Milton's Satan is not a very insipid personage.

Of Adam and Eve it has been said that the
ordinary reader can feel little interest in them,
because they have none of the passions, pursuits, or even relations of human life, except
that of man and wife, the least interesting of
all others, if not to the parties concerned, at
least to the by-standers.   The preference has
on this account been given to Homer, who, it
is said, has left very vivid and infinitely diver-
sified pictures of all the passions and affections, public and private, incident to human
nature — the relations of son, of brother,
parent, friend, citizen, and many others.—
Longinus preferred the Iliad to the Odyssey,

on account of the greater number of battles it
contains ; but I can neither agree to his criticism, nor assent to the present objection.   It
is true there is little action in this part of
Milton's poem ; but there is much repose,
and more enjoyment.   There are none of the
every-day occurrences, contentions, disputes,
wars, fightings, feuds, jealousies, trades, professions, liveries, and common handicrafts of
life ; " no kind of traffic ; letters are not
known ; no use of service, of riches, poverty,
contract, succession, bourne, bound of land,
tilth, vineyard, none ; no occupation, no trea-
son, felony, sword, pike, knife, gun, nor need
of any engine."   So much the better ; thank
Heaven, all these were yet to come.   But
still the die was cast, and in them our doom
was sealed.   In them

> " The generations were prepared ; the pangs,
>   The internal pangs, were ready, the dread strife
>   Of poor humanity's afflicted will,
>   Struggling in vain with ruthless destiny."

In their first false step we trace all our
future woe, with loss of Eden.   But there
was a short and precious interval between,
like the first blush of morning before the day
is overcast with tempest, the dawn of the
world, the birth of nature from " the unap-
parent deep," with its first dews and fresh-

ness on its cheek, breathing odours. Theirs was the first delicious taste of life, and on them depended all that was to come of it. In them hung trembling all our hopes and fears. They were as yet alone in the world, in the eye of nature, wondering at their new being, full of enjoyment, and enraptured with one another, with the voice of their Maker walking in the garden, and ministering angels attendant on their steps, winged messengers from heaven like rosy clouds descending in their sight. Nature played around them her virgin fancies wild; and spread for them a repast " where no crude surfeit reigned." Was there nothing in this scene, which God and nature alone witnessed, to interest a modern critic? What need was there of action, where the heart was full of bliss and innocence without it? They had nothing to do but feel their own happiness, and " know to know no more." " They toiled not, neither did they spin; yet Solomon in all his glory was not arrayed like one of these." All things seem to acquire fresh sweetness, and to be clothed with fresh beauty in their sight. They tasted as it were for themselves and us, of all that there ever was pure in human bliss. " In them the burthen of the mystery, the heavy and the weary weight of all this unintelligible

world, is lightened." They stood awhile
perfect, but they afterwards fell, and were
driven out of Paradise, tasting the first fruits
of bitterness as they had done of bliss. But
their pangs were such as a pure spirit might
feel at the sight — their tears " such as angels
weep." The pathos is of that mild contemplative kind which arises from regret for the
loss of unspeakable happiness, and resignation
to inevitable fate. There is none of the fierceness of intemperate passion, none of the agony
of mind and turbulence of action, which is the
result of the habitual struggle of the will with
circumstances, irritated by repeated disappointment, and constantly setting its desires
most eagerly on that which there is an impos-
sibility of attaining. This would have destroyed the beauty of the whole picture.—
They had received their unlooked-for happiness as a free gift from their Creator's hands,
and they submitted to its loss, not without
sorrow, but without impious and stubborn
repining.

> " In either hand the hast'ning angel caught
>   Our ling'ring parents, and to th' eastern gate
>   Led them direct, and down the cliff as fast
>   To the subjected plain ; then disappear'd.
>   They, looking back, all th' eastern side beheld
>   Of Paradise, so late their happy seat,
>   Wav'd over by that flaming brand, the gate

With dreadful faces throng'd, and fiery arms :
Some natural tears they dropt, but wip'd them soon ;
The world was all before them, where to choose
Their place of rest, and Providence their guide." *

---

* In the Appendix will be found the Author's criticisms
on Milton's "Eve" and "Lycidas."

LECTURE IV.

———◆———

ON DRYDEN AND POPE.

Dryden and Pope are the great masters of
the artificial style of poetry in our language,
as the poets of whom I have already treated,
Chaucer, Spenser, Shakspeare, and Milton,
were of the natural; and though this artificial
style is generally and very justly acknowledged
to be inferior to the other, yet those who stand
at the head of that class ought, perhaps, to
rank higher than those who occupy an inferior
place in a superior class. They have a clear
and independent claim upon our gratitude, as
having produced a kind and degree of excellence which existed equally nowhere else.
What has been done well by some later
writers of the highest style of poetry, is in-
cluded in, and obscured by, a greater degree
of power and genius in those before them :

what has been done best by poets of an entirely distinct turn of mind, stands by itself,
and tells for its whole amount.   Young, for
instance, Gray, or Akenside, only follow in
the train of Milton and Shakspeare : Pope
and Dryden walk by their side, though of an
unequal stature, and are entitled to a first
place in the lists of fame.   This seems to be
not only the reason of the thing, but the common sense of mankind, who, without any
regular process of reflection, judge of the
merit of a work not more by its inherent and
absolute worth than by its originality and
capacity of gratifying a different faculty of the
mind, or a different class of readers ; for it
should be recollected that there may be readers (as well as poets) not of the highest class,
though very good sort of people, and not
altogether to be despised.

   The question, whether Pope was a poet,
has hardly yet been settled, and is hardly
worth settling; for, if he was not a great poet,
he must have been a great prose-writer, that
is, he was a great writer of some sort.   He
was a man of exquisite faculties, and of the
most refined taste ; and as he chose verse (the
most obvious distinction of poetry) as the
vehicle to express his ideas, he has generally
passed for a poet, and a good one.   If, indeed,

by a great poet, we mean one who gives the
utmost grandeur to our conceptions of nature,
or the utmost force to the passions of the
heart, Pope was not in this sense a great
poet; for the bent, the characteristic power
of his mind, lay the clean contrary way;
namely, in representing things as they appear
to the indifferent observer, stripped of prejudice and passion, as in his Critical Essays; or
in representing them in the most contemptible
and insignificant point of view, as in his
Satires; or in clothing the little with mock-
dignity, as in his poems of Fancy; or in
adorning the trivial incidents and familiar
relations of life with the utmost elegance of
expression, and all the flattering illusions of
friendship or self-love, as in his Epistles. He
was not then distinguished as a poet of lofty
enthusiasm, of strong imagination, with a passionate sense of the beauties of nature, or a
deep insight into the workings of the heart;
but he was a wit, and a critic, a man of sense,
of observation, and the world, with a keen
relish for the elegances of art, or of nature
when embellished by art, a quick tact for
propriety of thought and manners as established by the forms and customs of society,
refined sympathy with the sentiments and
habitudes of human life, as he felt them

within the little circle of his family and friends. He was, in a word, the poet, not of nature, but of art; and the distinction between the two, as well as I can make it out, is this:—The poet of nature is one who, from the elements of beauty, of power, and of passion in his own breast, sympathises with whatever is beautiful, and grand, and impassioned in nature, in its simple majesty, in its immediate appeal to the senses, to the thoughts and hearts of all men; so that the poet of nature, by the truth, and depth, and harmony of his mind, may be said to hold communion with the very soul of nature; to be identified with, and to foreknow, and to record, the feelings of all men, at all times and places, as they are liable to the same impressions; and to exert the same power over the minds of his readers that nature does. He sees things in their eternal beauty, for he sees them as they are; he feels them in their universal interest, for he feels them as they affect the first principles of his and our common nature. Such was Homer, such was Shakspeare, whose works will last as long as nature, because they are a copy of the indestructible forms and everlasting impulses of nature, welling out from the bosom as from a perennial spring, or stamped upon the senses

by the hand of their Maker. The power of
the imagination in them is the representative
power of all nature. It has its centre in the
human soul, and makes the circuit of the
universe.

Pope was not assuredly a poet of this class,
or in the first rank of it. He saw nature
only dressed by art; he judged of beauty by
fashion; he sought for truth in the opinions
of the world; he judged of the feelings of
others by his own. The capacious soul of
Shakspeare had an intuitive and mighty sympathy with whatever could enter into the
heart of man in all possible circumstances:
Pope had an exact knowledge of all that he
himself loved or hated, wished or wanted.
Milton has winged his daring flight from heaven to earth, through Chaos and old Night.
Pope's Muse never wandered with safety, but
from his library to his grotto, or from his
grotto into his library back again. His mind
dwelt with greater pleasure on his own garden
than on the garden of Eden; he could describe the faultless whole-length mirror that
reflected his own person better than the
smooth surface of the lake that reflects the
face of heaven — a piece of cut glass or a
pair of paste buckles with more brilliance
and effect than a thousand dew-drops glittering in the sun. He would be more de-

lighted with a patent lamp than with " the
pale reflex of Cynthia's brow," that fills the
skies with its soft silent lustre, that trembles
through the cottage window, and cheers the
watchful mariner on the lonely wave. In
short, he was the poet of personality and of
polished life. That which was nearest to
him was the greatest ; the fashion of the day
bore sway in his mind over the immutable
laws of nature. He preferred the artificial to
the natural in external objects, because he had
a stronger fellow-feeling with the self-love of
the maker or proprietor of a gewgaw than
admiration of that which was interesting to all
mankind. He preferred the artificial to the
natural in passion, because the involuntary
and uncalculating impulses of the one hurried
him away with a force and vehemence with
which he could not grapple ; while he could
trifle with the conventional and superficial
modifications of mere sentiment at will, laugh
at or admire, put them on or off like a mas-
querade-dress, make much or little of them,
indulge them for a longer or a shorter time,
as he pleased; and because, while they amused
his fancy and exercised his ingenuity, they
never once disturbed his vanity, his levity, or
indifference. His mind was the antithesis of
strength and grandeur; its power was the power
of indifference. He had none of the enthusiasm

of poetry; he was in poetry what the sceptic is in religion.

It cannot be denied that his chief excellence lay more in diminishing than in aggrandizing objects; in checking, not in encouraging, our enthusiasm; in sneering at the extravagances of fancy or passion, instead of giving a loose to them; in describing a row of pins and needles rather than the embattled spears of Greeks and Trojans; in penning a lampoon or a compliment, and in praising Martha Blount.

Shakspeare says,

> "——— In Fortune's ray and brightness
> The herd hath more annoyance by the brize
> Than by the tyger: but when the splitting wind
> Makes flexible the knees of knotted oaks,
> And flies fled under shade, why then
> The thing of courage,
> As roused with rage, with rage doth sympathise;
> And, with an accent tuned in the self-same key,
> Replies to chiding Fortune."

There is none of this rough work in Pope. His Muse was on a peace-establishment, and grew somewhat effeminate by long ease and indulgence. He lived in the smiles of fortune, and basked in the favour of the great. In his smooth and polished verse we meet with no prodigies of nature, but with miracles of wit; the thunders of his pen are whispered

flatteries; its forked lightnings pointed sar-
casms; for " the gnarled oak," he gives us
" the soft myrtle:" for rocks, and seas, and
mountains, artificial grass-plats, gravel-walks,
and tinkling rills; for earthquakes and tempests, the breaking of a flower-pot, or the fall
of a china jar; for the tug and war of the
elements, or the deadly strife of the passions,
we have

> " Calm contemplation and poetic ease."

Yet within this retired and narrow circle how
much, and that how exquisite, was contained!
What discrimination, what wit, what delicacy,
what fancy, what lurking spleen, what elegance of thought, what pampered refinement
of sentiment! It is like looking at the world
through a microscope, where every thing assumes a new character and a new consequence,
where things are seen in their minutest circumstances and slightest shades of difference;
where the little becomes gigantic, the deformed
beautiful, and the beautiful deformed. The
wrong end of the magnifier is, to be sure, held
to every thing, but still the exhibition is highly
curious, and we know not whether to be most
pleased or surprised. Such, at least, is the
best account I am able to give of this extraordinary man, without doing injustice to him
or others. It is time to refer to particular

instances in his works. — The Rape of the
Lock is the best or most ingenious of these.
It is the most exquisite specimen of *fillagree*
work ever invented. It is admirable in proportion as it is made of nothng.

> " More subtle web Arachne cannot spin,
>   Nor the fine nets, which oft we woven see
>   Of scorched dew, do not in th' air more lightly flee."

It is made of gauze and silver spangles. The
most glittering appearance is given to every
thing, to paste, pomatum, billet-doux, and
patches. Airs, languid airs, breathe around ;
the atmosphere is perfumed with affectation.
A toilette is described with the solemnity of
an altar raised to the goddess of vanity, and
the history of a silver bodkin is given with all
the pomp of heraldry. No pains are spared,
no profusion of ornament, no splendour of
poetic diction, to set off the meanest things.
The balance between the concealed irony and
the assumed gravity is as nicely trimmed as
the balance of power in Europe. The little
is made great, and the great little. You
hardly know whether to laugh or weep. It is
the triumph of insignificance, the apotheosis
of foppery and folly. It is the perfection of
the mock-heroic ! I will give only the two
following passages in illustration of these remarks. Can any thing be more elegant and

graceful than the description of Belinda, in the
beginning of the second canto ?

> " Not with more glories, in the ethereal plain,
> The sun first rises o'er the purpled main,
> Than, issuing forth, the rival of his beams
> Launch'd on the bottom of the silver Thames,
> Fair nymphs, and well-drest youths around her shone,
> But ev'ry eye was fix'd on her alone.
> On her white breast a sparkling cross she wore,
> Which Jews might kiss and infidels adore.
> Her lively looks a sprightly mind disclose,
> Quick as her eyes, and as unfix'd as those ;
> Favours to none, to all she smiles extends ;
> Oft she rejects, but never once offends.
> Bright as the sun, her eyes the gazers strike ;
> And, like the sun, they shine on all alike,
> Yet graceful ease, and sweetness void of pride,
> Might hide her faults, if belles had faults to hide :
> If to her share some female errors fall,
> Look on her face, and you'll forget 'em all.
>
> This nymph, to the destruction of mankind,
> Nourish'd two locks, which graceful hung behind
> In equal curls, and well conspir'd to deck
> With shining ringlets the smooth iv'ry neck."

The following is the introduction to the
account of Belinda's assault upon the baron
bold, who had dissevered one of these locks
" from her fair head for ever and for ever."

> " Now meet thy fate, incens'd Belinda cry'd,
> And drew a deadly bodkin from her side.
> (The same his ancient personage to deck,
> Her great, great grandsire wore about his neck,
> In three seal-rings ; which after, melted down,
> Form'd a vast buckle for his widow's gown :

> Her infant grandame's whistle next it grew,
> The bells she jingled, and the whistle blew;
> Then in a bodkin grac'd her mother's hairs
> Which long she wore, and now Belinda wears.")

I do not know how far Pope was indebted for the original idea, or the delightful execution of this poem, to the Lutrin of Boileau.

The Rape of the Lock is a double-refined essence of wit and fancy, as the Essay on Criticism is of wit and sense. The quantity of thought and observation in this work, for so young a man as Pope was when he wrote it, is wonderful: unless we adopt the supposition that most men of genius spend the rest of their lives in teaching others what they themselves have learned under twenty. The conciseness and felicity of the expression are equally remarkable. Thus, on reasoning on the variety of men's opinion, he says —

> " 'Tis with our judgments, as our watches; none
> Go just alike, yet each believes his own."

Nothing can be more original and happy than the general remarks and illustrations in the Essay: the critical rules laid down are too much those of a school, and of a confined one. There is one passage in the Essay on Criticism in which the author speaks with that eloquent enthusiasm of the fame of ancient writers, which those will always feel who have

themselves any hope or chance of immortality.
I have quoted the passage elsewhere, but I
will repeat it here.

> " Still green with bays each ancient altar stands,
>   Above the reach of sacrilegious hands;
>   Secure from flames, from envy's fiercer rage,
>   Destructive war, and all-involving age.
>   Hail, bards triumphant, born in happier days,
>   Immortal heirs of universal praise !
>   Whose honours with increase of ages grow,
>   As streams roll down, enlarging as they flow."

These lines come with double force and beauty
on the reader, as they were dictated by the
writer's despair of ever attaining that lasting
glory which he celebrates with such disinterested enthusiasm in others, from the lateness
of the age in which he lived, and from his
writing in a tongue not understood by other
nations, and that grows obsolete and unintelligible to ourselves at the end of every second
century.   But he needed not have thus ante-
dated his own poetical doom—the loss and entire oblivion of that which can never die.   If
he had known, he might have boasted that " his
little bark" wafted down the stream of time,

> " ———— With *theirs* should sail,
>   Pursue the triumph and partake the gale "—

if those who know how to set a due value on
the blessing were not the last to decide confi-
dently on their own pretensions to it.

There is a cant in the present day about
genius, as every thing in poetry : there was a
cant in the time of Pope about sense, as performing all sorts of wonders. It was a kind
of watchword, the shibboleth of a critical
party of the day. As a proof of the exclusive
attention which it occupied in their minds, it
is remarkable that in the Essay on Criticism
(not a very long poem) there are no less than
half a score successive couplets rhyming to the
word *sense*. This appears almost incredible
without giving the instances, and no less so
when they are given.

" But of the two, less dangerous is the offence
 To tire our patience than mislead our sense."—*lines* 3, 4.
" In search of wit these lose their common sense,
 And then turn critics in their own defence."—*l.* 28, 29.
" Pride, where wit fails, steps in to our defence,
 And fills up all the mighty void of sense."—*l.* 209, 10.
" Some by old words to fame have made pretence,
 Ancients in phrase, mere moderns in their sense."—*l.* 324,5.
" 'Tis not enough no harshness gives offence ;
 The sound must seem an echo to the sense."—*l.* 364, 5.
" At every trifle scorn to take offence ;
 That always shows great pride or little sense."—*l.* 386, 7.
" Be silent always, when you doubt your sense,
 And speak, though sure, with seeming diffidence."—*l.*366,7
" Be niggards of advice on no pretence,
 For the worst avarice is that of sense."—*l.* 578, 9.
" Strain out the last dull dropping of their sense,
 And rhyme with all the rage of impotence."—*l.* 608, 9.
" Horace still charms with graceful negligence,
 And without method talks us into sense."—*l.* 633, 4.

I have mentioned this the more for the sake
of those critics who are bigotted idolisers of
our author, chiefly on the score of his correct-
ness.   These persons seem to be of opinion
that " there is but one perfect writer, even
Pope."   This is, however, a mistake : his
excellence is by no means faultlessness.   If he
had no great faults, he is full of little errors.
His grammatical construction is often lame
and imperfect.   In the Abelard and Eloise,
he says—

　　" There died the best of passions, Love and Fame."

This is not a legitimate ellipsis.   Fame is not
a passion, though love is : but his ear was
evidently confused by the meeting of the
sounds " love and fame," as if they of themselves immediately implied, " love, and love
of fame."   Pope's rhymes are constantly
defective, being rhymes to the eye instead of
the ear; and this to a greater degree, not only
than in later, but than in preceding, writers.
The praise of his versification must be confined to its uniform smoothness and harmony.
In the translation of the Iliad, which has been
considered as his masterpiece in style and
execution, he continually changes the tenses
in the same sentence for the purposes of the
rhyme, which shows either a want of tech-

nical resources, or great inattention to punctilious exactness. But to have done with this.

The epistle of Eloise to Abelard is the only exception, I can think of, to the general spirit of the foregoing remarks; and I should be disingenuous not to acknowledge that it is an exception. The foundation is in the letters themselves of Abelard and Eloise, which are quite as impressive, but still in a different way. It is fine as a poem: it is finer as a piece of high-wrought eloquence. No woman could be supposed to write a better love-letter in verse. Besides the richness of the historical materials, the high *gusto* of the original sentiments which Pope had to work upon, there were perhaps circumstances in his own situation which made him enter into the subject with even more than a poet's feeling. The tears shed are drops gushing from the heart: the words are burning sighs breathed from the soul of love. Perhaps the poem to which it bears the greatest similarity in our language is Dryden's Tancred and Sigismunda, taken from Boccaccio. Pope's Eloise will bear this comparison; and after such a test, with Boccaccio for the original author, and Dryden for the translator, it need shrink from no other. There is something exceedingly tender and beautiful in the sound of the concluding lines :

" If ever chance two wandering lovers brings
   To Paraclete's white walls and silver springs,'' &c.

The Essay on Man is not Pope's best work.
It is a theory which Bolingbroke is supposed
to have given him, and which he expanded
into verse. But " he spins the thread of his
verbosity finer than the staple of his argument." All that he says, " the very words,
and to the self-same tune," would prove just
as well that whatever is is *wrong,* as that
whatever is is *right.* The Dunciad has
splendid passages, but in general it is dull,
heavy, and mechanical. The sarcasm already
quoted on Settle, the Lord Mayor's poet (for
at that time there was a city, as well as a court,
poet),

" Now night descending, the proud scene is o'er,
  But lives in Settle's numbers one day more,"—

is the finest inversion of immortality conceivable. It is even better than his serious
apostrophe to the great heirs of glory, the
triumphant bards of antiquity !

The finest burst of severe moral invective
in all Pope is the prophetical conclusion of
the epilogue to the Satires :

" Virtue may chuse the high or low degree,
  'Tis just alike to virtue, and to me;
  Dwell in a monk, or light upon a king,
  She's still the same belov'd, contented thing.

Vice is undone, if she forgets her birth,
And stoops from angels to the dregs of earth.
But 'tis the fall degrades her to a whore :
Let greatness own her, and she's mean no more.
Her birth, her beauty, crowds and courts confess,
Chaste matrons praise her, and grave bishops bless ;
In golden chains the willing world she draws,
And hers the gospel is, and hers the laws ;
Mounts the tribunal, lifts her scarlet head,
And sees pale Virtue carted in her stead.
Lo ! at the wheels of her triumphal car,
Old England's Genius, rough with many a scar,
Dragg'd in the dust ! his arms hang idly round,
His flag inverted trains along the ground !
Our youth, all livery'd o'er with foreign gold,
Before her dance ; behind her crawl the old !
See thronging millions to the Pagod run,
And offer country, parent, wife, or son !
Hear her black trumpet through the land proclaim
That *not to be corrupted is the shame.*
In soldier, churchman, patriot, man in pow'r,
'Tis av'rice all, ambition is no more !
See all our nobles begging to be slaves !
See all our fools aspiring to be knaves !
The wit of cheats, the courage of a whore,
Are what ten thousand envy and adore :
All, all look up with reverential awe
At crimes that 'scape or triumph o'er the law ;
While truth, worth, wisdom, daily they decry :
Nothing is sacred now but villany.
Yet may this verse (if such a verse remain)
Show there was one who held it in disdain.''

His Satires are not in general so good as
his Epistles. His enmity is effeminate and
petulant from a sense of weakness, as his

friendship was tender from a sense of gratitude. I do not like, for instance, his character
of Chartres, or his characters of women. His
delicacy often borders upon sickliness; his
fastidiousness makes others fastidious. But
his compliments are divine; they are equal in
value to a house or an estate. Take the following. In addressing Lord Mansfield, he
speaks of the grave as a scene,

> " Where Murray, long enough his country's pride,
>   Shall be no more than Tully, or than Hyde."

To Bolingbroke he says —

> " Why rail they then if but one wreath of mine,
>   Oh all-accomplished St. John, deck thy shrine?"

Again, he has bequeathed this praise to Lord
Cornbury —

> " Despise low thoughts, low gains:
>   Disdain whatever Cornbury disdains;
>   Be virtuous and be happy for your pains."

One would think (though there is no knowing)
that a descendant of this nobleman, if there be
such a person living, could hardly be guilty of
a mean or paltry action.

The finest piece of personal satire in Pope
(perhaps in the world) is his character of
Addison; and this, it may be observed, is of
a mixed kind, made up of his respect for the
man, and a cutting sense of his failings. The

other finest one is that of Buckingham, and
the best part of that is the pleasurable.

> "——— Alas! how changed from him,
> That life of pleasure and that soul of whim,
> Gallant and gay, in Cliveden's proud alcove,
> The bower of wanton Shrewsbury and love!"

Among his happiest and most inimitable effusions are the Epistles to Arbuthnot, and to
Jervas the painter; amiable patterns of the
delightful unconcerned life, blending ease with
dignity, which poets and painters then led.
Thus he says to Arbuthnot:

> "Why did I write?   What sin to me unknown
> Dipp'd me in ink, my parents' or my own?
> As yet a child, nor yet a fool to fame,
> I lisped in numbers, for the numbers came.
> I left no calling for this idle trade,
> No duty broke, no father disobey'd:
> The muse but serv'd to ease some friend, not wife,
> To help me through this long disease, my life!
> To second, Arbuthnot! thy art and care,
> And teach the being you preserv'd to bear.
>
> But why then publish?   Granville the polite,
> And knowing Walsh, would tell me I could write;
> Well-natur'd Garth inflam'd with early praise,
> And Congreve lov'd, and Swift endur'd, my lays;
> The courtly Talbot, Somers, Sheffield, read;
> E'en mitred Rochester would nod the head;
> And St. John's self (great Dryden's friend before)
> With open arms receiv'd one poet more.
> Happy my studies, when by these approv'd!
> Happier their author, when by these belov'd!
> From these the world will judge of men and books,
> Not from the Burnets, Oldmixons, and Cooks."

I cannot help giving also the conclusion of the Epistle to Jervas.

> " Oh, lasting as those colours, may they shine,
> Free as thy stroke, yet faultless as thy line;
> New graces yearly, like thy works, display,
> Soft, without weakness, without glaring gay;
> Led by some rule, that guides, but not constrains;
> And finish'd more through happiness than pains,
> The kindred arts shall in their praise conspire,
> One dip the pencil, and one string the lyre.
> Yet should the Graces all thy figures place,
> And breathe an air divine on ev'ry face;
> Yet should the Muses bid my numbers roll
> Strong as their charms, and gentle as their soul;
> With Zeuxis' Helen thy Bridgewater vie,
> And these be sung till Granville's Myra die:
> Alas! how little from the grave we claim!
> Thou but preserv'st a face, and I a name."

And shall we cut ourselves off from beauties like these with a theory? Shall we shut up our books, and seal up our senses, to please the dull spite and inordinate vanity of those " who have eyes, but they see not—ears, but they hear not—and understandings, but they understand not,"—and go about asking our blind guides whether Pope was a poet or not? It will never do. Such persons, when you point out to them a fine passage in Pope, turn it off to something of the same sort in some other writer. Thus they say that the line, " I lisp'd in numbers, for the numbers came," is pretty, but taken from that of Ovid —*Et quum conabar scribere, versus erat.* They are safe in this mode of criticism : there is no danger of any one's tracing their writings to the classics.

Pope's letters and prose writings neither take away from, nor add to, his poetical reputation. There is, occasionally, a littleness of manner, and an unnecessary degree of caution. He appears anxious to say a good thing in every word, as well as every sentence. They, however, give a very favourable idea of his moral character in all respects ; and his letters to Atterbury, in his disgrace and exile, do equal honour to both. If I had to choose, there are one or two persons, and but one or two, that I should like to have been, better than Pope!

Dryden was a better prose-writer, and a bolder and more varied versifier, than Pope. He was a more vigorous thinker, a more correct and logical declaimer, and had more of what may be called strength of mind than Pope ; but he had not the same refinement and delicacy of feeling. Dryden's eloquence and spirit were possessed in a higher degree by others, and in nearly the same degree by Pope himself ; but that by which Pope was distinguished was an essence which he alone possessed, and of incomparable value on that sole account. Dryden's Epistles are excellent, but inferior to Pope's, though they appear

(particularly the admirable one to Congreve)
to have been the model on which the latter
formed his. His Satires are better than
Pope's. His Absalom and Achitophel is
superior, both in force of invective and discrimination of character, to any thing of Pope's
in the same way. The character of Achitophel is very fine; and breathes, if not a
sincere love for virtue, a strong spirit of
indignation against vice.

Mac Flecknoe is the origin of the idea of
the Dunciad; but it is less elaborately constructed, less feeble, and less heavy. The
difference between Pope's satirical portraits
and Dryden's appears to be this, in a good
measure, that Dryden seems to grapple with
his antagonists, and to describe real persons;
Pope seems to refine upon them in his own
mind, and to make them out just what he
pleases, till they are not real characters, but
the mere driveling effusions of his spleen and
malice. Pope describes the thing, and then
goes on describing his own description till he
loses himself in verbal repetitions. Dryden
recurs to the object often, takes fresh sittings
of nature, and gives us new strokes of character
as well as of his pencil. The Hind and
Panther is an allegory as well as a satire; and
so far it tells less home; the battery is not so

point-blank. But otherwise it has more genius,
vehemence, and strength of description, than
any other of Dryden's works, not excepting
the Absalom and Achitophel. It also contains
the finest examples of varied and sounding
versification. I will quote the following as an
instance of what I mean. He is complaining
of the treatment which the Papists, under
James II., received from the church of
England.

> " Besides these jolly birds, whose corpse impure
> Repaid their commons with their salt manure,
> Another farm he had behind his house,
> Not overstocked, but barely for his use ;
> Wherein his poor domestic poultry fed,
> And from his pious hand " received their bread."
> Our pampered pigeons, with malignant eyes,
> Beheld these inmates and their nurseries ;
> Though hard their fare, at evening, and at morn,
> (A cruise of water, and an ear of corn,)
> Yet still they grudged that *modicum*, and thought
> A sheaf in every single grain was brought.
> Fain would they filch that little food away,
> While unrestrained those happy gluttons prey ;
> And much they grieved to see so nigh their hall,
> The bird that warned St. Peter of his fall ;
> That he should raise his mitred crest on high,
> And clap his wings, and call his family
> To sacred rites ; and vex the ethereal powers
> With midnight matins at uncivil hours ;
> Nay more, his quiet neighbours should molest
> Just in the sweetness of their morning rest.
> Beast of a bird ! supinely when he might
> Lie snug and sleep, to rise before the light !

What if his dull forefathers us'd that cry,
Could he not let a bad example die ?
The world was fallen into an easier way :
This age knew better than to fast and pray.
Good sense in sacred worship would appear,
So to begin as they might end the year.
Such feats in former times had wrought the falls
Of crowing chanticleers in cloister'd walls.
Expell'd for this, and for their lands, they fled;
And sister Partlet with her hooded head
Was hooted hence, because she would not pray a-bed."

There is a magnanimity of abuse in some of these epithets, a fearless choice of topics of invective, which may be considered as the heroical in satire.

The *Annus Mirabilis* is a tedious perform-ance ; it is a tissue of far-fetched, heavy, lumbering conceits, and in the worst style of what has been denominated metaphysical poetry. His Odes in general are of the same stamp ; they are the hard-strained offspring of a meagre, meretricious fancy. The famous Ode on St. Cecilia deserves its reputation ; for, as a piece of poetical mechanism to be set to music, or recited in alternate strophe and antistrophe, with classical allusions, and flow-ing verse, nothing can be better. It is equally fit to be said or sung ; it is not equally good to read. It is lyrical, without being epic or dramatic. For instance, the description of Bacchus,

"The jolly god in triumph comes,
Sound the trumpets, beat the drums ;
Flush'd with a purple grace,
He shows his honest face,"—

does not answer, as it ought, to our idea of
the god, returning from the conquest of India,
with satyrs and wild beasts, that he had tamed,
following in his train; crowned with vine
leaves, and riding in a chariot drawn by leo-
pards — such as we have seen him painted by
Titian or Rubens! Lyrical poetry, of all
others, bears the nearest resemblance to painting : it deals in hieroglyphics and passing
figures, which depend for effect, not on the
working out, but on the selection. It is the
dance and pantomime of poetry. In variety
and rapidity of movement, the Alexander's
Feast has all that can be required in this
respect; it only wants loftiness and truth of
character.

Dryden's plays are better than Pope could
have written; for though he does not go out
of himself by the force of imagination, he goes
out of himself by the force of common-places
and rhetorical dialogue. On the other hand,
they are not so good as Shakspeare's ; but he
has left the best character of Shakspeare that
has ever been written.*

---

* "To begin, then, with Shakspeare: he was the man who
of all modern, and perhaps ancient, poets had the largest

His alterations from Chaucer and Boccaccio show a greater knowledge of the taste of his readers, and power of pleasing them, than acquaintance with the genius of his authors. He ekes out the lameness of the verse in the former, and breaks the force of the passion in both. The Tancred and Sigismunda is the only general exception, in which, I think, he has fully retained, if not improved upon, the impassioned declamation of the original. The Honoria has none of the bewildered, dreary, preternatural effect of Boccaccio's story. Nor has the Flower and the Leaf any thing of the enchanting simplicity and concentrated feeling of Chaucer's romantic

---

and most comprehensive soul. All the images of nature were still present to him, and he drew them not laboriously, but luckily : when he describes any thing, you more than see it, you feel it, too. Those who accuse him to have wanted learning give him the greater commendation : he was naturally learned ; he needed not the spectacles of books to read nature ; he looked inwards and found her there. I cannot say he is every where alike ; were he so, I should do him injury to compare him with the greatest of mankind. He is many times flat and insipid : his comic wit degenerating into clenches, his serious, swelling into bombast. But he is always great when some great occasion is presented to him. No man can say he ever had a fit subject for his wit, and did not then raise himself as high above the rest of poets,

Quantum lenta solent inter Viburna Cupressi."

fiction. Dryden, however, sometimes seemed
to indulge himself as well as his readers, as in
keeping entire that noble line in Palamon's
address to Venus :

" Thou gladder of the mount of Cithæron ! "

His Tales have been, upon the whole, the
most popular of his works ; and I should
think that a translation of some of the other
serious tales in Boccaccio and Chaucer, as
that of Isabella, the Falcon, of Constance,
the Prioress's Tale, and others, if executed
with taste and spirit, could not fail to succeed
in the present day.

It should appear, in tracing the history of
our literature, that poetry had, at the period
of which we are speaking, in general declined,
by successive gradations, from the poetry of
imagination, in the time of Elizabeth, to the
poetry of fancy (to adopt a modern distinction)
in the time of Charles I. ; and again from the
poetry of fancy to that of wit, as in the reign
of Charles II. and Queen Anne.   It degenerated into the poetry of mere common places,
both in style and thought, in the succeeding
reigns: as in the latter part of the last century,
it was transformed, by means of the French
Revolution, into the poetry of paradox.

Of Donne I know nothing but some beau-

tiful verses to his wife, dissuading her from
accompanying him on his travels abroad, and
some quaint riddles in verse, which the Sphinx
could not unravel.

Waller still lives in the name of Sacharissa;
and his lines on the death of Oliver Cromwell
show that he was a man not without genius
and strength of thought.

Marvel is a writer of nearly the same period,
and worthy of a better age. Some of his
verses are harsh as the words of Mercury;
others musical as is Apollo's lute. Of the
latter kind are his boat-song, his description
of a fawn, and his lines to Lady Vere. His
lines prefixed to Paradise Lost are by no
means the most favourable specimen of his
powers.

Butler's Hudibras is a poem of more wit
than any other in the language. The rhymes
have as much genius in them as the thoughts;
but there is no story in it, and but little humour. Humour is the making others act or
talk absurdly and unconsciously : wit is the
pointing out and ridiculing that absurdity
consciously, and with more or less ill-nature.
The fault of Butler's poem is not that it has
too much wit, but that it has not an equal
quantity of other things. One would suppose
that the starched manners and sanctified gri-

mace of the times in which he lived would of
themselves have been sufficiently rich in ludicrous incidents and characters; but they seem
rather to have irritated his spleen than to have
drawn forth his powers of picturesque imitation. Certainly, if we compare Hudibras with
Don Quixote in this respect, it seems rather
a meagre and unsatisfactory performance.

Rochester's poetry is the poetry of wit combined with the love of pleasure, of thought
with licentiousness. His extravagant heedless
levity has a sort of passionate enthusiasm in
it; his contempt for every thing that others
respect almost amounts to sublimity.   His
poem upon Nothing is itself no trifling work.
His epigrams were the bitterest, the least
laboured, and the truest, that ever were
written.

Sir John Suckling was of the same mer-
curial stamp, but with a greater fund of animal
spirits; as witty, but less malicious.   His
Ballad on a Wedding is perfect in its kind,
and has a spirit of high enjoyment in it, of
sportive fancy, a liveliness of description, and
a truth of nature, that never were surpassed.
It is superior to either Gay or Prior; for
with all their *naiveté* and terseness, it has a
Shakspearian grace and luxuriance about it
which they could not have reached.

Denham and Cowley belong to the same period, but were quite distinct from each other: the one was grave and prosing, the other melancholy and fantastical. There are a number of good lines and good thoughts in the "Cooper's Hill." And in Cowley there is an inexhaustible fund of sense and ingenuity, buried in inextricable conceits, and entangled in the cobwebs of the schools. He was a great man, not a great poet. But I shall say no more on this subject. I never wish to meddle with names that are sacred, unless when they stand in the way of things that are more sacred.

Withers is a name now almost forgotten, and his works seldom read; but his poetry is not unfrequently distinguished by a tender and pastoral turn of thought; and there is one passage of exquisite feeling, describing the consolations of poetry in the following terms:

> " She doth tell me where to borrow
> Comfort in the midst of sorrow;
> Makes the desolatest place *
> To her presence be a grace;
> And the blackest discontents
> Be her fairest ornaments,
> In my former days of bliss
> Her divine skill taught me this,

* Written in the Fleet Prison.

That from every thing I saw
I could some invention draw ;
And raise pleasure to her height,
Through the meanest object's sight ;—
By the murmur of a spring,
Or the least bough's rusteling,
By a daisy whose leaves spread
Shut when Titan goes to bed ;
Or a shady bush or tree,
She could more infuse in me
Than all Nature's beauties can
In some other wiser man.
By her help I also now
Make this churlish place allow
Some things that may sweeten gladness
In the very gall of sadness.
The dull loneness, the black shade,
That these hanging vaults have made,
The strange music of the waves,
Beating on these hollow caves,
This black den which rocks emboss,
Overgrown with eldest moss,
The rude portals that give light
More to terror than delight,
This my chamber of neglect,
Wall'd about with disrespect,
From all these and this dull air,
A fit object for despair,
She hath taught me by her might
To draw comfort and delight.
Therefore, thou best earthly bliss,
I will cherish thee for this.
Poesie, thou sweet'st content
That e'er Heaven to mortals lent,
Though they as a trifle leave thee,
Whose dull thoughts cannot conceive thee,
Though thou be to them a scorn,
That to nought but earth are born,

Let my life no longer be
Than I am in love with thee.
Though our wise ones call thee madness,
Let me never taste of sadness
If I love not thy maddest fits
Above all their greatest wits.
And though some too seeming holy
Do account thy raptures folly,
Thou dost teach me to contemn
What makes knaves and fools of them."

LECTURE V.

———◆———

ON THOMSON AND COWPER.

THOMSON, the kind-hearted Thomson, was the most indolent of mortals and of poets. But he was also one of the best both of mortals and of poets. Dr. Johnson makes it his praise that he wrote " no line which dying he would wish to blot." Perhaps a better proof of his honest simplicity, and inoffensive goodness of disposition, would be that he wrote no line which any other person living would wish that he should blot. Indeed, he himself wished, on his death-bed, formally to expunge his dedication of one of the Seasons to that finished courtier, and candid biographer of his own life, Bubb Doddington. As critics, however, not as moralists, we might say, on the other hand — " Would he had blotted a thousand !" The same suavity of temper and

sanguine warmth of feeling which threw such
a natural grace and genial spirit of enthusiasm
over his poetry was also the cause of his inherent vices and defects.   He is affected
through carelessness : pompous from unsus-
pecting simplicity of character.   He is frequently pedantic and ostentatious in his style,
because he had no consciousness of these
vices in himself.   He mounts upon stilts, not
out of vanity, but indolence.   He seldom
writes a good line but he makes up for it by
a bad one.   He takes advantage of all the
most trite and mechanical common-places of
imagery and diction as a kindly relief to his
Muse, and as if he thought them quite as
good, and likely to be quite as acceptable to
the reader, as his own poetry.   He did not
think the difference worth putting himself to
the trouble of accomplishing.   He had too
little art to conceal his art : or did not even
seem to know that there was any occasion for
it.   His art is as naked and undisguised as his
nature ; the one is as pure and genuine as the
other is gross, gaudy, and meretricious.   All
that is admirable in the Seasons is the emanation of a fine natural genius, and sincere
love of his subject, unforced, unstudied, that
comes uncalled for, and departs unbidden.
But he takes no pains, uses no self-correction ;

or if he seems to labour, it is worse than
labour lost. His genius " cannot be con-
strained by mastery." The feeling of nature,
of the changes of the seasons, was in his mind;
and he could not help conveying this feeling to
the reader, by the mere force of spontaneous
expression; but if the expression did not come
of itself, he left the whole business to chance;
or, willing to evade, instead of encountering
the difficulties of his subject, fills up the intervals of true inspiration with the most vapid
and worthless materials, pieces out a beautiful half line with a bombastic allusion, or
overloads an exquisitely natural sentiment or
image with a cloud of painted, pompous,
cumbrous phrases, like the shower of roses,
in which he represents the Spring, his own
lovely, fresh, and innocent Spring, as descending to the earth :

> " Come, gentle Spring ! ethereal Mildness ! come,
> And from the bosom of yon dropping cloud,
> While music wakes around, veil'd in a shower
> Of shadowing roses, on our plains descend."

Who, from such a flimsy, round-about, unmeaning commencement as this, would expect
the delightful, unexaggerated, home-felt descriptions of natural scenery, which are scattered in such unconscious profusion through
this and the following cantos ! For instance,

the very next passage is crowded with a set of
striking images.

> " And see where surly Winter passes off
>   Far to the north, and calls his ruffian blasts :
>   His blasts obey, and quit the howling hill,
>   The shatter'd forest, and the ravag'd vale ;
>   While softer gales succeed, at whose kind touch
>   Dissolving snows in livid torrents lost,
>   The mountains lift their green heads to the sky.
>   As yet the trembling year is unconfirm'd,
>   And Winter oft at eve resumes the breeze,
>   Chills the pale morn, and bids his driving sleets
>   Deform the day delightless ; so that scarce
>   The bittern knows his time with bill ingulpht
>   To shake the sounding marsh, or from the shore
>   The plovers when to scatter o'er the heath,
>   And sing their wild notes to the list'ning waste."

Thomson is the best of our descriptive
poets ; for he gives most of the poetry of
natural description. Others have been quite
equal to him, or have surpassed him, as Cowper
for instance, in the picturesque part of his art,
in marking the peculiar features and curious
details of objects ;—no one has yet come up
to him in giving the sum total of their effects,
their varying influences on the mind. He
does not go into the *minutiæ* of a landscape,
but describes the vivid impression which the
whole makes upon his own imagination ; and
thus transfers the same unbroken, unimpaired
impression to the imagination of his readers.

The colours with which he paints seem yet
wet and breathing, like those of the living
statue in the Winter's Tale. Nature in his
descriptions is seen growing around us, fresh
and lusty as in itself. We feel the effect of
the atmosphere, its humidity or clearness, its
heat or cold, the glow of summer, the gloom
of winter, the tender promise of the spring, the
full overshadowing foliage, the declining pomp
and deepening tints of autumn. He transports us to the scorching heat of vertical suns,
or plunges us into the chilling horrors and
desolation of the frozen zone. We hear the
snow drifting against the broken casement
without, and see the fire blazing on the hearth
within. The first scattered drops of a vernal
shower patter on the leaves above our heads,
or the coming storm resounds through the
leafless groves. In a word, he describes not
to the eye alone, but to the other senses, and
to the whole man. He puts his heart into his
subject, writes as he feels, and humanises
whatever he touches. He makes all his descriptions teem with life and vivifying soul.
His faults were those of his style — of the
author and the man ; but the original genius
of the poet, the pith and marrow of his imagination, the fine natural mould in which his
feelings were bedded, were too much for him

to counteract by neglect, or affectation, or
false ornaments. It is for this reason that he
is, perhaps, the most popular of all our poets,
treating of a subject that all can understand,
and in a way that is interesting to all alike, to
the ignorant or the refined, because he gives
back the impression which the things themselves make upon us in nature. " That," said
a man of genius, seeing a little shabby soiled
copy of Thomson's Seasons lying on the
window-seat of an obscure country alehouse
—" That is true fame !"

It has been supposed by some that the
Castle of Indolence is Thomson's best poem;
but that is not the case. He has in it, indeed,
poured out the whole soul of indolence, diffuse, relaxed, supine, dissolved into a voluptuous dream ; and surrounded himself with a
set of objects and companions in entire unison
with the listlessness of his own temper. Nothing can well go beyond the descriptions of
these inmates of the place, and their luxurious
pampered way of life — of him who came
among them like " a burnished fly in month
of June," but soon left them on his heedless
way ; and him,

> " For whom the merry bells had rung, I ween,
>   If in this nook of quiet bells had ever been."

The in-door quiet and cushioned ease, where

" all was one full-swelling bed ;" the out-of-
door stillness, broken only by "the stock-dove's
plaint amid the forest deep,

> " That drowsy rustled to the sighing gale,"—

are in the most perfect and delightful keeping.
But still there are no passages in this exquisite
little production of sportive ease and fancy,
equal to the best of those in the Seasons.
Warton, in his Essay on Pope, was the first
to point out and do justice to some of these;
for instance, to the description of the effects
of the contagion among our ships at Cartha-
gena — " of the frequent corse heard nightly
plunged amid the sullen waves," and to the
description of the pilgrims lost in the deserts
of Arabia. This last passage, profound and
striking as it is, is not free from those faults
of style which I have already noticed :

> "——— Breath'd hot
> From all the boundless furnace of the sky,
> And the wide-glitt'ring waste of burning sand,
> A suffocating wind the pilgrim smites
> With instant death. Patient of thirst and toil,
> Son of the desert, ev'n the camel feels
> Shot through his wither'd heart the fiery blast.
> Or from the black-red ether, bursting broad,
> Sallies the sudden whirlwind. Straight the sands,
> Commov'd around, in gath'ring eddies play ;
> Nearer and nearer still they dark'ning come,
> Till with the gen'ral all-involving storm
> Swept up, the whole continuous wilds arise,

And by their noon-day fount dejected thrown,
Or sunk at night in sad disastrous sleep,
Beneath descending hills the caravan
Is buried deep.   In Cairo's crowded streets,
Th' impatient merchant, wond'ring, waits in vain ;
And Mecca saddens at the long delay."

There are other passages of equal beauty with these ; such as that of the hunted stag, followed by " the inhuman rout,"

" ———That from the shady depth
Expel him, circling through his ev'ry shift.
He sweeps the forest oft, and, sobbing, sees
The glades mild op'ning to the golden day,
Where in kind contest with his butting friends
He wont to struggle, or his loves enjoy."

The whole of the description of the frozen zone, in the Winter, is perhaps even finer and more thoroughly felt, as being done from early associations, than that of the torrid zone in his Summer.   Any thing more beautiful than the following account of the Siberian exiles is, I think, hardly to be found in the whole range of poetry.

" There through the prison of unbounded wilds,
   Barr'd by the hand of nature from escape,
   Wide roams the Russian exile.   Nought around
   Strikes his sad eye but deserts lost in snow,
   And heavy-loaded groves, and solid floods,
   That stretch athwart the solitary vast
   Their icy horrors to the frozen main ;
   And cheerless towns far distant, never bless'd,
   Save when its annual course the caravan
   Bends to the golden coast of rich Cathay,
   With news of human kind.'

The feeling of loneliness, of distance, of lingering, slow-revolving years of pining expectation, of desolation within and without the heart, was never more finely expressed than it is here.

The account which follows of the employments of the Polar night—of the journeys of the natives by moonlight, drawn by rein-deer, and of the return of spring in Lapland—

> " Where pure Niemi's fairy mountains rise,
>   And fring'd with roses Tenglio rolls his stream,"

is equally picturesque and striking in a different way. The traveller lost in the snow, is a well known and admirable dramatic episode. I prefer, however, giving one example of our author's skill in painting common domestic scenery, as it will bear a more immediate comparison with the style of some later writers on such subjects. It is of little consequence what passage we take. The following description of the first setting in of winter is, perhaps as pleasing as any:

> " Through the hush'd air the whitening shower descends,
>   At first thin wav'ring, till at last the flakes
>   Fall broad and wide, and fast, dimming the day
>   With a continual flow. The cherish'd fields
>   Put on their winter-robe of purest white :
>   'Tis brightness all, save where the new snow melts
>   Along the mazy current. Low the woods
>   Bow their hoar head ; and ere the languid Sun,

Faint, from the West emits his ev'ning ray,
Earth's universal face, deep hid, and chill,
Is one wide dazzling waste, that buries wide
The works of man.   Drooping, the lab'rer-ox
Stands cover'd o'er with snow, and then demands
The fruit of all his toil.   The fowls of heav'n,
Tam'd by the cruel season, crowd around
The winnowing store, and claim the little boon
Which Providence assigns them.   One alone,
The red-breast, sacred to the household Gods,
Wisely regardful of the embroiling sky,
In joyless fields and thorny thickets leaves
His shivering mates, and pays to trusted man
His annual visit.   Half-afraid, he first
Against the window beats ; then, brisk, alights
On the warm hearth ; then hopping o'er the floor,
Eyes all the smiling family askance,
And pecks, and starts, and wonders where he is :
Till, more familiar grown, the table-crumbs
Attract his slender feet.   The foodless wilds
Pour forth their brown inhabitants.   The hare,
Though timorous of heart, and hard beset
By death in various forms, dark snares and dogs,
And more unpitying men, the garden seeks,
Urg'd on by fearless want.   The bleating kind
Eye the bleak heav'n, and next the glist'ning earth,
With looks of dumb despair ; then, sad dispers'd,
Dig for the wither'd herb through heaps of snow.''

It is thus that Thomson always give a *moral
sense* to nature.

Thomson's blank verse is not harsh, nor
utterly untuneable ; but it is heavy and
monotonous ; it seems always labouring up-
hill.   The selections which have been made
from his works in Enfield's Speaker, and

other books of extracts, do not convey the
most favourable idea of his genius or taste ;
such as Palemon and Lavinia, Damon and
Musidora, Celadon and Amelia. Those parts
of any author which are most liable to be
stitched in worsted, and framed and glazed, are
not by any means always the best. The moral
descriptions and reflections in the Seasons are
in an admirable spirit, and written with great
force and fervour.

His poem on Liberty is not equally good :
his Muse was too easy and good-natured for
the subject, which required as much indignation against unjust and arbitrary power, as
complacency in the constitutional monarchy,
under which, just after the expulsion of the
Stuarts and the establishment of the House
of Hanover, in contempt of the claims of
hereditary pretenders to the throne, Thomson
lived. Thomson was but an indifferent hater ;
and the most indispensable part of the love
of liberty has unfortunately hitherto been
the hatred of tyranny. Spleen is the soul
of patriotism, and of public good : but you
would not expect a man who has been seen
eating peaches off a tree with both hands in
his waistcoat pockets, to be " overrun with
the spleen," or to heat himself needlessly about
an abstract proposition.

His plays are liable to the same objection. They are never acted, and seldom read. The author could not, or would not, put himself out of his way, to enter into the situations and passions of others, particularly of a tragic kind. The subject of Tancred and Sigismunda, which is taken from a serious episode in Gil Blas, is an admirable one, but poorly handled : the ground may be considered as still unoccupied.

Cowper, whom I shall speak of in this connection, lived at a considerable distance of time after Thomson ; and had some advantages over him, particularly in simplicity of style, in a certain precision and minuteness of graphical description, and in a more careful and leisurely choice of such topics only as his genius and peculiar habits of mind prompted him to treat of. The Task has fewer blemishes than the Seasons ; but it has not the same capital excellence, the " unbought grace" of poetry, the power of moving and infusing the warmth of the author's mind into that of the reader. If Cowper had a more polished taste, Thomson had, beyond comparison, a more fertile genius, more impulsive force, a more entire forgetfulness of himself in his subject. If in Thomson you are sometimes offended with the slovenliness of the author

by profession, determined to get through his
task at all events; in Cowper you are no less
dissatisfied with the finicalness of the private
gentleman, who does not care whether he
completes his work or not; and, in whatever
he does, is evidently more solicitous to
please himself than the public.   There is an
effeminacy about him, which shrinks from
and repels common and hearty sympathy.
With all his boasted simplicity and love of the
country, he seldom launches out into general
descriptions of nature : he looks at her over
his clipped hedges, and from his well-swept
garden-walks; or if he makes a bolder experiment now and then, it is with an air of
precaution, as if he were afraid of being
caught in a shower of rain, or of not being
able, in case of any untoward accident, to
make good his retreat home.   He shakes
hands with nature with a pair of fashionable
gloves on, and leads " his Vashti" forth to
public view with a look of consciousness and
attention to etiquette, as a fine gentleman
hands a lady out to dance a minuet.   He is
delicate to fastidiousness, and glad to get back,
after a romantic adventure with crazy Kate, a
party of gypsies or a little child on a common,
to the drawing-room and the ladies again, to
the sofa and the tea-kettle—No, I beg his

pardon, not to the singing, well-scoured tea-kettle, but to the polished and loud-hissing urn. His walks and arbours are kept clear of worms and snails, with as much an appearance of *petit-maitreship* as of humanity. He has some of the sickly sensibility and pampered refinements of Pope ; but then Pope prided himself in them : whereas, Cowper affects to be all simplicity and plainness. He had neither Thomson's love of the unadorned beauties of nature, nor Pope's exquisite sense of the elegances of art. He was, in fact, a nervous man, afraid of trusting himself to the seductions of the one, and ashamed of putting forward his pretensions to an intimacy with the other : but to be a coward is not the way to succeed either in poetry, in war, or in love ! Still he is a genuine poet, and deserves all his reputation. His worst vices are amiable weaknesses, elegant trifling. Though there is a frequent dryness, timidity, and jejuneness in his manner, he has left a number of pictures of domestic comfort and social refinement, as well as of natural imagery and feeling, which can hardly be forgotten but with the language itself. Such, among others, are his memorable description of the post coming in, that of the preparations for tea in a winter's evening in the country, of the unexpected fall of snow,

of the frosty morning (with the fine satirical
transition to the Empress of Russia's palace
of ice), and, most of all, the winter's walk at
noon.   Every one of these may be considered
as distinct studies, or highly-finished cabinet-
pieces arranged without order or coherence. I
shall be excused for giving the last of them,
as what has always appeared to me one of the
most feeling, elegant, and perfect specimens
of this writer's manner.

> " The night was winter in his roughest mood ;
>   The morning sharp and clear.   But now at noon
>   Upon the southern side of the slant hills,
>   And where the woods fence off the northern blast,
>   The season smiles, resigning all its rage,
>   And has the warmth of May.   The vault is blue,
>   Without a cloud, and white without a speck
>   The dazzling splendour of the scene below.
>   Again the harmony comes o'er the vale ;
>   And through the trees I view th' embattled tow'r,
>   Whence all the music.   I again perceive
>   The soothing influence of the wafted strains,
>   And settle in soft musings as I tread
>   The walk, still verdant, under oaks and elms,
>   Whose outspread branches overarch the glade.
>   The roof, though moveable through all its length,
>   As the wind sways it, has yet well suffic'd,
>   And, intercepting in their silent fall
>   The frequent flakes, has kept a path for me.
>   No noise is here, or none that hinders thought.
>   The redbreast warbles still, but is content
>   With slender notes, and more than half suppress'd.
>   Pleas'd with his solitude, and flitting light
>   From spray to spray, where'er he rests he shakes

From many a twig the pendent drops of ice
That tinkle in the wither'd leaves below.
Stillness, accompanied with sounds so soft,
Charms more than silence.   Meditation here
May think down hours to moments.   Here the heart
May give a useful lesson to the head,
And Learning wiser grow without his books.
Knowledge and Wisdom, far from being one,
Have oft-times no connection.   Knowledge dwells
In heads replete with thoughts of other men ;
Wisdom in minds attentive to their own.
Books are not seldom talismans and spells,
By which the magic art of shrewder wits
Holds an unthinking multitude enthrall'd.
Some to the fascination of a name
Surrender judgment hood-wink'd.   Some the style
Infatuates, and through labyrinths and wilds
Of error leads them, by a tune entranc'd.
While sloth seduces more, too weak to bear
The insupportable fatigue of thought,
And swallowing therefore, without pause or choice,
The total grist unsifted, husks and all.
But trees, and rivulets whose rapid course
Defies the check of winter, haunts of deer,
And sheep-walks populous with bleating lambs,
And lanes, in which the primrose ere her time
Peeps through the moss that clothes the hawthorn root,
Deceive no student.   Wisdom there, and truth,
Not shy, as in the world, and to be won
By slow solicitation, seize at once
The roving thought, and fix it on themselves.''

His satire is also excellent.   It is pointed and
forcible, with the polished manners of the
gentleman, and the honest indignation of the
virtuous man.   His religious poetry, except
where it takes a tincture of controversial heat,

wants elevation and fire. His Muse had not a seraph's wing. I might refer, in illustration of this opinion, to the laboured anticipation of the Millennium at the end of the sixth book. He could describe a piece of shell-work as well as any modern poet : but he could not describe the New Jerusalem so well as John Bunyan ;—nor are his verses on Alexander Selkirk so good as Robinson Crusoe. The one is not so much like a vision, nor is the other so much like the reality.

The first volume of Cowper's poems has, however, been less read than it deserved. The comparison in these poems of the proud and humble believer to the peacock and the pheasant, and the parallel between Voltaire and the poor cottager, are exquisite pieces of eloquence and poetry, particularly the last :

> " Yon cottager, who weaves at her own door,
>   Pillow and bobbins all her little store ;
>   Content though mean, and cheerful if not gay,
>   Shuffling her threads about the live-long day,
>   Just earns a scanty pittance, and at night,
>   Lies down secure, her heart and pocket light ;
>   She, for her humble sphere by nature fit,
>   Has little understanding, and no wit,
>   Receives no praise ; but, though her lot be such,
>   (Toilsome and indigent) she renders much ;
>   Just knows, and knows no more, her Bible true—
>   A truth the brilliant Frenchman never knew ;
>   And in that charter reads with sparkling eyes
>   Her title to a treasure in the skies.

> O happy peasant ! Oh unhappy bard !
> His the mere tinsel, hers the rich reward ;
> He prais'd, perhaps, for ages yet to come,
> She never heard of half a mile from home :
> He lost in errors his vain heart prefers,
> She safe in the simplicity of hers.''

His character of Whitfield, in the poem on
Hope, is one of the most spirited and striking
things. It is written *con amore*.

> " But if, unblameable in word and thought,
> A man arise, a man whom God has taught,
> With all Elijah's dignity of tone,
> And all the love of the beloved John,
> To storm the citadels they build in air,
> To smite the untemper'd wall ('tis death to spare),
> To sweep away all refuges of lies,
> And place, instead of quirks themselves devise,
> Lama Sabachthani before their eyes ;
> To show that without Christ all gain is loss,
> All hope despair that stands not on his cross ;
> Except a few his God may have impress'd,
> A tenfold phrensy seizes all the rest.''

These lines were quoted, soon after their appearance, by the Monthly Reviewers, to show
that Cowper was no poet, though they afterwards took credit to themselves for having
been the first to introduce his verses to the
notice of the public. It is not a little remarkable that these same critics regularly damned,
at its first coming out, every work which has
since acquired a standard reputation with the
public. Cowper's verses on his mother's

picture, and his lines to Mary, are some of
the most pathetic that ever were written. His
stanzas on the loss of the Royal George have
a masculine strength and feeling beyond what
was usual with him. The story of John
Gilpin has perhaps given as much pleasure to
as many people as any thing of the same
length that ever was written.

His life was an unhappy one. It was em-
bittered by a morbid affection, and by his
religious sentiments. Nor are we to wonder
at this, or bring it as a charge against religion;
for it is the nature of the poetical temperament to carry every thing to excess, whether
it be love, religion, pleasure, or pain, as we
may see in the case of Cowper and of Burns,
and to find torment or rapture in that in which
others merely find a resource from *ennui*, or
a relaxation from common occupation.

There are two poets still living who belong
to the same class of excellence, and of whom
I shall here say a few words; I mean Crabbe,
and Robert Bloomfield, the author of the
Farmer's Boy. As a painter of simple natural
scenery, and of the still life of the country,
few writers have more undeniable and unas-
suming pretensions than the ingenious and
self-taught poet last mentioned. Among the
sketches of this sort I would mention, as

equally distinguished for delicacy, faithfulness,
and *naïveté*, his description of lambs racing,
of the pigs going out an acorning, of the boy
sent to feed his sheep before the break of day
in winter ; and I might add the innocently
told story of the poor bird-boy, who in vain
through the live-long day expects his promised
companions at his hut, to share his feast of
roasted sloes with him, as an example of that
humble pathos in which this author excels.
The fault indeed of his genius is that it is too
humble : his Muse has something not only
rustic, but menial in her aspect. He seems
afraid of elevating nature, lest she should be
ashamed of him. Bloomfield very beautifully
describes the lambs in spring-time as racing
round the hillocks of green turf : Thomson,
in describing the same image, makes the
mound of earth the remains of an old Roman
encampment. Bloomfield never gets beyond
his own experience ; and that is somewhat
confined. He gives the simple appearance of
nature, but he gives it naked, shivering, and
unclothed with the drapery of a moral imagination. His poetry has much the effect of
the first approach of spring, " while yet the
year is unconfirmed," where a few tender buds
venture forth here and there, but are chilled
by the early frosts and nipping breath of

poverty.   It should seem from this and other instances that have occurred within the last century, that we cannot expect from original genius alone, without education, in modern and more artificial periods, the same bold and independent results as in former periods. And one reason appears to be that, though such persons, from whom we might at first expect a restoration of the good old times of poetry, are not encumbered and enfeebled by the trammels of custom, and the dull weight of other men's ideas; yet they are oppressed by the consciousness of a want of the common advantages which others have; are looking at the tinsel finery of the age, while they neglect the rich unexplored mine in their own breasts; and, instead of setting an example for the world to follow, spend their lives in aping, or in the despair of aping, the hackneyed accomplishments of their inferiors.   Another cause may be, that original genius alone is not sufficient to produce the highest excellence, without a corresponding state of manners, passions, and religious belief : that no single mind can move in direct opposition to the vast machine of the world around it ; that the poet can do no more than stamp the mind of his age upon his works ; and that all that the ambition of the highest genius can hope to arrive at, after the lapse of one or two generations, is the perfection of that more refined and effeminate style of studied elegance and adventitious ornament, which is the result, not of nature, but of art. In fact, no other style of poetry has succeeded, or seems likely to succeed, in the present day. The public taste hangs like a millstone round the neck of all original genius that does not conform to established and exclusive models. The writer is not only without popular sympathy, but without a rich and varied mass of materials for his mind to work upon and assimilate unconsciously to itself; his attempts at originality are looked upon as affectation, and in the end degenerate into it from the natural spirit of contradiction, and the constant uneasy sense of disappointment and undeserved ridicule. But to return.

Crabbe is, if not the most natural, the most literal of our descriptive poets. He exhibits the smallest circumstances of the smallest things. He gives the very costume of meanness; the non-essentials of every trifling incident. He is his own landscape-painter, and engraver too. His pastoral scenes seem pricked on paper in little dotted lines. He describes the interior of a cottage like a person sent there to distrain for rent. He has an eye to the number of arms in an old worm-eaten chair, and takes care to inform himself and the reader whether a joint-stool stands upon three legs or upon four. If a settle by the fire-side stands awry, it gives him as much disturbance as a tottering world ; and he records the rent in a ragged counterpane as an event in history. He is equally curious in his back-grounds and in his figures. You know the christian and surnames of every one of his heroes, — the dates of their achievements, whether on a Sunday or a Monday, — their place of birth and burial, the colour of their clothes, and of their hair, and whether they squinted or not. He takes an inventory of the human heart exactly in the same manner as of the furniture of a sick room : his sentiments have very much the air of fixtures : he gives you the petrifaction of a sigh, and carves a tear, to the life, in stone. Almost all his characters are tired of their lives, and you heartily wish them dead. They remind one of anatomical preservations; or may be said to bear the same relation to actual life that a stuffed cat in a glass-case does to the real one purring on the hearth : the skin is the same, but the life and the sense of heat is gone. Crabbe's poetry is like a museum, or curiosity-shop: every thing has the same post-humous appearance, the same inanimateness

and identity of character. If Bloomfield is
too much of the Farmer's Boy, Crabbe is too
much of the parish beadle, an overseer of the
country poor. He has no delight beyond the
walls of a workhouse, and his officious zeal
would convert the world into a vast infirmary.
He is a kind of Ordinary, not of Newgate,
but of nature. His poetical morality is taken
from Burn's Justice, or the Statutes against
Vagrants. He sets his own imagination in
the stocks, and his Muse, like Malvolio,
" wears cruel garters." He collects all the
petty vices of the human heart, and superin-
tends, as in a panopticon, a select circle of
rural malefactors. He makes out the poor
to be as bad as the rich — a sort of vermin
for the others to hunt down and trample upon,
and this he thinks a good piece of work.
With him there are but two moral categories,
riches and poverty, authority and dependence.
His parish apprentice, Richard Monday, and
his wealthy baronet, Sir Richard Monday, of
Monday-place, are the same individual — the
extremes of the same character, and of his
whole system. " The latter end of his Commonwealth does not forget the beginning."
But his parish ethics are the very worst model
for a state : any thing more degrading and
helpless cannot well be imagined. He exhibits

just the contrary view of human life to that which Gay has done in his Beggar's Opera. In a word, Crabbe is the only poet who has attempted and succeeded in the *still life* of tragedy : who gives the stagnation of hope and fear—the deformity of vice without the temptation—the pain of sympathy without the interest—and who seems to rely, for the delight he is to convey to his reader, on the truth and accuracy with which he describes only what is disagreeable.

The best descriptive poetry is not, after all, to be found in our descriptive poets. There are set descriptions of the flowers, for instance, in Thomson, Cowper, and others ; but none equal to those in Milton's Lycidas, and in the Winter's Tale.

We have few good pastorals in the language. Our manners are not Arcadian ; our climate is not an eternal spring ; our age is not the age of gold. We have no pastoral-writers equal to Theocritus, nor any landscapes like those of Claude Lorraine. The best parts of Spenser's Shepherd's Calendar are two fables, Mother Hubberd's Tale, and the Oak and the Briar ; which last is as splendid a piece of oratory as any to be found in the records of the eloquence of the British senate ! Browne, who came after Spenser,

and Withers, have left some pleasing allegorical
poems of this kind. Pope's are as full of sense-
less finery and trite affectation as if a peer of
the realm were to sit for his picture with a
crook and cocked hat on, smiling with an
insipid air of no meaning, between nature and
fashion. Sir Philip Sydney's Arcadia is a
lasting monument of perverted power; where
an image of extreme beauty, as that of " the
shepherd boy piping as though he should
never be old," peeps out once in a hundred
folio pages, amidst heaps of intricate sophistry
and scholastic quaintness. It is not at all like
Nicholas Poussin's picture, in which he represents some shepherds wandering out in a
morning of the spring, and coming to a tomb
with this inscription — " I also was an Arcadian !" Perhaps the best pastoral in the
language is that prose-poem, Walton's Complete Angler. That well-known work has a
beauty and romantic interest equal to its simplicity, and arising out of it. In the description of a fishing-tackle you perceive the piety
and humanity of the author's mind. It is to
be doubted whether Sannazarius's Piscatory
Eclogues are equal to the scenes described by
Walton on the banks of the river Lea. He
gives the feeling of the open air: we walk
with him along the dusty road-side, or repose

on the banks of the river under a shady tree :
and in watching for the finny prey, imbibe
what he beautifully calls " the patience and
simplicity of poor honest fishermen." We
accompany them to their inn at night, and
partake of their simple but delicious fare ;
while Maud, the pretty milk-maid, at her
mother's desire, sings the classical ditties of
the poet Marlow ; " Come live with me, and
be my love." Good cheer is not neglected in
this work, any more than in Homer, or any
other history that sets a proper value on the
good things of this life. The prints in the
Complete Angler give an additional reality
and interest to the scenes it describes. While
Tottenham Cross shall stand, and longer, thy
work, amiable and happy old man, shall last !
—It is in the notes to it that we find that
character of " a fair and happy milk-maid,"
by Sir Thomas Overbury, which may vie in
beauty and feeling with Chaucer's character
of Griselda :

" A fair and happy milk-maid is a country wench that is
so far from making herself beautiful by art that one look of
her's is able to put all face-physic out of countenance. She
knows a fair look is but a dumb orator to commend virtue,
therefore minds it not. All her excellences stand in her so
silently as if they had stolen upon her without her knowledge. The lining of her apparel (which is herself) is far
better than outsides of tissue; for though she be not arrayed

in the spoil of the silk-worm, she is decked in innocency, a far better wearing. She doth not, with lying long in bed, spoil both her complexion and conditions. Nature hath taught her too immoderate sleep is rust to the soul: she rises therefore with chanticleer, her dame's clock, and at night makes the lamb her curfew. Her breath is her own, which scents all the year long of June, like a new-made haycock. She makes her hand hard with labour, and her heart soft with pity; and when winter evenings fall early (sitting at her merry wheel) she sings a defiance to the giddy wheel of Fortune. She doth all things with so sweet a grace, it seems ignorance will not suffer her to do ill, being her mind is to do well. She bestows her year's wages at next fair; and, in choosing her garments, counts no bravery in the world like decency. The garden and the bee-hive are all her physic and chirurgery, and she lives the longer for 't. She dares go alone, and unfold sheep in the night, and fears no manner of ill, because she means none: yet, to say the truth, she is never alone, for she is still accompanied with old songs, honest thoughts, and prayers, but short ones; yet they have their efficacy, in that they are not palled with ensuing idle cogitations. Lastly, her dreams are so chaste that she dare tell them; only a Friday's dream is all her superstition; that she conceals for fear of anger. Thus lives she; and all her care is she may die in the spring-time, to have store of flowers stuck upon her winding-sheet."

The love of the country has been sung by poets, and echoed by philosophers; but the first have not attempted, and the last have been greatly puzzled to account for it. I do not know that any one has ever explained, satisfactorily, the true source of this feeling, or of that soothing emotion which the sight of the country, or a lively description of rural objects hardly ever fails to infuse into the mind. Some have ascribed this feeling to the natural beauty of the objects themselves; others to the freedom from care, the silence and tranquillity which scenes of retirement afford ; others to the healthy and innocent employments of a country life ; others to the simplicity of country manners, and others to a variety of different causes ; but none to the right one. All these, indeed, have their effect; but there is another principal one which has not been touched upon, or only slightly glanced at. I will not, however, imitate Mr. Horne Tooke, who after enumerating seventeen different definitions of the verb, and laughing at them all as deficient and nugatory, at the end of two quarto volumes does not tell us what the verb really is, and has left posterity to pluck out " the heart of his mystery." I will say at once what it is that distinguishes this interest from others, and that is its *abstractedness*. The interest we feel in human nature is exclusive, and confined to the individual; the interest we feel in external nature is common, and transferable from one object to all others of the same class. Thus :

Rousseau in his Confessions relates that,

when he took possession of his room at
Annecy, he found that he could see " a little
spot of green" from his window, which en-
deared his situation the more to him because,
he says, it was the first time he had had this
object constantly before him since he left
Boissy, the place where he was at school when
a child.*   Some such feeling as that here described will be found lurking at the bottom of
all our attachments of this sort.   Were it not
for the recollections habitually associated with
them, natural objects could not interest the
mind in the manner they do.   No doubt, the
sky is beautiful, the clouds sail majestically
along its bosom; the sun is cheering; there
is something exquisitely graceful in the
manner in which a plant or tree puts forth its
branches; the motion with which they bend
and tremble in the evening breeze is soft and
lovely; there is music in the babbling of a
brook; the view from the top of a mountain
is full of grandeur; nor can we behold the
ocean with indifference.   Or, as the Minstrel
sweetly sings,

> " Oh how canst thou renounce the boundless store
> Of charms which Nature to her votary yields !

* Pope also declares that he had a particular regard for
an old post which stood in the court-yard before the house
where he was brought up.

The warbling woodland, the resounding shore,
  The pomp of groves, and garniture of fields ;
All that the genial ray of morning gilds,
  And all that echoes to the song of even,
All that the mountain's sheltering bosom shields,
  And all the dread magnificence of heaven,
Oh, how canst thou renounce, and hope to be forgiven !"

It is not, however, the beautiful and magnificent alone that we admire in Nature ; the
most insignificant and rudest objects are often
found connected with the strongest emotions ;
we become attached to the most common and
familiar images, as to the face of a friend whom
we have long known, and from whom we have
received many benefits.   It is because natural
objects have been associated with the sports
of our childhood, with air and exercise, with
our feelings in solitude, when the mind takes
the strongest hold of things, and clings with
the fondest interest to whatever strikes its attention ; with change of place, the pursuit of
new scenes, and thoughts of distant friends ;
it is because they have surrounded us in
almost all situations, in joy and in sorrow, in
pleasure and in pain ; because they have been
one chief source and nourishment of our
feelings, and a part of our being, that we love
them as we do ourselves.

There is, generally speaking, the same
foundation for our love of Nature as for all

our habitual attachments, namely, association
of ideas. But this is not all. That which
distinguishes this attachment from others is
the transferable nature of our feelings with
respect to physical objects; the associations
connected with any one object extending to
the whole class. Our having been attached
to any particular person does not make us feel
the same attachment to the next person we
may chance to meet; but, if we have once
associated strong feelings of delight with the
objects of natural scenery, the tie becomes
indissoluble, and we shall ever after feel the
same attachment to other objects of the same
sort. I remember, when I was abroad, the
trees, and grass, and wet leaves, rustling in
the walks of the Thuilleries, seemed to be as
much English, to be as much the same trees
and grass, that I had always been used to, as
the sun shining over my head was the same
sun which I saw in England; the faces only
were foreign to me. Whence comes this
difference? It arises from our always imper-
ceptibly connecting the idea of the individual
with man, and only the idea of the class
with natural objects. In the one case, the
external appearance or physical structure is
the least thing to be attended to; in the other,
it is every thing. The springs that move the

human form, and make it friendly or adverse
to me, lie hid within it.   There is an infinity
of motives, passions, and ideas, contained in
that narrow compass, of which I know nothing, and in which I have no share.   Each
individual is a world to himself, governed by
a thousand contradictory and wayward impulses.   I can, therefore, make no inference
from one individual to another; nor can my
habitual sentiments, with respect to any individual, extend beyond himself to others.   A
crowd of people presents a disjointed, confused and unsatisfactory appearance to the eye,
because there is nothing to connect the motley
assemblage into one continuous or general
impression, unless when there is some common
object of interest to fix their attention, as in
the case of a full pit at the play-house.   The
same principle will also account for that feeling of littleness, vacuity, and perplexity, which
a stranger feels on entering the streets of a
populous city.   Every individual he meets is
a blow to his personal identity.   Every new
face is a teazing, unanswered riddle.   He feels
the same wearisome sensation in walking from
Oxford Street to Temple Bar, as a person
would do who should be compelled to read
through the first leaf of all the volumes in a
library.   But it is otherwise with respect to

nature. A flock of sheep is not a contemptible, but a beautiful, sight. The greatest
number and variety of physical objects do not
puzzle the will, or distract the attention, but
are massed together under one uniform and
harmonious feeling. The heart reposes in
greater security on the immensity of Nature's
works, "expatiates freely there," and finds
elbow room and breathing space. We are
always at home with Nature. There is neither
hypocrisy, caprice, nor mental reservation in
her favours. Our intercourse with her is not
liable to accident or change, suspicion or
disappointment: she smiles on us still the
same. A rose is always sweet, a lily is always
beautiful : we do not hate the one, nor envy
the other. If we have once enjoyed the cool
shade of a tree, and been lulled into a deep
repose by the sound of a brook running at its
foot, we are sure that wherever we can find a
shady stream we can enjoy the same pleasure
again ; so that when we imagine these objects,
we can easily form a mystic personification of
the friendly power that inhabits them, Dryad
or Naiad, offering its cool fountain or its
tempting shade. Hence the origin of the
Grecian mythology. All objects of the same
kind being the same, not only in their appearance, but in their practical uses, we habitually

confound them together under the same general idea ; and whatever fondness we may have
conceived for one is immediately placed to
the common account.   The most opposite
kinds and remote trains of feeling gradually
go to enrich the same sentiment ; and in our
love of nature, there is all the force of individual attachment, combined with the most
airy abstraction. It is this circumstance which
gives that refinement, expansion, and wild
interest, to feelings of this sort, when strongly
excited, which every one must have experienced
who is a true lover of nature.

It is the same setting sun that we see and
remember year after year, through summer
and winter, seed-time and harvest. The moon
that shines above our heads, or plays through
the chequered shade, is the same moon that
we used to read of in Mrs. Radcliffe's romances. We see no difference in the trees
first covered with leaves in the spring.   The
dry reeds rustling on the side of a stream—
the woods swept by the loud blast—the dark
massy foliage of autumn—the grey trunks and
naked branches of the trees in winter—the
sequestered copse, and wide-extended heath—
the glittering sunny showers, and December
snows — are still the same, or accompanied
with the same thoughts and feelings : there is

no object, however trifling or rude, that does not in some mood or other find its way into the heart, as a link in the chain of our living being ; and this it is that makes good that saying of the poet —

> " To me the meanest flower that blows can give
> Thoughts that do often lie too deep for tears."

Thus nature is a kind of universal home, and every object it presents to us an old acquaintance with unaltered looks ; for there is that consent and mutual harmony among all her works, one undivided spirit pervading them throughout, that, to him who has well acquainted himself with them, they speak always the same well-known language, striking on the heart, amidst unquiet thoughts and the tumult of the world, like the music of one's native tongue heard in some far-off country.

> " My heart leaps up when I behold
> A rainbow in the sky :
> So was it when my life began,
> So is it now I am a man,
> So shall it be when I grow old and die.
> The child's the father of the man,
> And I would have my years to be
> Linked each to each by natural piety."

The daisy that first strikes the child's eye, in trying to leap over his own shadow, is the same flower that with timid upward glance implores the grown man not to tread upon it.

Rousseau, in one of his botanical excursions, meeting with the periwinkle, fell upon his knees, crying out—*Ah! voila de la pervenche!* It was because he had, thirty years before, brought home the same flower with him in one of his rambles with Madame de Warens, near Chambery. It struck him as the same identical little blue flower that he remembered so well; and thirty years of sorrow and bitter regret were effaced from his memory. That, or a thousand other flowers of the same name, were the same to him, to the heart, and to the eye; but there was but one Madame Warens in the world, whose image was never absent from his thoughts; with whom flowers and verdure sprung up beneath his feet, and without whom all was cold and barren in nature and in his own breast. The cuckoo, " that wandering voice," that comes and goes with the spring, mocks our ears with one note from youth to age; and the lapwing, screaming round the traveller's path, repeats for ever the same sad story of Tereus and Philomel!

LECTURE VI.

———✦———

ON SWIFT, YOUNG, GRAY, COLLINS, &c.

I SHALL in the present Lecture go back to the age of Queen Anne, and endeavour to give a cursory account of the most eminent of our poets, of whom I have not already spoken, from that period to the present.

The three principal poets among the wits of Queen Anne's reign, next to Pope, were Prior, Swift, and Gay. Parnell, though a good-natured, easy man, and a friend to poets and the Muses, was himself little more than an occasional versifier; and Arbuthnot, who had as much wit as the best of them, chose to show it in prose, and not in verse. He had a very notable share in the immortal History of John Bull, and the inimitable and praise-worthy Memoirs of Martinus Scriblerus.— There has been a great deal said and written

about the plagiarisms of Sterne; but the only
real plagiarism he has been guilty of (if such
theft were a crime), is in taking Tristram
Shandy's father from Martin's, the elder
Scriblerus. The original idea of the character,
that is, of the opinionated, captious old gentleman, who is pedantic, not from profession,
but choice, belongs to Arbuthnot. Arbuthnot's style is distinguished from that of his
contemporaries, even by a greater degree of
terseness and conciseness. He leaves out
every superfluous word; is sparing of connecting particles, and introductory phrases;
uses always the simplest forms of construction; and is more a master of the idiomatic
peculiarities and internal resources of the language than almost any other writer. There
is a research in the choice of a plain, as well
as of an ornamented or learned, style; and, in
fact, a great deal more. Among common
English words, there may be ten expressing
the same thing with different degrees of force
and propriety, and only one of them the very
word we want, because it is the only one that
answers exactly with the idea we have in our
minds. Each word in familiar use has a set
of associations and shades of meaning attached
to it, and distinguished from each other by
inveterate custom; and it is in having the

whole of these at our command, and in knowing which to choose, as they are called for by the occasion, that the perfection of a pure conversational prose-style consists. But in writing a florid and artificial style, neither the same range of invention, nor the same quick sense of propriety—nothing but learning is required. If you know the words, and their general meaning, it is sufficient : it is impossible you should know the nicer inflections of signification, depending on an endless variety of application, in expressions borrowed from a foreign or dead language. They all impose upon the ear alike, because they are not familiar to it ; the only distinction left is between the pompous and the plain; the *sesquipedalia verba* have this advantage, that they are all of one length ; and any words are equally fit for a learned style, so that we have never heard them before. Themistocles thought that the same sounding epithets could not suit all subjects, as the same dress does not fit all persons. The style of our modern prose-writers is very fine in itself; but it wants variety of inflection and adaptation ; it hinders us from seeing the differences of the things it undertakes to describe.

What I have here insisted on will be found to be the leading distinction between the style

of Swift, Arbuthnot, Steele, and the other
writers of the age of Queen Anne, and the
style of Dr. Johnson, which succeeded to it.
The one is English, and the other is not.
The writers first mentioned, in order to express their thoughts, looked about them for
the properest word to convey any idea, that
the language which they spoke, and which
their countrymen understood, afforded : Dr.
Johnson takes the first English word that
offers, and, by translating it at a venture into
the first Greek or Latin word he can think of,
only retaining the English termination, produces an extraordinary effect upon the reader,
by much the same sort of mechanical process
that Trim converted the old jack-boots into a
pair of new mortars.

Dr. Johnson was a lazy learned man, who
liked to think and talk better than to read or
write ; who, however, wrote much and well,
but too often by rote. His long compound
Latin phrases required less thought, and took
up more room than others. What shows the
facilities afforded by this style of imposing
generalization is that it was instantly adopted
with success by all those who were writers by
profession, or who were not; and that, at present, we cannot see a lottery puff or a quack
advertisement pasted against a wall, that is

not perfectly Johnsonian in style. Formerly, the learned had the privilege of translating their notions into Latin; and a great privilege it was, as it confined the reputation and emoluments of learning to themselves. Dr. Johnson may be said to have naturalised this privilege, by inventing a sort of jargon translated half-way out of one language into the other, which raised the Doctor's reputation, and confounded all ranks in literature.

In the short period above alluded to, authors professed to write as other men spoke ; every body now affects to speak as authors write ; and any one who retains the use of his mother tongue, either in writing or conversation, is looked upon as a very illiterate character.

Prior and Gay belong, in the characteristic excellences of their style, to the same class of writers with Suckling, Rochester, and Sedley : the former imbibed most of the licentious levity of the age of Charles II. and carried it on beyond the Revolution under King William. Prior has left no single work equal to Gay's Fables, or the Beggar's Opera. But in his lyrical and fugitive pieces he has shown even more genius, more playfulness, more mischievous gaiety. No one has exceeded him in the laughing grace with which he

glances at a subject that will not bear exami-
ning, with which he gently hints at what
cannot be directly insisted on, with which he
half conceals, and half draws aside, the veil
from some of the Muses' nicest mysteries.
His Muse is, in fact, a giddy wanton flirt, who
spends her time in playing at snap-dragon and
blind-man's buff, who tells what she should
not, and knows more than she tells. She
laughs at the tricks she shows us, and blushes,
or would be thought to do so, at what she
keeps concealed. Prior has translated several
of Fontaine's Tales from the French; and
they have lost nothing in the translation,
either of their wit or malice. I need not
name them: but the one I like the most is
that of Cupid in search of Venus's doves. No
one could insinuate a knavish plot, a tender
point, a loose moral, with such unconscious
archness, and careless raillery, as if he gained
new self-possession and adroitness from the
perplexity and confusion into which he throws
scrupulous imaginations, and knew how to
seize on all the ticklish parts of his subject,
from their involuntarily shrinking under his
grasp. Some of his imitations of Boileau's
servile addresses to Louis XIV. which he has
applied with a happy mixture of wit and

patriotic enthusiasm to King William, or as he familiarly calls him, to

> " Little Will, the scourge of France,
>   No Godhead, but the first of men,"

are excellent, and show the same talent for *double-entendre* and the same gallantry of spirit, whether in the softer lyric, or the more lively heroic. Some of Prior's *bon mots* are the best that are recorded. His serious poetry, as his *Solomon*, is as heavy as his familiar style was light and agreeable. His moral Muse is a Magdalen, and should not have obtruded herself on public view. Henry and Emma is a paraphrase of the old ballad of the Nut-brown Maid, and not so good as the original. In short, as we often see in other cases, where men thwart their own genius, Prior's senti-mental and romantic productions are mere affectation, the result not of powerful impulse or real feeling, but of a consciousness of his deficiencies, and a wish to supply their place by labour and art.

Gay was sometimes grosser than Prior, not systematically, but inadvertently — from not being so well aware of what he was about; nor was there the same necessity for caution, for his grossness is by no means so seductive or inviting.

Gay's Fables are certainly a work of great merit, both as to the quantity of invention implied, and as to the elegance and facility of the execution. They are, however, spun out too long; the descriptions and narrative are too diffuse and deusltory ; and the moral is sometimes without point. They are more like Tales than fables. The best are, perhaps, the Hare with Many Friends, the Monkeys, and the Fox at the Point of Death. His Pastorals are pleasing and poetical. But his capital work is his Beggar's Opera. It is indeed a masterpiece of wit and genius, not to say of morality. In composing it, he chose a very unpromising ground to work upon, and he has prided himself in adorning it with all the graces, the precision, and brilliancy of style. It is a vulgar error to call this a vulgar play. So far from it that I do not scruple to say that it appears to me one of the most refined productions in the language. The elegance of the composition is in exact proportion to the coarseness of the materials : by " happy alchemy of mind," the author has extracted an essence of refinement from the dregs of human life, and turns its very dross into gold. The scenes, characters, and incidents are, in themselves, of the lowest and most disgusting kind : but, by the sentiments

and reflections which are put into the mouths
of highwaymen, turnkeys, their mistresses,
wives, or daughters, he has converted this
motley group into a set of fine gentlemen and
ladies, satirists and philosophers.   He has
also effected this transformation without once
violating probability, or " o'erstepping the
modesty of nature."   In fact, Gay has turned
the tables on the critics ; and by the assumed
license of the mock-heroic style, has enabled
himself to *do justice to nature*, that is, to give
all the force, truth, and locality of real feeling
to the thoughts and expressions, without being
called to the bar of false taste and affected
delicacy.   The extreme beauty and feeling of
the song, " Woman is like the fair flower in
its lustre," are only equalled by its characteristic propriety and *naïveté*.   *Polly* describes
her lover going to the gallows with the same
touching simplicity, and with all the natural
fondness of a young girl in her circumstances,
who sees, in his approaching catastrophe,
nothing but the misfortunes and the personal
accomplishments of the object of her affections.   " I see him sweeter than the nosegay
in his hand ; the admiring crowd lament that
so lovely a youth should come to an untimely
end : even butchers weep, and Jack Ketch
refuses his fee rather than consent to tie the

fatal knot." The preservation of the character and costume is complete. It has been said by a great authority—" There is some soul of goodness in things evil :" and the *Beggar's Opera* is a good-natured but instructive comment on this text. The poet has thrown all the gaiety and sunshine of the imagination, all the intoxication of pleasure, and the vanity of despair, round the short-lived existence of his heroes ; while *Peachum* and *Lockitt* are seen in the back-ground, parcelling out their months and weeks between them. The general view exhibited of human life is of the most subtle and abstracted kind. The author has, with great felicity, brought out the good qualities and interesting emotions almost inseparable from the lowest conditions; and, with the same penetrating glance, has detected the disguises which rank and circumstances lend to exalted vice. Every line in this sterling comedy sparkles with wit, and is fraught with the keenest sarcasm. The very wit, however, takes off from the offensiveness of the satire ; and I have seen great statesmen, very great statesmen, heartily enjoying the joke, laughing most immoderately at the compliments paid to them, as not much worse than pickpockets and cut-throats in a different line of life, and pleased, as it were, to see themselves humanised by some sort of fellowship with their kind. Indeed, it may be said that the moral of the piece is *to show the vulgarity of vice;* or that the same violations of integrity and decorum, the same habitual sophistry in palliating their want of principle, are common to the great and powerful, with the meanest and most contemptible of the species. What can be more convincing than the arguments used by these would-be politicians, to show that, in hypocrisy, selfishness and treachery, they do not come up to many of their betters? The exclamation of *Mrs. Peachum,* when her daughter marries *Macheath,* " Hussy, hussy, you will be as ill used, and as much neglected, as if you had married a lord," is worth all Miss Hannah More's laboured invectives on the laxity of the manners of high life!

I shall conclude this account of Gay with his verses on Sir Richard Blackmore, which may serve at once as a specimen of his own manner, and as a character of a voluminous contemporary poet, who was admired by Mr. Locke and knighted by King William III.

" See who ne'er was nor will be half-read,
Who first sung Arthur, then sung Alfred ;
Praised great Eliza in God's anger,
Till all true Englishmen cried, ' Hang her !'"—

> Maul'd human wit in one thick satire ;
> Next in three books spoil'd human nature :
> Undid Creation at a jerk,
> And of Redemption made damn'd work.
> Then took his Muse at once, and dipt her
> Full in the middle of the Scripture.
> What wonders there the man, grown old, did !
> Sternhold himself he out-Sternholded.
> Made David seem so mad and freakish,
> All thought him just what thought King Achish.
> No mortal read his Solomon
> But judg'd Re'boam his own son.
> Moses he serv'd as Moses Pharaoh,
> And Deborah as she Siserah ;
> Made Jeremy full sore to cry,
> And Job himself curse God and die.
> What punishment all this must follow ?
> Shall Arthur use him like King Tollo ?
> Shall David as Uriah slay him ?
> Or dextrous Deborah Siserah him ?
> No !—none of these ! Heaven spare his life !
> But send him, honest Job, thy wife !"

Gay's Trivia, or Art of Walking the Streets, is as pleasant as walking the streets must have been at the time when it was written. His ballad of Black Eyed Susan is one of the most delightful that can be imagined ; nor do I see that it is a bit the worse for Mr. Jekyll's parody on it.

Swift's reputation as a poet has been in a manner obscured by the greater splendour, by the natural force and inventive genius of his prose writings ; but if he had never written either the Tale of a Tub or Gulliver's Travels, his name merely as a poet would have come down to us, and have gone down to posterity, with well-earned honours. His imitations of Horace, and still more his Verses on his own Death, place him in the first rank of agreeable moralists in verse. There is not only a dry humour, an exquisite tone of irony, in these productions of his pen, but there is a touching, unpretending pathos, mixed up with the most whimsical and eccentric strokes of pleasantry and satire. His Description of the Morning in London, and of a City Shower, which were first published in the Tatler, are among the most delightful of the contents of that very delightful work. Swift shone as one of the most sensible of the poets; he is also distinguished as one of the most nonsensical of them. No man has written so many lack-a-daisical, slip-shod, tedious, trifling, foolish, fantastical verses as he, which are so little an imputation on the wisdom of the writer; and which, in fact, only show his readiness to oblige others, and to forget himself. He has gone so far as to invent a new stanza of fourteen and sixteen syllable lines for Mary the cookmaid to vent her budget of nothings, and for Mrs. Harris to gossip with the deaf old housekeeper. Oh, when shall we have such

another Rector of Laracor!—The Tale of a
Tub is one of the most masterly compositions
in the language, whether for thought, wit, or
style.   It is so capital and undeniable a proof
of the author's talents, that Dr. Johnson, who
did not like Swift, would not allow that he
wrote it.   It is hard that the same performance
should stand in the way of a man's promotion
to a bishopric, as wanting gravity, and at the
same time be denied to be his, as having too
much wit.   It is a pity the Doctor did not
find out some graver author, for whom he felt
a critical kindness, on whom to father this
splendid, but unacknowledged, production.—
Dr. Johnson could not deny that Gulliver's
Travels were his ; he therefore disputed their
merits, and said that, after the first idea of them
was conceived, they were easy to execute ; all
the rest followed mechanically.   I do not know
how that may be ; but the mechanism em-
ployed is something very different from any
that the author of Rasselas was in the habit of
bringing to bear on such occasions.   There is
nothing more futile, as well as invidious, than
this mode of criticising a work of original
genius.   Its greatest merit is supposed to be
in the invention ; and you say, very wisely,
that it is not *in the execution.*   You might as
well take away the merit of the invention of

the telescope, by saying that, after its uses
were explained and understood, any ordinary
eyesight could look through it.   Whether the
excellence of Gulliver's Travels is in the
conception or the execution, is of little consequence ; the power is somewhere, and it is a
power that has moved the world. The power
is not that of big words and vaunting common
places.   Swift left these to those who wanted
them ; and has done what his acuteness and
intensity of mind alone could enable any one
to conceive or to perform. His object was to
strip empty pride and grandeur of the imposing
air which external circumstances throw around
them ; and for this purpose he has cheated
the imagination of the illusions which the
prejudices of sense and of the world put upon
it, by reducing every thing to the abstract
predicament of size. He enlarges or dimi-
nishes the scale, as he wishes, to show the
insignificance or the grossness of our over-
weening self-love. That he has done this
with mathematical precision, with complete
presence of mind and perfect keeping, in a
manner that comes equally home to the understanding of the man and of the child, does not
take away from the merit of the work or the
genius of the author. He has taken a new
view of human nature, such as a being of a

higher sphere might take of it; he has torn
the scales from off his moral vision; he has
tried an experiment upon human life, and
sifted its pretensions from the alloy of circumstances; he has measured it with a rule, has
weighed it in a balance, and found it, for the
most part, wanting and worthless, in substance
and in show. Nothing solid, nothing valuable
is left in his system but virtue and wisdom.
What a libel is this upon mankind! What
a convincing proof of misanthropy! What
presumption and what *malice prepense*, to
show men what they are, and to teach them
what they ought to be! What a mortifying
stroke, aimed at national glory, is that unlucky
incident of Gulliver's wading across the chan-
nel and carrying off the whole fleet of Blefuscu!
After that, we have only to consider which of
the contending parties was in the right. What
a shock to personal vanity is given in the
account of Gulliver's nurse Glumdalclitch!
Still, notwithstanding the disparagement to
her personal charms, her good nature remains
the same amiable quality as before. I cannot
see the harm, the misanthropy, the immoral
and degrading tendency of this. The moral
lesson is as fine as the intellectual exhibition
is amusing. It is an attempt to tear off the
mask of imposture from the world; and no-

thing but imposture has a right to complain
of it. It is, indeed, the way with our quacks
in morality to preach up the dignity of human
nature, to pamper pride and hypocrisy with
the idle mockeries of the virtues they pretend
to, and which they have not : but it was not
Swift's way to cant morality, or any thing
else; nor did his genius prompt him to write
unmeaning panegyrics on mankind !

I do not, therefore, agree with the estimate
of Swift's moral or intellectual character,
given by an eminent critic, who does not seem
to have forgotten the party politics of Swift.
I do not carry my political resentments so far
back : I can at this time of day forgive Swift
for having been a Tory. I feel little disturbance (whatever I might think of them) at his
political sentiments, which died with him,
considering how much else he has left behind
him of a more solid and imperishable nature !
If he had, indeed, (like some others) merely
left behind him the lasting infamy of a de-
stroyer of his country, or the shining example
of an apostate from liberty, I might have
thought the case altered.

The determination with which Swift per-
sisted in a preconcerted theory, savoured of
the morbid affection of which he died. There
is nothing more likely to drive a man mad

than the being unable to get rid of the idea
of the distinction between right and wrong,
and an obstinate, constitutional preference of
the true to the agreeable. Swift was not a
Frenchman. In this respect he differed from
Rabelais and Voltaire. They have been ac-
counted the three greatest wits in modern
times ; but their wit was of a peculiar kind
in each. They are little beholden to each
other ; there is some resemblance between
Lord Peter in the Tale of a Tub, and
Rabelais' Friar John ; but in general they are
all three authors of a substantive character in
themselves. Swift's wit (particularly in his
chief prose works) was serious, saturnine, and
practical ; Rabelais' was fantastical and
joyous ; Voltaire's was light, sportive, and
verbal. Swift's wit was the wit of sense ;
Rabelais', the wit of nonsense ; Voltaire's, of
indifference to both. The ludicrous in Swift
arises out of his keen sense of impropriety,
his soreness and impatience of the least
absurdity. He separates, with a severe and
caustic air, truth from falsehood, folly from
wisdom, " shews vice her own image, scorn
her own feature ;" and it is the force, the
precision, and the honest abruptness with
which the separation is made, that excites our
surprise, our admiration, and laughter. He

sets a mark of reprobation on that which offends good sense and good manners, which cannot be mistaken, and which holds it up to our ridicule and contempt ever after. His occasional disposition to trifling (already noticed) was a relaxation from the excessive earnestness of his mind. *Indignatio facit versus.* His better genius was his spleen. It was the biting acrimony of his temper that sharpened his other faculties. The truth of his perceptions produced the pointed coruscations of his wit; his playful irony was the result of inward bitterness of thought; his imagination was the product of the literal, dry, incorrigible tenaciousness of his understanding. He endeavoured to escape from the persecution of realities into the regions of fancy, and invented his Lilliputians and Brobdignagians, Yahoos, and Houynhyms, as a diversion to the more painful knowledge of the world around him : *they* only made him laugh, while men and women made him angry. His feverish impatience made him view the infirmities of that great baby the world with the same scrutinizing glance and jealous irritability that a parent regards the failings of its offspring ; but, as Rousseau has well observed, parents have not on this account been supposed to have more affection

for other people's children than their own.
In other respects, and except from the sparkling effervescence of his gall, Swift's brain was
as " dry as the remainder biscuit after a
voyage." He hated absurdity—Rabelais loved
it, exaggerated it with supreme satisfaction,
luxuriated in its endless varieties, rioted in
nonsense, " reigned there and revelled." He
dwelt on the absurd and ludicrous for the
pleasure they gave him, not for the pain. He
lived upon laughter, and died laughing. He
indulged his vein, and took his full swing of
folly. He did not baulk his fancy or his
readers. His wit was to him " as riches fine-
less;" he saw no end of his wealth in that
way, and set no limits to his extravagance : he
was communicative, prodigal, boundless, and
inexhaustible. His were the Saturnalia of wit,
the riches and the royalty, the health and long
life. He is intoxicated with gaiety, mad with
folly. His animal spirits drown him in a
flood of mirth: his blood courses up and
down his veins like wine. His thirst of enjoyment is as great as his thirst of drink : his
appetite for good things of all sorts is unsa-
tisfied, and there is a never-ending supply.
Discourse is dry ; so they moisten their words
in their cups, and relish their dry jests with
plenty of Botargos and dried neats' tongues.

It is like Camacho's wedding in Don Quixote,
where Sancho ladled out whole pullets and
fat geese from the soup - kettles at a pull.
The flagons are set a running, their tongues
wag at the same time, and their mirth flows
as a river.   How Friar John roars and lays
about him in the vineyard!   How Panurge
whines in the storm, and how dexterously he
contrives to throw the sheep overboard!   How
much Pantagruel behaves like a wise king!
How Gargantua mewls, and pules, and
slabbers his nurse, and demeans himself most
like a royal infant!   what provinces he de-
vours!   what seas he drinks up!   How he
eats, drinks, and sleeps — sleeps, eats, and
drinks!   The style of Rabelais is no less
prodigious than his matter.   His words are of
marrow, unctuous, dropping fatness.   He was
a mad wag, the king of good fellows, and
prince of practical philosophers!

Rabelais was a Frenchman of the old
school—Voltaire of the new.   The wit of
the one arose from an exuberance of enjoyment—of the other, from an excess of indifference, real or assumed.   Voltaire had no
enthusiasm for one thing or another : he made
light of every thing.   In his hands all things
turn to chaff and dross, as the pieces of silver
money in the Arabian Nights were changed

by the hands of the enchanter into little dry
crumbling leaves! He is a Parisian. He
never exaggerates, is never violent : he treats
things with the most provoking *sang froid;*
and expresses his contempt by the most indirect hints, and in the fewest words, as if he
hardly thought them worth even his contempt.
He retains complete possession of himself and
of his subject. He does not effect his pur-
by the eagerness of his blows, but by the
delicacy of his tact. The poisoned wound he
inflicted was so fine as scarcely to be felt till
it rankled and festered in its "mortal consequences." His callousness was an excellent
foil for the antagonists he had mostly to deal
with. He took knaves and fools on his shield
well. He stole away its cloak from grave imposture. If he reduced other things below
their true value, making them seem worthless
and hollow, he did not degrade the pretensions
of tyranny and superstition below their true
value, by making them seem utterly worthless
and hollow, as contemptible as they were
odious. This was the service he rendered to
truth and mankind ! His *Candide* is a masterpiece of wit. It has been called " the dull
product of a scoffer's pen." It is, indeed,
" the product of a scoffer's pen ;" but after
reading the Excursion, few people will think

it *dull*. It is in the most perfect keeping,
and without any appearance of effort. Every
sentence tells, and the whole reads like one
sentence.   There is something sublime in
Martin's   sceptical   indifference   to   moral
good and evil.   It is the repose of the grave.
It is better to suffer this living death than a
living martyrdom.   " Nothing can touch him
further."   The moral of Candide (such as it
is) is the same as that of Rasselas : the execution is different.   Voltaire says, " A great
book is a great evil."   Dr. Johnson would have
laboured this short apophthegm into a voluminous commonplace.   Voltaire's traveller (in
another work) being asked " whether he likes
black or white mutton best," replies that " he
is indifferent, provided it is tender."   Dr.
Johnson did not get at a conclusion by so
short a way as this.   If Voltaire's licentiousness is objected to me, I say, let it be placed
to its true account, the manners of the age
and court in which he lived.   The lords and
ladies of the bedchamber in the reign of
Louis XV. found no fault with the immoral
tendency of his writings.   Why then should
our modern *purists* quarrel with them ?—But
to return.

Young is a gloomy epigrammatist. He has
abused great powers both of thought and

language.   His moral reflections are sometimes excellent; but he spoils their beauty by
overloading them with a religious horror, and
at the same time giving them all the smart
turns and quaint expressions of an enigma or
repartee in verse.   The well-known lines on
Procrastination are in his best manner:

> " Be wise to-day; 'tis madness to defer;
> Next day the fatal precedent will plead;
> Thus on, till wisdom is push'd out of life.
> Procrastination is the thief of time;
> Year after year it steals, till all are fled,
> And to the mercies of a moment leaves
> The vast concerns of an eternal scene.

> " Of man's miraculous mistakes, this bears
> The palm, ' That all men are about to live,'
> For ever on the brink of being born.
> All pay themselves the compliment to think
> They, one day, shall not drivel; and their pride
> On this reversion takes up ready praise;
> At least, their own; their future selves applauds;
> How excellent that life they ne'er will lead!
> Time lodg'd in their own hands is Folly's vails:
> That lodg'd in Fate's, to Wisdom they consign;
> The thing they can't but purpose they postpone.
> 'Tis not in Folly not to scorn a fool;
> And scarce in human Wisdom to do more.
> All promise is poor dilatory man,
> And that through every stage.   When young, indeed,
> In full content, we, sometimes, nobly rest,
> Un-anxious for ourselves; and only wish,
> As duteous sons, our fathers were more wise.
> At thirty man suspects himself a fool;
> Knows it at forty, and reforms his plan;

At fifty chides his infamous delay,
Pushes his prudent purpose to resolve ;
In all the magnanimity of thought
Resolves, and re-resolves ; then dies the same.

"And why ? Because he thinks himself immortal.
All men think all men mortal, but themselves ;
Themselves, when some alarming shock of fate
Strikes through their wounded hearts the sudden dread ;
But their hearts wounded, like the wounded air,
Soon close ; where, past the shaft, no trace is found.
As from the wing no scar the sky retains ;
The parted wave no furrow from the keel ;
So dies in human hearts the thought of death.
Ev'n with the tender tear which nature sheds
O'er those we love, we drop it in their grave."

His Universal Passion is a keen and powerful satire ; but the effort takes from the effect, and oppresses attention by perpetual and violent demands upon it.   His tragedy of the Revenge is monkish and scholastic.   Zanga is a vulgar caricature of Iago.   The finest lines in it are the burst of triumph at the end, when his revenge is completed :

"Let Europe and her pallid sons go weep,
Let Afric on her hundred thrones rejoice," &c.

Collins is a writer of a very different stamp, who had perhaps less general power of mind than Young ; but he had that true *vivida vis*, that genuine inspiration, which alone can give birth to the highest efforts of poetry.   He

leaves stings in the minds of his readers, certain traces of thought and feeling, which
never wear out, because nature had left them
in his own mind. He is the only one of the
minor poets of whom, if he had lived, it cannot be said that he might not have done the
greatest things. The germ is there. He is
sometimes affected, unmeaning, and obscure ;
but he also catches rich glimpses of the
bowers of Paradise, and has lofty aspirations
after the highest seats of the Muses. With a
great deal of tinsel and splendid patch-work,
he has not been able to hide the solid sterling
ore of genius. In his best works there is an
attic simplicity, a pathos, and fervour of
imagination, which make us the more lament
that the efforts of his mind were at first de-
pressed by neglect and pecuniary embarrass-
ment, and at length buried in the gloom of
an unconquerable and fatal malady. How
many poets have gone through all the horrors
of poverty and contempt, and ended their
days in moping melancholy or moody madness !

" We poets in our youth begin in gladness,
    But thereof comes in the end despondency and madness."

Is this the fault of themselves, of nature in
tempering them of too fine a clay, or of the
world, that spurner of living, and patron of

dead merit? Read the account of Collins—
with hopes frustrated, with faculties blighted,
at last when it was too late for himself or
others, receiving the deceitful favours of re-
lenting Fortune, which served only to throw
their sunshine on his decay, and to light him
to an early grave. He was found sitting with
every spark of imagination extinguished, and
with only the faint traces of memory and
reason left — with only one book in his room,
the Bible; " but that," he said, " was the
best. " A melancholy damp hung like an
unwholesome mildew upon his faculties — a
canker had consumed the flower of his life.
He produced works of genius, and the public
regarded them with scorn : he aimed at excellence that should be his own, and his friends
treated his efforts as the wanderings of fatuity.
The proofs of his capacity are, his Ode on
Evening, his Ode on the Passions (particularly the fine personification of Hope),
his Ode to Fear, the Dirge in Cymbe-
line, the Lines on Thomson's Grave, and
his Eclogues, parts of which are admirable. But perhaps his Ode on the Poetical
Character is the best of all. A rich distilled
perfume emanates from it like the breath of
genius; a golden cloud envelopes it; a honeyed
paste of poetic diction encrusts it, like the

candied coat of the auricula. His Ode to
Evening shows equal genius in the images and
versification. The sounds steal slowly over
the ear, like the gradual coming on of evening
itself :

" If aught of oaten stop or pastoral song
    May hope, chaste Eve, to soothe thy modest ear,
        Like thy own solemn springs,
        Thy springs and dying gales,

O nymph reserv'd, while now the bright-haired sun
Sits on yon western tent, whose cloudy skirts
        With brede ethereal wove,
        O'erhang his wavy bed :

Now air is hush'd, save where the weak-ey'd bat,
With short shrill shriek, flits by on leathern wing,
        Or where the beetle winds
        His small but sullen horn,

As oft he rises midst the twilight path,
Against the pilgrim borne in heedless hum.
        Now teach me, maid compos'd,
        To breathe some soften'd strain,

Whose numbers, stealing through thy darkling vale,
May not unseemly with its stillness suit,
        As, musing slow, I hail
        Thy genial, lov'd return !

For when thy folding star arising shows
His paly circlet, at his warning lamp
        The fragrant Hours and Elves
        Who slept in flow'rs the day,

And many a nymph who wreathes her brows with sedge
And sheds the fresh'ning dew, and, lovelier still,
        The pensive Pleasures sweet
        Prepare thy shadowy car ;

Then lead, calm Votress, where some sheety lake
Cheers the lone heath, or some time-hallow'd pile,
  Or upland fallows grey
  Reflect its last cool gleam.

But when chill blust'ring winds, or driving rain,
Forbid my willing feet, be mine the hut,
  That from the mountain's side
  Views wilds and swelling floods,

And hamlets brown, and dim discover'd spires,
And hears their simple bell, and marks o'er all
  Thy dewy fingers draw
  The gradual dusky veil.

While Spring shall pour his show'rs, as oft he wont,
And bathe thy breathing tresses, meekest Eve!
  While Summer loves to sport
  Beneath thy lingering light;

While sallow Autumn fills thy lap with leaves;
Or Winter yelling through the troublous air,
  Affrights thy shrinking train,
  And rudely rends thy robes;

So long, sure-found beneath the sylvan shed,
Shall Fancy, Friendship, Science, rose-lipp'd Health,
  Thy gentlest influence own,
  And hymn thy favourite name."

Hammond, whose poems are bound up with Collins's, in Bell's pocket edition, was a young gentleman, who appears to have fallen in love about the year 1740, and who translated Tibullus into English verse, to let his mistress and the public know of it.

I should conceive that Collins had a much greater poetical genius than Gray: he had more of that fine madness which is inseparable from it, of its turbid effervescence, of all that pushes it to the verge of agony or rapture. Gray's Pindaric Odes are, I believe, generally given up at present : they are stately and pedantic, a kind of methodical borrowed phrenzy. But I cannot so easily give up, nor will the world be in any haste to part with, his Elegy in a Country Church-yard : it is one of the most classical productions that ever was penned by a refined and thoughtful mind, moralising on human life. Mr. Coleridge (in his Literary Life) says that his friend Mr. Wordsworth had undertaken to show that the language of the Elegy is unintelligible : it has, however, been understood ! The Ode on a Distant Prospect of Eton College is more mechanical and common-place; but it touches on certain strings about the heart, that vibrate in unison with it to our latest breath. No one ever passes by Windsor's " stately heights," or sees the distant spires of Eton College below, without thinking of Gray. He deserves that we should think of him ; for he thought of others, and turned a trembling, ever-watchful ear to " the still sad music of humanity."— His letters are inimitably fine. If his poems are sometimes finical and pedantic, his prose is quite free from affectation. He pours his thoughts out upon paper as they arise in his mind; and they arise in his mind without pretence, or constraint, from the pure impulse of learned leisure and contemplative indolence. He is not here on stilts or in buckram; but smiles in his easy chair, as he moralises through the loopholes of retreat, on the bustle and raree-show of the world, or on " those reverend bedlams, colleges, and schools !"— He had nothing to do but to read and to think, and to tell his friends what he read and thought. His life was a luxurious thoughtful dream. " Be mine," he says in one of his Letters, " to read eternal new romances of Marivaux and Crebillon." And in another, to show his contempt for action and the turmoils of ambition, he says to some one, " Don't you remember Lords —— and ——, who are now great statesmen, little dirty boys playing at cricket? For my part, I do not feel a bit wiser, or bigger, or older than I did then." What an equivalent for not being wise or great, to be always young ! What a happiness never to lose or gain any thing in the game of human life, by being never any thing more than a looker-on !

How different from Shenstone, who only wanted to be looked at : who withdrew from the world to be followed by the crowd, and

courted popularity by affecting privacy! His
Letters show him to have lived in a continual
fever of petty vanity, and to have been a
finished literary coquet.   He seems always
to say, " You will find nothing in the world
so amiable as Nature and me : come, and
admire us."   His poems are indifferent and
tasteless, except his Pastoral Ballad, his Lines
on Jemmy Dawson, and his School-mistress,
which last is a perfect piece of writing.

Akenside had in him the materials of poetry,
but he was hardly a great poet. He improved
his Pleasures of the Imagination in the subse-
quent editions, by pruning away a great many
redundances of style and ornament.   Arm-
strong is better, though he has not chosen
a very exhilarating subject — The Art of Pre-
serving Health.   Churchill's Satires on the
Scotch, and Characters of the Players, are as
good as the subject deserved : they are strong,
coarse, and full of an air of hardened assu-
rance.   I ought not to pass over without
mention Green's Poem on the Spleen, or
Dyer's Grongar Hill.

The principal name of the period we are
now come to is that of Goldsmith, than which
few names stand higher or fairer in the annals
of modern literature.   One should have his
own pen to describe him as he ought to be

described — amiable, various, and bland, with
careless inimitable grace touching on every
kind of excellence — with manners unstudied,
but a gentle heart — performing miracles of
skill from pure happiness of nature, and whose
greatest fault was ignorance of his own worth.
As a poet, he is the most flowing and elegant
of our versifiers since Pope, with traits of
artless nature which Pope had not, and with
a peculiar felicity in his turns upon words,
which he constantly repeated with delightful
effect : such as —

> "———— His lot, though small,
> He sees that little lot, the lot of all."
>
> *   *   *   *
> " And turn'd and look'd, and turn'd to look again."

As a novelist, his Vicar of Wakefield has
charmed all Europe.   What reader is there in
the civilised world who is not the better for
the story of the washes which the worthy Dr.
Primrose demolished so deliberately with the
poker — for the knowledge of the guinea
which the Miss Primroses kept unchanged in
their pockets — the adventure of the picture
of the Vicar's family, which could not be got
into the house—and that of the Flamborough
family, all painted with oranges in their hands
—or for the story of the case of shagreen
spectacles and the cosmogony ?

As a comic writer, his Tony Lumpkin

draws forth new powers from Mr. Liston's face. That alone is praise enough for it. Poor Goldsmith! how happy he has made others! how unhappy he was in himself! He never had the pleasure of reading his own works! He had only the satisfaction of good-naturedly relieving the necessities of others, and the consolation of being harassed to death with his own! He is the most amusing and interesting person, in one of the most amusing and interesting books in the world, Boswell's Life of Johnson. His peach-coloured coat shall always bloom in Boswell's writings, and his fame survive in his own!—His genius was a mixture of originality and imitation : he could do nothing without some model before him, and he could copy nothing that he did not adorn with the graces of his own mind.—Almost all the latter part of the Vicar of Wakefield, and a great deal of the former, is taken from Joseph Andrews; but the circumstances I have mentioned above are not.

The finest things he has left behind him in verse are his character of a country schoolmaster, and that prophetic description of Burke in the Retaliation. His moral Essays, in the Citizen of the World, are as agreeable chit-chat as can be conveyed in the form of didactic discourses.

Warton was a poet and a scholar, studious with ease, learned without affectation. He had a happiness which some have been prouder of than he, who deserved it less— he was poet-laureat.

> " And that green wreath which decks the bard when dead,
> That laurel garland, crown'd his living head."

But he bore his honours meekly, and performed his half-yearly task regularly. 1 should not have mentioned him for this distinction alone (the highest which a poet can receive from the state), but for another circumstance; I mean his being the author of some of the finest sonnets in the language — at least so they appear to me; and as this species of composition has the necessary advantage of being short (though it is also sometimes both " tedious and brief,") I will here repeat two or three of them, as treating pleasing subjects in a pleasing and philosophical way.

Written in a blank leaf of Dugdale's Monasticon.

> " Deem not, devoid of elegance, the sage,
> By Fancy's genuine feelings unbeguil'd,
> Of painful pedantry the poring child ;
> Who turns of these proud domes the historic page,
> Now sunk by Time, and Henry's fiercer rage.
> Think'st thou the warbling Muses never smil'd
> On his lone hours ? Ingenuous views engage
> His thoughts, on themes unclassic falsely styl'd,
> Intent. While cloister'd piety displays

Her mouldering roll, the piercing eye explores
New manners, and the pomp of elder days,
Whence culls the pensive bard his pictur'd stores.
Not rough nor barren are the winding ways
Of hoar Antiquity, but strewn with flowers."

Sonnet.   Written at Stonehenge.

" Thou noblest monument of Albion's isle,
    Whether, by Merlin's aid, from Scythia's shore
    To Amber's fatal plain Pendragon bore,
    Huge frame of giant hands, the mighty pile,
    T' entomb his Britons slain by Hengist's guile:
    Or Druid priests, sprinkled with human gore,
    Taught 'mid thy massy maze their mystic lore:
    Or Danish chiefs, enrich'd with savage spoil,
    To victory's idol vast, an unhewn shrine,
    Rear'd the rude heap, or in thy hallow'd ground
    Repose the kings of Brutus' genuine line;
    Or here those kings in solemn state were crown'd;
    Studious to trace thy wondrous origin,
    We muse on many an ancient tale renown'd."

Nothing can be more admirable than the
learning here displayed, or the inference from
it, that it is of no use but as it leads to interesting thought and reflection.

That written after seeing Wilton House is
in the same style, but I prefer concluding
with that to the river Lodon, which has a
personal, as well as poetical, interest about it.

" Ah ! what a weary race my feet have run,
    Since first I trod thy banks with alders crown'd,
    And thought my way was all through fairy ground,
    Beneath the azure sky and golden sun :
    When first my Muse to lisp her notes begun !

While pensive memory traces back the round
Which fills the varied interval between ;
Much pleasure, more of sorrow, marks the scene
Sweet native stream ! those skies and suns so pure
No more return, to cheer my evening road !
Yet still one joy remains, that not obscure
Nor useless all my vacant days have flow'd
From youth's gay dawn to manhood's prime mature,
Nor with the Muse's laurel unbestow'd."

I have thus gone through all the names of
this period I could think of, but I find that
there are others still waiting behind that I had
never thought of.   Here is a list of some of
them — Pattison, Tickell, Hill, Somerville,
Browne, Pitt, Wilkie, Dodsley, Shaw, Smart,
Langhorne, Bruce, Greame, Glover, Lovi-
bond, Penrose, Mickle, Jago, Scott, White-
head, Jenyns, Logan, Cotton, Cunningham,
and Blacklock.   I think it will be best to let
them pass and say nothing about them.   It
will be hard to persuade so many respectable
persons that they are dull writers, and if we
give them any praise, they will send others.

But here comes one whose claims cannot
be so easily set aside : they have been sanctioned by learning, hailed by genius, and
hallowed by misfortune — I mean Chatterton.
Yet I must say what I think of him, and that
is not what is generally thought.   I pass over
the disputes between the learned antiquaries,
Dr. Mills, Herbert Croft, and Dr. Knox,

whether he was to be placed after Shakspeare
and Dryden, or to come after Shakspeare
alone.   A living poet has borne a better testimony to him —

> " I thought of Chatterton, the marvellous boy,
>   The sleepless soul that perished in his pride ;
> And him* who walked in glory and in joy
>   Beside his plough along the mountain side."

I am loth to put asunder whom so great an
authority has joined together; but I cannot
find in Chatterton's works any thing so extraordinary as the age at which they were written.
They have a facility, vigour, and knowledge,
which were prodigious in a boy of sixteen,
but which would not have been so in a man
of twenty.   He did not shew extraordinary
powers of genius, but extraordinary precocity.
Nor do I believe he would have written better
had he lived.   He knew this himself, or he
would have lived.   Great geniuses, like great
kings, have too much to think of to kill themselves ; for their mind to them also " a kingdom is."   With an unaccountable power
coming over him at an unusual age, and with
the youthful confidence it inspired, he per-

---

* Burns.—These lines are taken from the introduction
to Mr. Wordsworth's poem of the LEECH-GATHERER.

formed wonders, and was willing to set a seal
on his reputation by a tragic catastrophe.
He had done his best; and, like another
Empedocles, threw himself into Ætna, to
ensure immortality. The brazen slippers alone
remain!—

LECTURE VII.

---◆---

ON BURNS, AND THE OLD ENGLISH BALLADS.

I AM sorry that what I said in the conclusion of the last Lecture, respecting Chatterton, should have given dissatisfaction to some persons, with whom I would willingly agree on all such matters. What I meant was less to call in question Chatterton's genius than to object to the common mode of estimating its magnitude by its prematureness. The lists of fame are not filled with the dates of births or deaths; and the side-mark of the age at which they were done wears out in works destined for immortality. Had Chatterton really done more, we should have thought less of him, for our attention would then have been fixed on the excellence of the works themselves, instead of the singularity of the circumstances in which they are produced. But because he attained to the full powers of manhood at an early age, I do not see that he would have attained to more than those powers, had he lived to be a man. He was a prodigy, because in him the ordinary march of nature was violently precipitated; and it is therefore inferred that he would have continued to hold on his course, " unslacked of motion." On the contrary, who knows but he might have lived to be poet-laureat? It is much better to let him remain as he was. Of his actual productions, any one may think as highly as he pleases; I would only guard against adding to the account of his *quantum meruit* those possible productions by which the learned rhapsodists of his time raised his gigantic pretensions to an equality with those of Homer and Shakspeare. It is amusing to read some of these exaggerated descriptions, each rising above the other in extravagance. In Anderson's Life, we find that Mr. Warton speaks of him " as a prodigy of genius," as " a singular instance of prematurity of abilities :" that may be true enough, and Warton was at any rate a competent judge; but Mr. Malone " believes him to have been the greatest genius that England has produced since the days of Shakspeare." Dr. Gregory says, " he must rank, as a universal genius, above Dryden, and perhaps only second to Shakspeare." Mr. Herbert Croft is still more unqualified in his praises ; he asserts that " no such being, at any period of life, has ever been known, or possibly ever will be known." He runs a parallel between Chatterton and Milton ; and asserts that "an army of Macedonian and Swedish mad butchers fly before him," meaning, I suppose, that Alexander the Great and Charles the Twelfth were nothing to him ; " nor," he adds, " does my memory supply me with any human being, who, at such an age, with such advantages, has produced such compositions. Under the heathen mythology, superstition and admiration would have explained all, by bringing Apollo on earth ; nor would the God ever have descended with more credit to himself." — Chatterton's physiognomy would at least have enabled him to pass *incognito*. It is quite different from the look of timid wonder and delight with which Annibal Caracci has painted a young Apollo listening to the first sounds he draws from a Pan's pipe, under the tutelage of the old Silenus ! If Mr. Croft is sublime on the occasion, Dr. Knox is no less pathetic. " The testimony of Dr. Knox," says Dr. Anderson, (essays, p. 144.) " does equal credit to the classical taste and amiable benevo-

lence of the writer, and the genius and reputation of Chatterton." "When I read," says
the Doctor, " the researches of those learned
antiquaries who have endeavoured to prove
that the poems attributed to Rowley were
really written by him, I observe many ingenious remarks in confirmation of their opinion,
which it would be tedious, if not difficult, to
controvert."

Now this is so far from the mark that the
whole controversy might have been settled by
any one but the learned antiquaries themselves,
who had the smallest share of their learning,
from this single circumstance, that the poems
read as smooth as any modern poems, if you
read them as modern compositions; and that
you cannot read them, or make verse of them
at all, if you pronounce or accent the words
as they were spoken at the time when the
poems were pretended to have been written.
The whole secret of the imposture, which
nothing but a deal of learned dust, raised by
collecting and removing a great deal of learned
rubbish, could have prevented our laborious
critics from seeing through, lies on the face
of it (to say nothing of the burlesque air
which is scarcely disguised throughout) in the
repetition of a few obsolete words, and in the
mis-spelling of common ones.

" No sooner," proceeds the Doctor, " do I turn to the poems, than the labour of the antiquaries appears only waste of time ; and I am involuntarily forced to join in placing that laurel, which he seems so well to have deserved, on the brow of Chatterton. The poems bear so many marks of superior genius that they have deservedly excited the general attention of polite scholars, and are considered as the most remarkable productions in modern poetry. We have many instances of poetical eminence at an early age ; but neither Cowley, Milton, nor Pope, ever produced any thing while they were boys, which can justly be compared to the poems of Chatterton. The learned antiquaries do not indeed dispute their excellence. They extol it in the highest terms of applause. They raise their favourite Rowley to a rivalry with Homer : but they make the very merits of the works an argument against their real author. ' Is it possible,' say they, ' that a boy should produce compositions so beautiful and masterly ?' That a common boy should produce them is not possible," rejoins the Doctor; " but that they should be produced by a boy of an extraordinary genius, such as was that of Homer or Shakspeare, though a prodigy, is such a one as by no means exceeds the bounds of rational credibility."

Now it does not appear that Shakspeare or Homer were such early prodigies ; so that by this reasoning he must take precedence of them too, as well as of Milton, Cowley, and Pope.   The reverend and classical writer then breaks out into the following melancholy raptures :—

" Unfortunate boy ! short and evil were thy days, but thy fame shall be immortal.   Hadst thou been known to the munificent patrons of genius........

" Unfortunate boy ! poorly wast thou accommodated during thy short sojourning here among us ;—rudely wast thou treated—sorely did thy feelings suffer from the scorn of the unworthy ; and there at last those who wish to rob thee of thy only meed, thy posthumous glory.   Severe too are the censures of thy morals.   In the gloomy moments of despondency, I fear thou hast uttered impious and blasphemous thoughts.   But let thy more rigid censors reflect that thou wast literally and strictly but a boy.   Let many of thy bitterest enemies reflect what were their own religious principles, and whether they had any, at the age of fourteen, fifteen, and sixteen.   Surely it is a severe and an unjust surmise that thou wouldst probably have ended thy life as a victim to the laws, if thou hadst not ended it as thou didst."

Enough, enough, of the learned antiquaries, and of the classical and benevolent testimony of Dr. Knox. Chatterton was, indeed, badly enough off; but he was at least saved from the pain and shame of reading this woful lamentation over fallen genius, which circulates, splendidly bound, in the fourteenth edition, while he is a prey to worms. As to those who are really capable of admiring Chatterton's genius, or of feeling an interest in his fate, I would only say that I never heard any one speak of any one of his works as if it were an old well-known favourite, and had become a faith and a religion in his mind. It is his name, his youth, and what he might have lived to have done, that excite our wonder and admiration. He has the same sort of posthumous fame that an actor of the last age has — an abstracted reputation which is independent of any thing we know of his works. The admirers of Collins never think of him without recalling to their minds his Ode on the Evening, or on the Poetical Character. Gray's Elegy, and his popularity, are identified together, and inseparable even in imagination. It is the same with respect to Burns: when you speak of him as a poet, you mean his works, his Tam o' Shanter, or his Cotter's Saturday Night.

But the enthusiasts for Chatterton, if you ask
for the proofs of his extraordinary genius, are
obliged to turn to the volume, and perhaps
find there what they seek ; but it is not in
their minds ; and it is of *that* I spoke.

The Minstrel's song in Ælla is, I think,
the best.

> " O ! synge untoe my roundelaie,
>   O ! droppe the brynie teare wythe mee,
>   Daunce ne moe atte hallie daie,
>   Lycke a rennynge ryver bee.
>   Mie love ys dedde,
>   Gonne to hys deathe-bedde,
>   Al under the wyllowe-tree.
>
> Black hys cryne as the wyntere nyght,
> Whyte hys rode as the sommer snowe,
> Rodde hys face as the mornynge lyghte,
> Cale he lyes ynne the grave belowe.
>   Mie love ys dedde,
>   Gonne to hys deathe-bedde,
>   Al under the wyllowe-tree.
>
> Swote hys tongue as the throstles note,
> Quycke ynne daunce as thought cann bee,
> Defte his taboure, codgelle stote,
> O ! hee lys bie the wyllowe-tree.
>   Mie love ys dedde,
>   Gonne to hys deathe-bedde,
>   Al under the wyllowe-tree.
>
> Harke ! the ravenne flappes hys wynge,
> In the briered dell belowe ;
> Harke ! the dethe-owle loude dothe synge,
> To the nyghte-mares as theie goe.
>   Mie love ys dedde,
>   Gonne to hys deathe-bedde,
>   Al under the wyllowe-tree.

See! the whyte moone sheenes onne hie;
Whyterre ys mie true loves shroude;
Whyterre yanne the mornynge skie,
Whyterre yanne the evenynge cloude.
        Mie love ys dedde,
        Gone to hys deathe-bedde,
        Al under the wyllowe-tree.

Heere, upon mie true loves grave,
Schalle the baren fleurs be layde,
Ne one hallie seyncte to save
Al the celness of a mayde.
        Mie love ys dedde,
        Gonne to hys deathe-bedde,
        Al under the wyllowe-tree.

Wythe mie hondes I'll dent the brieres
Rounde hys hallie corse to gre,
Ouphante fairies, lyghte your fyres,
Heere mie boddie stille schalle bee.
        Mie love ys dedde,
        Gonne to hys deathe-bedde,
        Al under the wyllowe-tree.

Comme, wythe acorne-coppe and thorne,
Drayne my hartys blodde awaie;
Lyfe and all yttes goode I scorne,
Daunce bie nete, or feaste by daie.
        Mie love ys dedde,
        Gonne to hys deathe-bedde,
        Al under the wyllowe-tree.

Water wytches, crownede wythe reytes,
Bere mee to yer leathalle tyde.
I die; I comme; mie true love waytes.
Thos the damselle spake, and dyed."

To proceed to the more immediate subject
of the present Lecture, the character and

writings of Burns.—Shakspeare says of some
one, that " he was like a man made after
supper of a cheese-paring." Burns, the poet
was not such a man.   He had a strong mind,
and a strong body, the fellow to it.   He had
a real heart of flesh and blood beating in his
bosom—you can almost hear it throb.   Some
one said, that if you had shaken hands with
him, his hand would have burnt yours.   The
gods, indeed, " made him poetical ;" but
nature had a hand in him first.   His heart
was in the right place.   He did not " create
a soul under the ribs of death," by tinkling
siren sounds, or by piling up centos of poetic
diction; but for the artificial flowers of poetry,
he plucked the mountain-daisy under his feet;
and a field-mouse, hurrying from its ruined
dwelling, could inspire him with the sentiments of terror and pity.   He held the plough
or the pen with the same firm, manly grasp ;
nor did he cut out poetry as we cut out watch-
papers, with finical dexterity, nor from the
same flimsy materials.   Burns was not like
Shakspeare in the range of his genius ; but
there is something of the same magnanimity,
directness, and unaffected character about
him.   He was not a sickly sentimentalist, a
namby-pamby poet, a mincing metre ballad-
monger, any more than Shakspeare.   He

would as soon hear " a brazen candlestick tuned, or a dry wheel grate on the axletree.' He was as much of a man — not a twentieth part as much of a poet—as Shakspeare. With but little of his imagination or inventive power, he had the same life of mind : within the narrow circle of personal feeling or domestic incidents, the pulse of his poetry flows as healthily and vigorously. He had an eye to see ; a heart to feel : — no more. His pictures of good fellowship, of social glee, of quaint humour, are equal to any thing ; they come up to nature, and they cannot go beyond. The sly jest collected in his laughing eye at the sight of the grotesque and ludicrous in manners — the large tear rolled down his manly cheek at the sight of another's distress. He has made us as well acquainted with himself as it is possible to be ; has let out the honest impulses of his native disposition, the unequal conflict of the passions in his breast, with the same frankness and truth of description. His strength is not greater than his weakness : his virtues were greater than his vices. His virtues belonged to his genius : his vices to his situation, which did not correspond to his genius.

It has been usual to attack Burns's moral character, and the moral tendency of his

writings at the same time ; and Mr. Wordsworth, in a letter to Mr. Gray, Master of the
High School at Edinburgh, in attempting to
defend, has only laid him open to a more serious and unheard-of responsibility.   Mr. Gray
might very well have sent him back, in return
for his epistle, the answer of Holofernes in
Love's Labour Lost :—" *Via* goodman Dull,
thou hast spoken no word all this while."
The author of this performance, which is as
weak in effect as it is pompous in pretension,
shows a great dislike of Robespierre, Buona-
parte, and of Mr. Jeffrey, whom he, by some
unaccountable fatality, classes together as the
three most formidable enemies of the human
race that have appeared in his (Mr. Wordsworth's) remembrance ; but he betrays very
little liking to Burns.   He is, indeed, anxious
to get him out of the unhallowed clutches of
the Edinburgh Reviewers (as a mere matter
of poetical privilege), only to bring him before
a graver and higher tribunal, which is his
own ; and, after repeating and insinuating
ponderous charges against him, shakes his
head, and declines giving any opinion in so
tremendous a case ; so that, though the judgment of the former critic is set aside, poor
Burns remains just where he was, and nobody
gains any thing by the cause but Mr. Words-

worth, in an increasing opinion of his own
wisdom and purity. " Out upon this half-
faced fellowship !" The author of the Lyrical Ballads has thus missed a fine opportunity
of doing Burns justice and himself honour.
He might have shown himself a philosophical
prose-writer, as well as a philosophical poet.
He might have offered as amiable and as
gallant a defence of the Muses as my uncle
Toby, in the honest simplicity of his heart,
did of the army. He might have said at once,
instead of making a parcel of wry faces over
the matter, that Burns had written Tam o'
Shanter, and that that alone was enough ; that
he could hardly have described the excesses of
mad, hairbrained, roaring mirth, and convivial
indulgence, which are the soul of it, if he
himself had not " drunk full ofter of the tun
than of the well " — unless " the act and
practique part of life had been the mistress of
his theorique." Mr. Wordsworth might have
quoted such lines as —

> " The landlady and Tam grew gracious,
> Wi' favours, secret, sweet, and precious ;"—

or,

> " Care, mad to see a man so happy,
> E'en drowned himself amang the nappy ;"—

and fairly confessed that he could not have

written such lines from a want of proper
habits and previous sympathy; and that, till
some great puritanical genius should arise
to do these things equally well without any
knowledge of them, the world might forgive
Burns the injuries he had done his health
and fortune in his poetical apprenticeship to
experience, for the pleasure he had afforded
them. Instead of this, Mr. Wordsworth hints
that, with different personal habits and greater
strength of mind, Burns would have written
differently, and almost as well as *he* does. He
might have taken that line of Gay's,

" The fly that sips treacle is lost in the sweets,"—

and applied it in all its force and pathos to the
poetical character. He might have argued that
poets are men of genius, and that a man of
genius is not a machine; that they live in a
state of intellectual intoxication, and that it is
too much to expect them to be distinguished
by peculiar *sang froid*, circumspection, and
sobriety. Poets are by nature men of stronger
imagination and keener sensibilities than others;
and it is a contradiction to suppose them at
the same time governed only by the cool, dry,
calculating dictates of reason and foresight.
Mr. Wordsworth might have ascertained the
boundaries that part the provinces of reason

and imagination : — that it is the business of the understanding to exhibit things in their relative proportions and ultimate consequences —of the imagination to insist on their immediate impressions, and to indulge their strongest impulses; but it is the poet's office to pamper the imagination of his readers and his own with the extremes of present ecstacy or agony, to snatch the swift-winged golden minutes, the torturing hour, and to banish the dull, prosaic, monotonous realities of life, both from his thoughts and from his practice. Mr. Wordsworth might have shown how it is that all men of genius, or of originality and independence of mind, are liable to practical errors, from the very confidence their superiority inspires, which makes them fly in the face of custom and prejudice, always rashly, sometimes unjustly ; for, after all, custom and prejudice are not without foundation in truth and reason, and no one individual is a match for the world in power, very few in knowledge. The world may altogether be set down as older and wiser than any single person in it.

Again, our philosophical letter-writer might have enlarged on the temptations to which Burns was exposed from his struggles with fortune and the uncertainty of his fate. He might have shown how a poet, not born to

wealth or title, was kept in a constant state of
feverish anxiety with respect to his fame and
the means of a precarious livelihood : that,
" from being chilled with poverty, steeped in
contempt, he had passed into the sunshine of
fortune, and was lifted to the very pinnacle of
public favour ; " yet even there could not
count on the continuance of success, but was,
" like the giddy sailor on the mast, ready
with every blast to topple down into the fatal
bowels of the deep !"   He might have traced
his habit of ale-house tippling to the last long
precious draught of his favourite usquebaugh,
which he took in the prospect of bidding
farewel for ever to his native land ; and his
conjugal infidelities to his first disappointment
in love, which would not have happened to
him if he had been born to a small estate in
land, or bred up behind a counter !

Lastly, Mr. Wordsworth might have shown
the incompatibility between the Muses and
the Excise, which never agreed well together,
or met in one seat, till they were unaccount-
ably reconciled on Rydal Mount.   He must
know (no man better) the distraction created
by the opposite calls of business and of fancy,
the torment of extents, the plague of receipts
laid in order or mislaid, the disagreeableness
of exacting penalties or paying the forfeiture ;

and how all this (together with the broaching of casks and the splashing of beer-barrels) must have preyed upon a mind like Burns', with more than his natural sensibility and none of his acquired firmness.

Mr. Coleridge, alluding to this circumstance of the promotion of the Scottish Bard to be "a gauger of ale-firkins," in a poetical epistle to his friend Charles Lamb, calls upon him, in a burst of heart-felt indignation, to gather a wreath of henbane, nettles, and nightshade,

> "———— To twine
> The illustrious brow of Scotch nobility."

If, indeed, Mr. Lamb had undertaken to write a letter in defence of Burns, how different would it have been from this of Mr. Wordsworth ! How much better than I can even imagine it to have been done !

It is hardly reasonable to look for a hearty or genuine defence of Burns from the pen of Mr. Wordsworth ; for there is no common link of sympathy between them. Nothing can be more different or hostile than the spirit of their poetry. Mr. Wordsworth's poetry is the poetry of mere sentiment and pensive contemplation : Burns's is a very highly sub-limated essence of animal existence. With Burns, " self-love and social are the same"—

" And we'll tak a cup of kindness yet,
    For auld lang syne."

Mr. Wordsworth is " himself alone," a recluse
philosopher, or a reluctant spectator of the
scenes of many-coloured life ; moralising on
them, not describing, not entering into them.
Robert Burns has exerted all the vigour of
his mind, all the happiness of his nature, in
exalting the pleasures of wine, of love, and
good fellowship : but in Mr. Wordsworth
there is a total disunion and divorce of the
faculties of the mind from those of the body :
the banns are forbid, or a separation is au-
sterely pronounced from bed and board —
a mensâ et thoro.   From the Lyrical Ballads,
it does not appear that men eat or drink,
marry or are given in marriage.   If we lived
by every sentiment that proceeded out of
mouths, and not by bread or wine, or if the
species were continued like trees (to borrow
an expression from the great Sir Thomas
Brown), Mr. Wordsworth's poetry would be
just as good as ever.   It is not so with Burns :
he is " famous for the keeping it up," and
in his verse is ever fresh and gay.   For this,
it seems, he has fallen under the displeasure
of the Edinburgh Reviewers, and the still
more formidable patronage of Mr. Wordsworth's pen.

" This, this was the unkindest cut of all."

I was going to give some extracts out of this composition in support of what I have said, but I find them too tedious. Indeed (if I may be allowed to speak my whole mind, under correction) Mr. Wordsworth could not be in any way expected to tolerate or give a favourable interpretation to Burns's constitutional foibles — even his best virtues are not good enough for him. He is repelled and driven back into himself, not less by the worth than by the faults of others. His taste is as exclusive and repugnant as his genius. It is because so few things give him pleasure that he gives pleasure to so few people. It is not every one who can perceive the sublimity of a daisy, or the pathos to be extracted from a withered thorn !

To proceed from Burns's patrons to his poetry, than which no two things can be more different. His " Twa Dogs" is a very spirited piece of description, both as it respects the animal and human creation, and conveys a very vivid idea of the manners both of high and low life. The burlesque panegyric of the first dog,

" His locked, lettered, braw brass collar
Show'd him the gentleman and scholar,"—

reminds one of Launce's account of his dog
Crabbe, where he is said, as an instance of his
being in the way of promotion, " to have got
among three or four gentleman-like dogs under
the Duke's table." The " Halloween" is
the most striking and picturesque description
of local customs and scenery. The Brigs of
Ayr, the Address to a Haggis, Scotch Drink,
and innumerable others, are, however, full of
the same kind of characteristic and comic
painting. But his masterpiece in this way is
his Tam o' Shanter. I shall give the beginning of it, but I am afraid I shall hardly know
when to leave off.

> " When chapman billies leave the street,
> And drouthy neebours neebours meet,
> As market-days are wearing late,
> And folk begin to tak' the gate ;
> While we sit bousing at the nappy,
> And getting fou and unco happy,
> We think na on the lang Scots miles,
> The mosses, waters, slaps, and styles,
> That lie between us and our hame,
> Where sits our sulky, sullen dame,
> Gathering her brows like gathering storm,
> Nursing her wrath to keep it warm.
>
> This truth fand honest Tam o' Shanter,
> As he frae Ayr ae night did canter ;
> (Auld Ayr, wham ne'er a town surpasses
> For honest men and bonny lasses).
>
> O Tam ! hadst thou but been sae wise,
> As ta'en thy ain wife Kate's advice !
> She tauld thee weel thou was a skellum,
> A blethering, blustering, drunken blellum ;

That frae November till October
Ae market-day thou was na sober;
That ilka melder, wi' the miller,
Thou sat as lang as thou had siller;
That ev'ry naig was ca'd a shoe on,
The smith and thee gat roaring fou on;
That at the Lord's house, ev'n on Sunday,
Thou drank wi' Kirton Jean till Monday —
She prophesy'd, that, late or soon,
Thou wad be found deep drown'd in Doon;
Or catch't wi' warlocks in the mirk,
By Alloway's auld haunted kirk.

   Ah, gentle dames! it gars me greet,
To think how mony counsels sweet,
How mony lengthen'd, sage advices,
The husband frae the wife despises!

   But to our tale: Ae market night,
Tam had got planted unco right
Fast by an ingle, bleezing finely,
Wi' reaming swats, that drank divinely;
And at his elbow, Souter Johnny,
His ancient, trusty, drouthy crony;
Tam lo'ed him like a vera brither;
They had been fou for weeks thegither.
The night drave on wi' sangs and clatter,
And aye the ale was growing better:
The landlady and Tam grew gracious
Wi' favours secret, sweet, and precious:
The Souter tauld his queerest stories;
The landlord's laugh was ready chorus:
The storm without might rair and rustle,
Tam did na mind the storm a whistle.

   Care, mad to see a man sae happy,
E'en drown'd himsel amang the nappy;
As bees flee hame wi' lades o' treasure,
The minutes wing'd their way wi' pleasure:
Kings may be blest, but Tam was glorious,
O'er a' the ills of life victorious!

But pleasures are like poppies spread,
You seize the flow'r—its bloom is shed ;
Or like the snow, falls in the river,
A moment white—then melts for ever ;
Or like the Borealis race,
That flit ere you can point their place ;
Or like the rainbow's lovely form,
Evanishing amid the storm.—
Nae man can tether time or tide,
The hour approaches, Tam maun ride ;
That hour o' night's black arch the key-stane,
That dreary hour he mounts his beast in,
And sic a night he taks the road in,
As ne'er poor sinner was abroad in.

The wind blew as 'twad blawn its last ;
The rattling showers rose on the blast,
The speedy gleams the darkness swallow'd,
Loud, deep, and lang, the thunder bellow'd :
That night a child might understand
The Deil had business on his hand.

Weel mounted on his grey mare, Meg,
A better never lifted leg,
Tam skelpit on thro' dub and mire,
Despising wind, and rain, and fire ;
Whiles haulding fast his gude blue bonnet ;
Whiles crooning o'er some auld Scots sonnet ;
Whiles glowring round wi' prudent cares,
Lest bogles catch him unawares ;
Kirk-Alloway was drawing nigh,
Whare ghaists and houlets nightly cry.—

By this time Tam was cross the ford,
Whare in the snaw, the chapman smoor'd ;
And past the birks and meikle stane,
Whare drunken Charlie brak's neck-bane;
And thro' the whins, and by the cairn,
Where hunters fand the murder'd bairn ;
And near the thorn, aboon the well,

Whare Mungo's mither hang'd hersel.—
Before him Doon pours all his floods ;
The doubling storm roars thro' the woods ;
The lightnings flash from pole to pole ;
Near and more near the thunders roll :
Whan, glimmering thro' the groaning trees,
Kirk-Alloway seem'd in a bleeze ;
Thro' ilka bore the beams were glancing ;
And loud resounded mirth and dancing.

   Inspiring bold John Barleycorn !
What dangers thou canst make us scorn !
Wi' Tippenny, we fear nae evil,
Wi' Usqueba, we'll face the devil !
The swats sae ream'd in Tammie's noddle,
Fair play, he car'd na de'ils a boddle.
But Maggie stood right sair astonish'd,
Till, by the heel and hand admonish'd,
She ventur'd forward on the light,
And, wow ! Tam saw an unco sight !
Warlocks and witches in a dance,
Nae light cotillion new frae France,
But hornpipes, jigs, strathspeys, and reels,
Put life and mettle in their heels.
As winnock-bunker, in the east,
There sat auld Nick, in shape o' beast ;
A touzie tyke, black, grim, and large,
To gie them music was his charge ;
He screw'd the pipes, and gart them skirl,
Till roof and rafters a' did dirl.—
Coffins stood round like open presses,
That shaw'd the dead in their last dresses ;
And, by some devilish cantrip slight,
Each in its cauld hand held a light—
By which heroic Tam was able
To note upon the haly table
A murderer's banes in gibbet-airns ;
Twa span-lang, wee, unchristen'd bairns ;

A thief, new cutted frae a rape,
Wi' his last gasp his gab did gape ;
Five tomahawks, wi' bluid red rusted ;
Five scimitars, wi' murder crusted ;
A garter, which a babe had strangled ;
A knife, a father's throat had mangled,
Whom his ain son o' life bereft,
The grey hairs yet stack to the heft ;
Wi' mair o' horrible and awfu',
Which e'en to name wad be unlawfu'.

As Tammie glowr'd, amaz'd and curious,
The mirth and fun grew fast and furious :
The Piper loud and louder blew ;
The dancers quick and quicker flew ;
They reel'd, they set, they cross'd, they cleekit,
Till ilka Carlin swat and reekit,
And coost her duddies to the wark,
And linket at it in her sark !

Now Tam, O Tam ! had they been queans
A' plump and strapping in their teens ;
Their sarks, instead o' creeshie flannen,
Been snaw-white seventeen hundred linen !
Thir breeks o' mine, my only pair,
That ance were plush, o' gude blue hair,
I wad hae gi'en them aff my hurdies,
For ae blink o' the bonnie burdies !

But wither'd beldams, auld and droll,
Rigwoodie hags wad spean a foal,
Louping and flinging on a crummock,
I wonder did na turn thy stomach.

But Tam ken'd what was what fu' brawly,
There was ae winsome wench and waly,
That night enlisted in the core,
(Lang after ken'd on Carrick shore ;
For mony a beast to dead she shot,
And perish'd mony a bonnie boat,
And shook baith meikle corn and bear,

And kept the country-side in fear—)
Her cutty sark o' Paisely harn,
That while a lassie she had worn,
In longitude tho' sorely scanty,
It was her best, and she was vaunty.—
Ah ! little ken'd thy reverend grannie,
That sark she coft for her wee Nannie,
Wi' twa pund Scots ('twas a' her riches),
Wad ever grac'd a dance of witches !

But here my Muse her wing maun cour ;
Sic flights are far beyond her power :
To sing how Nannie lap and flang,
(A souple jade she was, and strang)
And how Tam stood like ane bewitch'd,
And thought his very een enrich'd ;
Ev'n Satan glowr'd and fidg'd fu' fain,
And hotch't, and blew wi' might and main ;
Till first ae caper, syne anither,
Tam tint his reason a' thegither,
And roars out, " Weel done, Cutty Sark !"
And in an instant all was dark ;
And scarcely had he Maggie rallied,
When out the hellish legion sallied.

As bees biz out wi' angry fyke
When plundering herds assail their byke ;
As open pussie's mortal foes,
When, pop ! she starts before their nose ;
As eager rins the market-crowd,
When "Catch the thief!" resounds aloud ;
So Maggie rins—the witches follow,
Wi' mony an eldritch skreech and hollow,

Ah, Tam ! ah, Tam ! thou'll get thy fairin' !
In hell they'll roast thee like a herrin' !
In vain thy Kate awaits thy comin' !
Kate soon will be a waefu' woman !
Now, do thy speedy utmost, Meg,
And win the key-stane o' the brig ;

There, at them thou thy tail may toss,
A running stream they dare na cross;
But ere the key-stane she could make,
The fient a tail she had to shake !
For Nannie, far before the rest,
Hard upon noble Maggie prest,
And flew at Tam wi' furious ettle :
But little wist she Maggie's mettle—
Ae spring brought aff her master hale,
But left behind her ain grey tail :
The Carlin claught her by the rump,
And left poor Maggie scarce a stump.

　Now, wha this tale of truth shall read,
Ilk man and mother's son tak heed :
Whane'er to drink you are inclin'd,
Or Cutty Sarks rin in your mind,
Think, ye may buy the joys owre dear ;
Remember Tam o' Shanter's mare."

Burns has given the extremes of licentious
eccentricity and convivial enjoyment, in the
story of this scape-grace, and of patriarchal
simplicity and gravity in describing the old
national character of the Scottish peasantry.
The Cotter's Saturday Night is a noble and
pathetic picture of human manners, mingled
with a fine religious awe.　It comes over the
mind like a slow and solemn strain of music.
The soul of the poet aspires from this scene
of low-thoughted care, and reposes, in trembling hope, on " the bosom of its Father and
its God."　Hardly any thing can be more
touching than the following stanzas, for in-

stance, whether as they describe human interests, or breathe a lofty devotional spirit.

" The toil-worn Cotter frae his labour goes,
 This night his weekly moil is at an end,
Collects his spades, his mattocks, and his hoes,
 Hoping the morn in ease and rest to spend,
And weary, o'er the moor, his course does hameward bend.

 At length his lonely cot appears in view,
  Beneath the shelter of an aged tree ;
 Th' expectant wee-things, toddlin, stacher through
  To meet their dad, wi' flichterin noise and glee.
 His wee-bit ingle, blinkin bonilie,
  His clean hearth-stane, his thriftie wifie's smile,
 The lisping infant, prattling on his knee,
  Does a' his weary carking cares beguile,
And makes him quite forget his labour and his toil.

 Belyve, the elder bairns come drapping in
  At service out, amang the farmers roun',
 Some ca' the pleugh, some herd, some tentie rin
  A cannie errand to a neebor town ;
 Their eldest hope, their Jenny, woman-grown,
  In youthfu' bloom, love sparkling in her e'e,
 Comes hame, perhaps, to show a braw new gown,
  Or deposite her sair-won penny-fee,
To help her parents dear, if they in hardship be.

 Wi' joy unfeign'd, brothers and sisters meet,
  And each for other's welfare kindly spiers ;
 The social hours, swift-wing'd, unnotic'd fleet ;
  Each tells the uncos that he sees or hears :
 The parents, partial, eye their hopeful years ;
  Anticipation forward points the view ;
 The mither, wi' her needle and her shears,
  Gars auld claes look amaist as weel's the new ;
The father mixes a' wi' admonition due.

  *   *   *   *

But, hark ! a rap comes gently to the door ;
    Jenny, wha kens the meaning o' the same,
Tells how a neebor lad cam o'er the moor,
    To do some errands, and convoy her hame.
The wily mother sees the conscious flame
    Sparkle in Jenny's e'e, and flush her cheek ;
With heart-struck, anxious care, inquires his name,
    While Jenny hafflins is afraid to speak ;
Weel pleas'd the mother hears it's nae wild, worthless rake.

Wi' kindly welcome, Jenny brings him ben ;
    A strappan youth ; he taks the mother's eye ;
Blithe Jenny sees the visit's no ill ta'en ;
    The father cracks of horses, pleughs, and kye.
The youngster's artless heart o'erflows wi' joy,
    But blate an' laithfu', scarce can weel behave ;
The mother, wi' a woman's wiles, can spy
    What makes the youth sae bashfu' an' sae grave ;
Weel-pleas'd to think her bairn's respected like the lave.

But now the supper crowns their simple board,
    The halesome parritch, chief o' Scotia's food :
The soupe their only hawkie does afford,
    That 'yont the hallan snugly chows her cood :
The dame brings forth, in complimental mood,
    To grace the lad, her weel-hained kebbuck, fell,
An' aft he's prest, an' aft he ca's it guid ;
    The frugal wifie, garrulous, will tell,
How 'twas a towmond auld, sin' lint was i' the bell.

The cheerfu' supper done, wi' serious face,
    They, round the ingle, form a circle wide ;
The sire turns o'er, with patriarchal grace,
    The big ha'-Bible, ance his father's pride :
His bonnet rev'rently is laid aside,
    His lyart haffets wearing thin an' bare ;
Those strains that once did sweet in Zion glide,
    He wales a portion wi' judicious care ;
And " Let us worship God !" he says, with solemn air.

They chant their artless notes in simple guise;
    They tune their hearts, by far the noblest aim:
Perhaps Dundee's wild-warbling measures rise,
    Or plaintive Martyrs, worthy of the name;
Or noble Elgin beets the heav'nward flame,
    The sweetest far of Scotia's holy lays:
Compar'd with these, Italian trills are tame;
    The tickled ears no heart-felt raptures raise;
Nae unison hae they with our Creator's praise."

Burns's poetical epistles to his friends are admirable, whether for the touches of satire, the painting of character, or the sincerity of friendship they display. Those to Captain Grose, and to Davie, a brother poet, are among the best: they are " the true pathos and sublime of human life." His prose-letters are sometimes tinctured with affectation. They seem written by a man who has been admired for his wit, and is expected on all occasions to shine. Those in which he expresses his ideas of natural beauty in reference to Alison's Essay on Taste, and advocates the keeping up the remembrances of old customs and seasons, are the most powerfully written. His English serious odes and moral stanzas are, in general, failures, such as The Lament, Man was made to Mourn, &c.; nor do I much admire his " Scots wha hae wi' Wallace bled." In this strain of didactic or sentimental moralising, the lines to Glencairn are the most happy and impressive.

His imitations of the old humorous ballad
style of Ferguson's songs are no whit inferior
to the admirable originals, such as " John
Anderson, my Joe," and many more. But of
all his productions, the pathetic and serious
love-songs which he has left behind him, in
the manner of the old ballads, are perhaps
those which take the deepest and most lasting
hold of the mind. Such are the lines to Mary
Morison, and those entitled Jessy.

> " Here's a health to ane I lo'e dear—
>   Here's a health to ane I lo'e dear—
> Thou art sweet as the smile when fond lovers meet,
>   And soft as their parting tear—Jessy!
>
> Altho' thou maun never be mine,
>   Altho' even hope is denied;
> 'Tis sweeter for thee despairing
>   Than aught in the world beside—Jessy !"

The conclusion of the other is as follows :

> " Yestreen, when to the trembling string
>   The dance gaed through the lighted ha',
> To thee my fancy took its wing,
>   I sat, but neither heard nor saw.
> Tho' this was fair, and that was braw,
>   And yon the toast of a' the town,
> I sighed, and said among them a',
>   Ye are na Mary Morison."

That beginning, " Oh gin my love were a
bonny red rose," is a piece of rich and fantastic description. One would think that

nothing could surpass these in beauty of
expression, and in true pathos : and nothing
does or can, but some of the old Scotch
ballads themselves. There is in them a still
more original cast of thought, a more romantic
imagery — the thistle's glittering down, the
gilliflower on the old garden-wall, the horse-
man's silver bells, the hawk on its perch —
a closer intimacy with nature, a firmer reliance on it, as the only stock of wealth which
the mind has to resort to, a more infantine
simplicity of manners, a greater strength of
affection, hopes longer cherished and longer
deferred, sighs that the heart dare hardly
heave, and " thoughts that often lie too deep
for tears." We seem to feel that those who
wrote and sung them (the early minstrels)
lived in the open air, wandering on from
place to place with restless feet and thoughts,
and lending an ever-open ear to the fearful
accidents of war or love, floating on the breath
of old tradition or common fame, and moving
the strings of their harp with sounds that sank
into a nation's heart. How fine an illustration of this is that passage in Don Quixote,
where the knight and Sancho, going in search
of Dulcinea, inquire their way of the countryman, who was driving his mules to plough
before break of day, " singing the ancient

ballad of Roncesvalles." Sir Thomas Overbury describes his country girl as still accompanied with fragments of old songs. One of
the best and most striking descriptions of the
effects of this mixture of national poetry and
music is to be found in one of the letters of
Archbishop Herring, giving an account of a
confirmation-tour in the mountains of Wales.

"That pleasure over, our work became very arduous,
for we were to mount a rock, and in many places of the
road, over natural stairs of stone. I submitted to this,
which they told me was but a taste of the country, and to
prepare me for worse things to come. However, worse
things did not come that morning, for we dined soon after
out of our own wallets; and, though our inn stood in a
place of the most frightful solitude, and the best formed
for the habitation of monks (who once possessed it) in the
world, yet we made a cheerful meal. The novelty of the
thing gave me spirits, and the air gave me appetite much
keener than the knife I ate with. We had our music too ;
for there came in a harper, who soon drew about us a group
of figures that Hogarth would have given any price for.
The harper was in his true place and attitude ; a man and
woman stood before him, singing to his instrument wildly,
but not disagreeably ; a little dirty child was playing with
the bottom of the harp ; a woman in a sick night-cap hanging over the stairs ; a boy with crutches, fixed in a staring
attention, and a girl carding wool in the chimney, and rock-
ing a cradle with her naked feet, interrupted in her business
by the charms of the music ; all ragged and dirty, and all
silently attentive. These figures gave us a most entertaining picture, and would please you or any man of observation ; and one reflection gave me a particular comfort, that
the assembly before us demonstrated that even here the

influential sun warmed poor mortals, and inspired them
with love and music."

I could wish that Mr. Wilkie had been recom-
mended to take this group as the subject of his
admirable pencil; he has painted a picture of
Bathsheba, instead.

In speaking of the old Scotch ballads, I
need do no more than mention the name of
Auld Robin Gray. The effect of reading
this old ballad is as if all our hopes and fears
hung upon the last fibre of the heart, and we
felt that giving way. What silence, what
loneliness, what leisure for grief and despair!

> " My father pressed me sair,
>   Though my mother did na' speak;
> But she looked in my face
>   Till my heart was like to break."

The irksomeness of the situations, the sense
of painful dependence, is excessive; and yet
the sentiment of deep-rooted, patient affection
triumphs over all, and is the only impression
that remains. Lady Ann Bothwell's Lament
is not, I think, quite equal to the lines beginning—

> " O waly, waly, up the bank,
>   And waly, waly, down the brae,
> And waly, waly, yon burn side,
>   Where I and my love wont to gae.
> I leant my back unto an aik,
>   I thought it was a trusty tree;

But first it bow'd, and syne it brak,
  Sae my true-love's forsaken me.

O waly, waly, love is bonny,
  A little time while it is new ;
But when it's auld, it waxeth cauld.
  And fades awa' like the morning dew.
Whan cockle-shells turn siller bells,
  And muscles grow on every tree,
Whan frost and snaw sall warm us aw,
  Then sall my love prove true to me.

Now Arthur seat sall be my bed,
  The sheets sall ne'er be fyld by me :
Saint Anton's well sall be my drink,
  Since my true-love's forsaken me.
Martinmas wind, when wilt thou blaw,
  And shake the green leaves aff the tree ?
O gentle death, whan wilt thou cum
  And tak' a life that wearies me ?

'Tis not the frost that freezes sae,
  Nor blawing snaw's inclemencie,
'Tis not sic cauld, that makes me cry,
  But my love's heart grown cauld to me.
Whan we came in by Glasgow town,
  We were a comely sight to see,
My love was clad in black velvet,
  And I myself in cramasie.

But had I wist, before I kist,
  That love had been sae hard to win ;
I'd lockt my heart in case of gowd,
  And pinn'd it with a siller pin.
And oh ! if my poor babe were born,
  And set upon the nurse's knee,
And I mysel in the cold grave !
  Since my true-love's forsaken me."

The finest modern imitation of this style is
the Braes of Yarrow ; and perhaps the finest
subject for a story of the same kind, in any
modern book, is that told in Turner's History
of England, of a Mahometan woman, who,
having fallen in love with an English merchant,
the father of Thomas à Becket, followed him
all the way to England, knowing only the
word London, and the name of her lover,
Gilbert.

But to have done with this, which is rather
too serious a subject.—The old English ballads
are of a gayer and more lively turn.   They
are adventurous and romantic ; but they relate
chiefly to good living and good fellowship,
to drinking and hunting scenes.   Robin Hood
is the chief of these, and he still, in imagination, haunts Sherwood Forest.   The archers
green glimmer under the waving branches ;
the print on the grass remains where they have
just finished their noontide meal under the
green-wood tree ; and the echo of their bugle-
horn and twanging bows resounds through the
tangled mazes of the forest, as the tall slim
deer glances startled by.

    " The trees in Sherwood Forest are old and good
        The grass beneath them now is dimly green :
        Are they deserted all ? Is no young mien,
    With loose-slung bugle, met within the wood ?

No arrow found—foil'd of its antler'd food—
   Struck in the oak's rude side ?—Is there nought seen
   To mark the revelries which there have been,
In the sweet days of merry Robin Hood ?

Go there with summer, and with evening—go
   In the soft shadows, like some wand'ring man—
   And thou shalt far amid the forest know
The archer-men in green, with belt and bow,
   Feasting on pheasant, river-fowl, and swan,
   With Robin at their head, and Marian."*

---

* Sonnet on Sherwood Forest, by J. H. Reynolds.

LECTURE VIII.

———◆———

ON THE LIVING POETS.

" No more of talk where God or Angel guest
    With man, as with his friend, familiar us'd
    To sit indulgent."————

GENIUS is the heir of fame; but the hard
condition on which the bright reversion must
be earned is the loss of life. Fame is the
recompense not of the living, but of the dead.
The temple of fame stands upon the grave :
the flame that burns upon its altars is kindled
from the ashes of great men. Fame itself is
immortal, but it is not begot till the breath
of genius is extinguished. For fame is not
popularity, the shout of the multitude, the
idle buzz of fashion, the venal puff, the soothing flattery of favour or of friendship; but it
is the spirit of a man surviving himself in the
minds and thoughts of other men, undying
and imperishable. It is the power which the

intellect exercises over the intellect, and the
lasting homage which is paid to it, as such,
independently of time and circumstances,
purified from partiality and evil-speaking.—
Fame is the sound which the stream of high
thoughts, carried down to future ages, makes
as it flows—deep, distant, murmuring evermore like the waters of the mighty ocean.
He who has ears truly touched to this music
is in a manner deaf to the voice of popularity.
The love of fame differs from mere vanity in
this,—that the one is immediate and personal,
the other ideal and abstracted. It is not the
direct and gross homage paid to himself, that
the lover of true fame seeks or is proud of;
but the indirect and pure homage paid to the
eternal forms of truth and beauty as they are
reflected in his mind, that gives him confidence
and hope. The love of nature is the first
thing in the mind of the true poet : the admiration of himself the last. A man of genius
cannot well be a coxcomb; for his mind is
too full of other things to be much occupied
with his own person. He who is conscious
of great powers in himself has also a high
standard of excellence with which to compare
his efforts : he appeals also to a test and
judge of merit, which is the highest, but
which is too remote, grave, and impartial, to

flatter his self-love extravagantly, or puff him up with intolerable and vain conceit. This, indeed, is one test of genius and of real greatness of mind, whether a man can wait patiently and calmly for the award of posterity, satisfied with the unwearied exercise of his faculties, retired within the sanctuary of his own thoughts; or whether he is eager to forestal his own immortality, and mortgage it for a newspaper puff. He who thinks much of himself will be in danger of being forgotten by the rest of the world: he who is always trying to lay violent hands on reputation will not secure the best and most lasting. If the restless candidate for praise takes no pleasure, no sincere and heartfelt delight in his works, but as they are admired and applauded by others, what should others see in them to admire or applaud? They cannot be expected to admire them because they are *his;* but for the truth and nature contained in them, which must first be inly felt and copied with severe delight, from the love of truth and nature, before it can ever appear there. Was Raphael, think you, when he painted his pictures of the Virgin and Child in all their inconceivable truth and beauty of expression, thinking most of his subject or of himself? Do you suppose that Titian, when

he painted a landscape, was pluming himself
on being thought the finest colourist in the
world, or making himself so by looking at
nature? Do you imagine that Shakspeare,
when he wrote Lear or Othello, was thinking
of any thing but Lear and Othello? Or that
Mr. Kean, when he plays these characters, is
thinking of the audience?— No: he who
would be great in the eyes of others must
first learn to be nothing in his own. The
love of fame, as it enters at times into his
mind, is only another name for the love of
excellence; or it is the ambition to attain the
highest excellence, sanctioned by the highest
authority — that of time.

Those minds, then, which are the most
entitled to expect it, can best put up with
the postponement of their claims to lasting
fame. They can afford to wait. They are
not afraid that truth and nature will ever wear
out; will lose their gloss with novelty, or
their effect with fashion. If their works have
the seeds of immortality in them, they will
live; if they have not, they care little about
them as theirs. They do not complain of
the start which others have got of them in the
race of everlasting renown, or of the impossi-
bility of attaining the honours which time
alone can give, during the term of their

natural lives. They know that no applause, however loud and violent, can anticipate or over-rule the judgment of posterity; that the opinion of no one individual, nor of any one generation can have the weight, the authority (to say nothing of the force of sympathy and prejudice), which must belong to that of successive generations. The brightest living reputation cannot be equally imposing to the imagination with that which is covered and rendered venerable with the hoar of innumerable ages. No modern production can have the same atmosphere of sentiment around it as the remains of classical antiquity. But then our moderns may console themselves with the reflection that they will be old in their turn, and will either be remembered with still increasing honours, or quite forgotten !

I would speak of the living poets as I have spoken of the dead (for I think highly of many of them); but I cannot speak of them with the same reverence, because I do not feel it ; with the same confidence, because I cannot have the same authority to sanction my opinion. I cannot be absolutely certain that any body, twenty years hence, will think any thing about any of them; but we may be pretty sure that Milton and Shakspeare will be remembered twenty years hence. We are, therefore, not without excuse if we husband our enthusiasm a little, and do not prematurely lay out our whole stock in untried ventures, and what may turn out to be false bottoms. I have myself out-lived one generation of favourite poets, the Darwins, the Hayleys, the Sewards. Who reads them now?—If, however, I have not the verdict of posterity to bear me out in bestowing the most unqualified praises on their immediate successors, it is also to be remembered that neither does it warrant me in condemning them. Indeed, it was not my wish to go into this ungrateful part of the subject; but something of the sort is expected from me, and I must run the gauntlet as well as I can. Another circumstance that adds to the difficulty of doing justice to all parties is that I happen to have had a personal acquaintance with some of these jealous votaries of the Muses; and that is not the likeliest way to imbibe a high opinion of the rest. Poets do not praise one another in the language of hyperbole. I am afraid, therefore, that I labour under a degree of prejudice against some of the most popular poets of the day, from an early habit of deference to the critical opinions of some of the least popular. I cannot say that I ever learnt much about

Shakspeare or Milton, Spenser or Chaucer,
from these professed guides; for I never heard
them say much about them.   They were
always talking of themselves and one another.
Nor am I certain that this sort of personal
intercourse with living authors, while it takes
away all real relish or freedom of opinion with
regard to their contemporaries, greatly enhances our respect for themselves.   Poets are
not ideal beings; but have their prose-sides,
like the commonest of the people.   We often
hear persons say, What they would have given
to have seen Shakspeare!   For my part, I
would give a great deal not to have seen him;
at least, if he was at all like any body else
that I have ever seen.   But why should he?
for his works are not!   This is, doubtless, one
great advantage which the dead have over the
living.   It is always fortunate for ourselves
and others, when we are prevented from
exchanging admiration for knowledge.   The
splendid vision that in youth haunts our idea
of the poetical character, fades, upon acquaintance, into the light of common day; as
the azure tints that deck the mountain's brow
are lost on a nearer approach to them.   It is
well, according to the moral of one of the
Lyrical Ballads, — "To leave Yarrow un-
visited."   But to "leave this face-making,"
and begin.

I am a great admirer of the female writers of the present day ; they appear to me like so many modern muses. I could be in love with Mrs. Inchbald, romantic with Mrs. Radcliffe, and sarcastic with Madame D'Arblay : but they are novel-writers, and, like Audrey, may " thank the gods for not having made them poetical." Did any one here ever read Mrs. Leicester's School ? If they have not, I wish they would ; there will be just time before the next three volumes of the Tales of My Landlord come out. That is not a school of affectation, but of humanity. No one can think too highly of the work, or highly enough of the author.

The first poetess I can recollect is Mrs. Barbauld, with whose works I became acquainted before those of any other author, male or female, when I was learning to spell words of one syllable in her story-books for children. I became acquainted with her poetical works long after in Enfield's Speaker; and remember being much divided in my opinion, at that time, between her Ode to Spring and Collins's Ode to Evening. I wish I could repay my childish debt of gratitude in terms of appropriate praise. She is a very pretty poetess ; and, to my fancy, strews the flowers of poetry most agreeably round the

borders of religious controversy. She is a neat
and pointed prose-writer. Her " Thoughts
on the Inconsistency of Human Expectations"
is one of the most ingenious and sensible essays
in the language. There is the same idea in
one of Barrow's Sermons.

Mrs. Hannah More is another celebrated
modern poetess, and I believe still living. She
has written a great deal which I have never
read.

Miss Baillie must make up this trio of female poets. Her tragedies and comedies, one
of each to illustrate each of the passions.
separately, from the rest, are heresies in the
dramatic art. She is a Unitarian in poetry.
With her the passions are, like the French
republic, one and indivisible : they are not so
in nature, or in Shakspeare. Mr. Southey
has, I believe, somewhere expressed an
opinion that the Basil of Miss Baillie is
superior to Romeo and Juliet. I shall not
stay to contradict him. On the other hand, I
prefer her De Montfort, which was condemned on the stage, to some later tragedies, which
have been more fortunate—to the Remorse,
Bertram, and lastly, Fazio. There is in the
chief character of that play a nerve, a continued unity of interest, a setness of purpose
and precision of outline which John Kemble

alone was capable of giving; and there is all
the grace which women have in writing. In
saying that De Montfort was a character which
just suited Mr. Kemble, I mean to pay a
compliment to both. He was not "a man of
no mark or likelihood:" and what he could
be supposed to do particularly well must have
a meaning in it. As to the other tragedies
just mentioned, there is no reason why any
common actor should not "make mouths in
them at the invisible event,"—one as well as
another. Having thus expressed my sense of
the merits of this authoress, I must add that
her comedy of the Election, performed last
summer at the Lyceum with indifferent success, appears to me the perfection of baby-
house theatricals. Every thing in it has such
a *do-me-good* air, is so insipid and amiable.
Virtue seems such a pretty playing at make-
believe, and vice is such a naughty word. It
is a theory of some French author that little
girls ought not to be suffered to have dolls to
play with, to call them *pretty dears*, to admire
their black eyes and cherry cheeks, to lament
and bewail over them if they fall down and
hurt their faces, to praise them when they are
good, and scold them when they are naughty.
It is a school of affectation: Miss Baillie has
profited of it. She treats her grown men and

women as little girls treat their dolls—makes
moral puppets of them, pulls the wires, and
they talk virtue and act vice, according to their
cue and the title prefixed to each comedy or
tragedy, not from any real passions of their
own, or love either of virtue or vice.

The transition from these to Mr. Rogers's
Pleasures of Memory is not far : he is a very
lady-like poet. He is an elegant, but feeble
writer. He wraps up obvious thoughts in a
glittering cover of fine words ; is full of
enigmas with no meaning to them ; is studi-
ously inverted, and scrupulously far-fetched ;
and his verses are poetry, chiefly because no
particle, line, or syllable of them reads like
prose. He differs from Milton in this respect,
who is accused of having inserted a number
of prosaic lines in Paradise Lost. This kind of
poetry, which is a more minute and inoffensive species of the Della Cruscan, is like the
game of asking what one's thoughts are like.
It is a tortuous, tottering, wriggling, fidgetty
translation of every thing from the vulgar
tongue, into all the tantalizing, teasing,
tripping, lisping *mimminee-pimminee* of the
highest brilliancy and fashion of poetical
diction. You have nothing like truth of
nature or simplicity of expression. The
fastidious and languid reader is never shocked

by meeting, from the rarest chance in the world, with a single homely phrase or intelligible idea. You cannot see the thought for the ambiguity of the language, the figure for the finery, the picture for the varnish. The whole is refined, and frittered away into an appearance of the most evanescent brilliancy and tremulous imbecility.—There is no other fault to be found with the Pleasures of Memory than a want of taste and genius. The sentiments are amiable, and the notes at the end highly interesting, particularly the one relating to the Countess Pillar (as it is called) between Appleby and Penrith, erected (as the inscription tells the thoughtful traveller) by Anne Countess of Pembroke, in the year 1648, in memory of her last parting with her good and pious mother in the same place in the year 1616—

> " To shew that power of love, how great
> Beyond all human estimate."

This story is also told in the poem, but with so many artful inuendos and tinsel words that it is hardly intelligible, and still less does it reach the heart.

Campbell's Pleasures of Hope is of the same school, in which a painful attention is paid to the expression in proportion as there

is little to express, and the decomposition of
prose is substituted for the composition of
poetry. How much the sense and keeping
in the ideas are sacrificed to a jingle of words
and epigrammatic turn of expression, may be
seen in such lines as the following :---one of
the characters, an old invalid, wishes to end
his days under

> " Some hamlet shade, to yield his sickly form
> Health in the breeze, and shelter in the storm."

Now the antithesis here totally fails : for it is
the breeze, and not the tree, or, as it is
quaintly expressed, *hamlet shade,* that affords
health, though it is the tree that affords shelter
in or from the storm. Instances of the same
sort of *curiosa infelicitas* are not rare in this
author. His verses on the Battle of Hohen-
linden have considerable spirit and animation.
His Gertrude of Wyoming is his principal
performance. It is a kind of historical paraphrase of Mr. Wordsworth's poem of Ruth.
It shows little power, or power enervated by
extreme fastidiousness. It is

> " ——— Of outward show
> Elaborate ; of inward less exact."

There are painters who trust more to the
setting of their pictures than to the truth of
the likeness. Mr. Campbell always seems to

me to be thinking how his poetry will look
when it comes to be hot-pressed on superfine
wove paper, to have a disproportionate eye to
points and commas, and dread of errors of the
press. He is so afraid of doing wrong, of
making the smallest mistake, that he does
little or nothing. Lest he should wander
irretrievably from the right path, he stands
still. He writes according to established
etiquette. He offers the Muses no violence.
If he lights upon a good thought, he immediately drops it for fear of spoiling a good
thing. When he launches a sentiment that
you think will float him triumphantly for once
to the bottom of the stanza, he stops short at
the end of the first or second line, and stands
shivering on the brink of beauty, afraid to
trust himself to the fathomless abyss. *Tutus
nimium, timidusque procellarum.* His very
circumspection betrays him. The poet, as
well as the woman, that deliberates, is undone.
He is much like a man whose heart fails him
just as he is going up in a balloon, and who
breaks his neck by flinging himself out of it
when it is too late. Mr. Campbell too often
maims and mangles his ideas before they are full
formed, to form them to the Procrustes' bed
of criticism; or strangles his intellectual offspring in the birth, lest they should come to

an untimely end in the Edinburgh Review. He plays the hypercritic on himself, and starves his genius to death from a needless apprehension of a plethora. No writer who thinks habitually of the critics, either to tremble at their censures or set them at defiance, can write well. It is the business of reviewers to watch poets, not of poets to watch reviewers. There is one admirable simile in this poem, of the European child brought by the sooty Indian in his hand, " like morning brought by night." The love-scenes of Gertrude of Wyoming breathe a balmy voluptuousness of sentiment ; but they are generally broken off in the middle ; they are like the scent of a bank of violets, faint and rich, which the gale suddenly conveys in a different direction. Mr. Campbell is careful of his own reputation, and economical of the pleasures of his readers. He treats them as the fox in the fable treated his guest the stork ; or, to use his own expression, his fine things are

" Like angels' visits, few, and far between."*

---

* There is the same idea in Blair's Grave.
" ———— Its visits,
Like those of angels, short, and far between."
Mr. Campbell, in altering the expression, has spoiled it. " Few," and " far between," are the same thing.

There is another fault in this poem, which is the mechanical structure of the fable. The most striking events occur in the shape of antitheses. The story is cut into the form of a parallelogram. There is the same systematic alternation of good and evil, of violence and repose, that there is of light and shade in a picture. The Indian, who is the chief agent in the interest of the poem, vanishes and returns after long intervals, like the periodical revolutions of the planets. He unexpectedly appears just in the nick of time, after years of absence, and without any known reason but the convenience of the author and the astonishment of the reader; as if nature were a machine constructed on a principle of complete contrast, to produce a theatrical effect. *Nec Deus intersit, nisi dignus vindice nodus.* Mr. Campbell's savage never appears but upon great occasions, and then his punctuality is preternatural and alarming. He is the most wonderful instance on record of poetical *reliability*. The most dreadful mischiefs happen at the most mortifying moments; and when your expectations are wound up to the highest pitch, you are sure to have them knocked on the head by a premeditated and remorseless stroke of the poet's pen. This is done so often for the convenience of the author, that in the end it ceases to be for the satisfaction of the reader.

Tom Moore is a poet of a quite different stamp. He is as heedless, gay, and prodigal of his poetical wealth, as the other is careful, reserved, and parsimonious. The genius of both is national. Mr. Moore's Muse is another Ariel, as light, as tricksy, as indefatigable, and as humane a spirit. His fancy is for ever on the wing, flutters in the gale, glitters in the sun. Every thing lives, moves, and sparkles in his poetry, while over all love waves his purple light. His thoughts are as restless, as many, and as bright, as the insects that people the sun's beam. " So work the honey-bees," extracting liquid sweets from opening buds; so the butterfly expands its wings to the idle air ; so the thistle's silver down is wafted over summer seas. An airy voyager on life's stream, his mind inhales the fragrance of a thousand shores, and drinks of endless pleasures under halcyon skies.— Wherever his footsteps tend over the enamelled ground of fairy fiction —

> " Around him the bees in play flutter and cluster,
>   And gaudy butterflies frolic around."

The fault of Mr. Moore is an exuberance of involuntary power. His facility of production lessens the effect of, and hangs as a dead weight upon, what he produces. His levity at last oppresses. The infinite delight he takes in such an infinite number of things, creates indifference in minds less susceptible of pleasure than his own. He exhausts attention by being inexhaustible. His variety cloys; his rapidity dazzles and distracts the sight. The graceful ease with which he lends himself to every subject, the genial spirit with which he indulges in every sentiment, prevents him from giving their full force to the masses of things, from connecting them into a whole. He wants intensity, strength, and grandeur. His mind does not brood over the great and permanent; it glances over the surfaces, the first impressions of things, instead of grappling with the deep-rooted prejudices of the mind, its inveterate habits, and that " perilous stuff that weighs upon the heart." His pen, as it is rapid and fanciful, wants momentum and passion. It requires the same principle to make us thoroughly like poetry that makes us like ourselves so well the feeling of continued identity. The impressions of Mr. Moore's poetry are detached, desultory, and physical. Its gorgeous colours brighten and fade like the rainbow's. Its sweetness evaporates like the effluvia exhaled from beds of flowers! His gay laughing style, which relates to the immediate pleasures of love or wine, is better than his sentimental and romantic vein. His Irish melodies are not free from affectation and a certain sickliness of pretension. His serious descriptions are apt to run into flowery tenderness. His pathos sometimes melts into a mawkish sensibility, or crystallizes into all the prettinesses of allegorical language, and glittering hardness of external imagery. But he has wit at will, and of the first quality. His satirical and burlesque poetry is his best : it is first-rate. His Twopenny Post-Bag is a perfect " nest of spicery ;" where the Cayenne is not spared. The politician there sharpens the poet's pen. In this, too, our bard resembles the bee—he has its honey and its sting.

Mr. Moore ought not to have written Lalla Rookh, even for three thousand guineas. His fame is worth more than that. He should have minded the advice of Fadladeen. It is not, however, a failure, so much as an evasion and a consequent disappointment of public expectation. He should have left it to others to break conventions with nations, and faith with the world. He should, at any rate, have kept his with the public. Lalla Rookh is not what people wanted to see whether Mr.

Moore could do—namely, whether he could write a long epic poem. It is four short tales. The interest, however, is often high-wrought and tragic, but the execution still turns to the effeminate and voluptuous side.   Fortitude of mind is the first requisite of a tragic or epic writer.   Happiness of nature and felicity of genius are the pre-eminent characteristics of the bard of Erin.   If he is not perfectly contented with what he is, all the world beside is.   He had no temptation to risk any thing in adding to the love and admiration of his age, and more than one country.

> " Therefore to be possessed with double pomp,
>   To guard a title that was rich before,
>   To gild refined gold, to paint the lily,
>   To throw a perfume on the violet,
>   To smooth the ice, or add another hue
>   Unto the rainbow, or with taper light
>   To seek the beauteous eye of heav'n to garnish,
>   Is wasteful and ridiculous excess."

The same might be said of Mr. Moore's seeking to bind an epic crown, or the shadow of one, round his other laurels.

If Mr. Moore has not suffered enough personally, Lord Byron (judging from the tone of his writings) might be thought to have suffered too much to be a truly great poet. If Mr. Moore lays himself too open to all the various impulses of things, the outward shows of earth and sky, to every breath that blows, to every stray sentiment that crosses his fancy ; Lord Byron shuts himself up too much in the impenetrable gloom of his own thoughts, and buries the natural light of things in " nook monastic." The Giaour, the Corsair, Childe Harold, are all the same person, and they are apparently all himself. The everlasting repetition of one subject, the same dark ground of fiction, with the darker colours of the poet's mind spread over it, the unceasing accumulation of horrors on horror's head, steels the mind against the sense of pain as inevitably as the unwearied Siren sounds and luxurious monotony of Mr. Moore's poetry make it inaccessible to pleasure.

Lord Byron's poetry is as morbid as Mr. Moore's is careless and dissipated. He has more depth of passion, more force and impetuosity, but the passion is always of the same unaccountable character, at once violent and sullen, fierce and gloomy. It is not the passion of a mind struggling with misfortune, or the hopelessness of its desires, but of a mind preying upon itself, and disgusted with, or indifferent to, all other things. There is nothing less poetical than this sort of unaccommodating selfishness. There is nothing more repulsive than this sort of ideal absorp-

tion of all the interests of others, of the good
and ills of life, in the ruling passion and
moody abstraction of a single mind, as if it
would make itself the centre of the universe,
and there was nothing worth cherishing but
its intellectual diseases. It is like a cancer,
eating into the heart of poetry. But still
there is power; and power rivets attention
and forces admiration. " He hath a demon :"
and that is the next thing to being full of the
God. His brow collects the scattered gloom:
his eye flashes livid fire that withers and con-
sumes. But still we watch the progress of
the scathing bolt with interest, and mark the
ruin it leaves behind with awe. Within the
contracted range of his imagination, he has
great unity and truth of keeping. He chooses
elements and agents congenial to his mind, the
dark and glittering ocean, the frail bark hurrying before the storm, pirates and men that
" house on the wild sea with wild usages."
He gives the tumultuous eagerness of action,
and the fixed despair of thought. In vigour
of style and force of conception, he in one
sense surpasses every writer of the present
day. His indignant apothegms are like oracles
of misanthropy. He who wishes for " a curse
to kill with," may find it in Lord Byron's
writings. Yet he has beauty lurking under-

neath his strength, tenderness sometimes joined with the phrenzy of despair. A flash of golden light sometimes follows from a stroke of his pencil, like a falling meteor. The flowers that adorn his poetry bloom over charnel-houses and the grave !

There is one subject on which Lord Byron is fond of writing, on which I wish he would not write — Bonaparte. Not that I quarrel with his writing for him, or against him, but but with his writing both for him and against him. What right has he to do this? Bonaparte's character, be it what else it may, does not change every hour according to his Lordship's varying humour. He is not a pipe for Fortune's finger, or for his Lordship's Muse, to play what stop she pleases on. Why should Lord Byron now laud him to the skies in the hour of his success, and then peevishly wreak his disappointment on the god of his idolatry? The man he writes of does not rise or fall with circumstances : but " looks on tempests and is never shaken." Besides, he is a subject for history, and not for poetry.

> " Great princes' favourites their fair leaves spread,
>   But as the marigold at the sun's eye,
>   And in themselves their pride lies buried ;
>   For at a frown they in their glory die.
>   The painful warrior, famoused for fight,
>   After a thousand victories once foil'd,

Is from the book of honour razed quite,
  And all the rest forgot for which he toil'd."

If Lord Byron will write any thing more on
this hazardous theme, let him take these lines
of Shakspeare for his guide, and finish them
in the spirit of the original — they will then
be worthy of the subject.

Walter Scott is the most popular of all the
poets of the present day, and deservedly so.
He describes that which is most easily and
generally understood with more vivacity and
effect than any body else. He has no excellences, either of a lofty or recondite kind,
which lie beyond the reach of the most ordinary capacity to find out ; but he has all the
good qualities which all the world agree to
understand. His style is clear, flowing, and
transparent : his sentiments, of which his style
is an easy and natural medium, are common
to him with his readers. He has none of
Mr. Wordsworth's *idiosyncracy*. He differs
from his readers only in a greater range of
knowledge and facility of expression. His
poetry belongs to the class of *improvisatori*
poetry. It has neither depth, height, nor
breadth in it ; neither uncommon strength,
nor uncommon refinement of thought, sentiment, or language. It has no originality.
But if this author has no research, no moving

power in his own breast, he relies with the greater safety and success on the force of his subject. He selects a story such as is sure to please, full of incidents, characters, peculiar manners, costume, and scenery ; and he tells it in a way that can offend no one. He never wearies or disappoints you. He is communicative and garrulous ; but he is not his own hero. He never obtrudes himself on your notice to prevent your seeing the subject. What passes in the poem passes much as it would have done in reality. The author has little or nothing to do with it. Mr. Scott has great intuitive power of fancy, great vividness of pencil in placing external objects and events before the eye. The force of his mind is picturesque, rather than *moral*. He gives more of the features of nature than the soul of passion. He conveys the distinct outlines and visible changes in outward objects, rather than " their mortal consequences." He is very inferior to Lord Byron in intense passion, to Moore in delightful fancy, to Mr. Wordsworth in profound sentiment : but he has more picturesque power than any of them ; that is, he places the objects themselves, about which *they* might feel and think, in a much more striking point of view, with greater variety of dress and attitude, and with

more local truth of colouring. His imagery
is Gothic and grotesque. The manners and
actions have the interest and curiosity belonging to a wild country and a distant period of
time. Few descriptions have a more complete reality, a more striking appearance of
life and motion, than that of the warriors in
the Lady of the Lake, who start up at the
command of Roderick Dhu, from their con-
cealment under the fern, and disappear again
in an instant. The Lay of the Last Minstrel
and Marmion are the first, and perhaps the
best, of his works. The Goblin Page, in
the first of these, is a very interesting and
inscrutable little personage. In reading these
poems, I confess I am a little disconcerted,
in turning over the page, to find Mr. Westall's
pictures, which always seem *fac-similes* of
the persons represented, with ancient costume
and a theatrical air. This may be a compliment to Mr. Westall, but it is not one to
Walter Scott. The truth is, there is a
modern air in the midst of the antiquarian
research of Mr. Scott's poetry. It is history
or tradition in masquerade. Not only the
crust of old words and images is worn off
with time,—the substance is grown comparatively light and worthless. The forms are old
and uncouth ; but the spirit is effeminate and

frivolous. This is a deduction from the praise
I have given to his pencil for extreme fidelity,
though it has been no obstacle to its drawing-
room success. He has just hit the town
between the romantic and the fashionable ;
and, between the two, secured all classes of
readers on his side. In a word, I conceive
that he is to the great poet what an excellent
mimic is to a great actor. There is no de-
terminate impression left on the mind by
reading his poetry. It has no results. The
reader rises up from the perusal with new
images and associations, but he remains the
same man that he was before. A great mind
is one that moulds the minds of others. Mr.
Scott has put the Border Minstrelsy and
scattered traditions of the country into easy,
animated verse. But the Notes to his poems
are just as entertaining as the poems themselves, and his poems are only entertaining.

Mr. Wordsworth is the most original poet
now living. He is the reverse of Walter
Scott in his defects and excellences. He has
nearly all that the other wants, and wants all
that the other possesses. His poetry is not
external, but internal ; it does not depend
upon tradition, or story, or old song ; he fur-
nishes it from his own mind, and is his own
subject. He is the poet of mere sentiment.

Of many of the Lyrical Ballads, it is not
possible to speak in terms of too high praise,
such as Hart-leap Well, the Banks of the
Wye, Poor Susan, parts of the Leech-gatherer,
the lines to a Cuckoo, to a Daisy, the Complaint, several of the Sonnets, and a hundred
others of inconceivable beauty, of perfect
originality and pathos.   They open a finer
and deeper vein of thought and feeling than
any poet in modern times has done, or attempted.   He has produced a deeper impression, and on a smaller circle, than any other
of his contemporaries.   His powers have
been mistaken by the age, nor does he exactly
understand them himself.   He cannot form a
whole.   He has not the constructive faculty.
He can give only the fine tones of thought,
drawn from his mind by accident or nature,
like the sounds drawn from the Æolian harp
by the wandering gale.—He is totally deficient
in all the machinery of poetry.   His *Excursion*, taken as a whole, notwithstanding the
noble materials thrown away in it, is a proof
of this.   The line labours, the sentiment
moves slow, but the poem stands stock-still.
The reader makes no way from the first line
to the last.   It is more than any thing in the
world like Robinson Crusoe's boat, which
would have been an excellent good boat, and

would have carried him to the other side of
the globe, but that he could not get it out of
the sand where it stuck fast. I did what little
I could to help to launch it at the time, but
it would not do. I am not, however, one of
those who laugh at the attempts or failures of
men of genius. It is not my way to cry
" Long life to the conqueror." Success and
desert are not with me synonymous terms;
and the less Mr. Wordsworth's general merits
have been understood, the more necessary is
it to insist upon them. This is not the place
to repeat what I have already said on the subject. The reader may turn to it in the Round
Table.* I do not think, however, there is any
thing in the larger poem equal to many of the
detached pieces in the Lyrical Ballads. As
Mr. Wordsworth's poems have been little
known to the public, or chiefly through garbled
extracts from them, I will here give an entire
poem (one that has always been a favourite
with me), that the reader may know what it is
that the admirers of this author find to be
delighted with in his poetry. Those who
do not feel the beauty and the force of it
may save themselves the trouble of inquiring
farther.

* The criticism referred to will be found in the Appendix.

HART-LEAP WELL.

" The knight had ridden down from Wensley moor
    With the slow motion of a summer's cloud ;
He turned aside towards a vassal's door,
    And, ' Bring another horse !' he cried aloud.

' Another horse !'—That shout the vassal heard,
    And saddled his best steed, a comely gray ;
Sir Walter mounted him ; he was the third
    Which he had mounted on that glorious day.

Joy sparkled in the prancing courser's eyes :
    The horse and horseman are a happy pair ;
But, though Sir Walter like a falcon flies,
    There is a doleful silence in the air.

A rout this morning left Sir Walter's hall,
    That as they galloped made the echoes roar ;
But horse and man are vanished, one and all ;
    Such race, I think, was never seen before.

Sir Walter, restless as a veering wind,
    Calls to the few tired dogs that yet remain :
Brach, Swift, and Music, noblest of their kind,
    Follow, and up the weary mountain strain.

The knight hallooed, he chid and cheered them on
    With suppliant gestures and upbraidings stern ;
But breath and eye-sight fail ; and, one by one,
    The dogs are stretched among the mountain fern.

Where is the throng, the tumult of the race ?
    The bugles that so joyfully were blown ?
—This chase it looks not like an earthly chase ;
    Sir Walter and the hart are left alone.

The poor hart toils along the mountain side ;
  I will not stop to tell how far he fled,
Nor will I mention by what death he died ;
  But now the knight beholds him lying dead.

Dismounting then, he leaned against a thorn ;
  He had no follower, dog, nor man, nor boy :
He neither smacked his whip nor blew his horn,
  But gazed upon the spoil with silent joy.

Close to the thorn on which Sir Walter leaned,
  Stood his dumb partner in this glorious act ;
Weak as a lamb the hour that it is yeaned ;
  And foaming like a mountain cataract.

Upon his side the hart was lying stretched :
  His nose half-touched a spring beneath a hill,
And with the last deep groan his breath had fetched
  The waters of the spring were trembling still.

And now, too happy for repose or rest,
  (Was never man in such a joyful case !)
Sir Walter walked all round, north, south, and west,
  And gazed, and gazed upon that darling place.

And climbing up the hill—(it was at least,
  Nine roods of sheer ascent) Sir Walter found,
Three several hoof-marks which the hunted beast
  Had left imprinted on the verdant ground.

Sir Walter wiped his face and cried, ' Till now
  Such sight was never seen by living eyes :
Three leaps have borne him from this lofty brow,
  Down to the very fountain where he lies.

I'll build a pleasure-house upon this spot,
  And a small arbour, made for rural joy ;
'Twill be the traveller's shed, the pilgrim's cot,
  A place of love for damsels that are coy.

A cunning artist will I have to frame
  A bason for that fountain in the dell ;
And they, who do make mention of the same
  From this day forth, shall call it HART-LEAP WELL.

And, gallant brute ! to make thy praises known,
  Another monument shall here be raised ;
Three several pillars, each a rough-hewn stone,
  And planted where thy hoofs the turf have grazed.

And, in the summer-time when days are long,
  I will come hither with my paramour ;
And with the dancers, and the minstrel's song,
  We will make merry in that pleasant bower.

Till the foundations of the mountains fail,
  My mansion with its arbour shall endure ;—
The joy of them who till the fields of Swale,
  And them who dwell among the woods of Ure !'

Then home he went, and left the hart, stone dead,
  With breathless nostrils stretched above the spring,
—Soon did the knight perform what he had said,
  And far and wide the fame thereof did ring.

Ere thrice the moon into her port had steered,
  A cup of stone received the living well ;
Three pillars of rude stone Sir Walter reared,
  And built a house of pleasure in the dell.

And near the fountain, flowers of stature tall
  With trailing plants and trees were intertwined,—
Which soon composed a little sylvan hall,
  A leafy shelter from the sun and wind.

And thither, when the summer-days were long,
  Sir Walter journeyed with his paramour ;
And with the dancers and the minstrel's song
  Made merriment within that pleasant bower.

The knight, Sir Walter, died in course of time,
    And his bones lie in his paternal vale.—
But there is matter for a second rhyme,
    And I to this would add another tale."

PART SECOND.

" The moving accident is not my trade:
    To freeze the blood I have no ready arts:
'Tis my delight, alone in summer shade,
    To pipe a simple song for thinking hearts.

As I from Hawes to Richmond did repair,
    It chanced that I saw standing in a dell
Three aspens at three corners of a square,
    And one, not four yards distant, near a well.

What this imported I could ill divine:
    And, pulling now the rein my horse to stop,
I saw three pillars standing in a line,
    The last stone pillar on a dark hill-top.

The trees were grey, with neither arms nor head;
    Half-wasted the square mound of tawny green;
So that you just might say, as then I said,
    ' Here in old time the hand of man hath been.'

I looked upon the hill both far and near,
    More doleful place did never eye survey;
It seemed as if the spring-time came not here,
    And Nature here were willing to decay.

I stood in various thoughts and fancies lost,
    When one, who was in shepherd's garb attired,
Came up the hollow:—Him did I accost,
    And what this place might be I then inquired.

The shepherd stopped, and that same story told
  Which in my former rhyme I have rehearsed.
'A jolly place,' said he, ' in times of old !
  But something ails it now ; the spot is curst.

You see these lifeless stumps of aspen wood—
  Some say that they are beeches, others elms—
These were the bower ; and here a mansion stood,
  The finest palace of a hundred realms !

The arbour does its own condition tell ;
  You see the stones, the fountain, and the stream ;
But as to the great lodge ! you might as well
  Hunt half a day for a forgotten dream.

There's neither dog nor heifer, horse nor sheep,
  Will wet his lips within that cup of stone;
And oftentimes, when all are fast asleep,
  This water doth send forth a dolorous groan.

Some say that here a murder has been done,
  And blood cries out for blood : but, for my part,
I've guessed, when I've been sitting in the sun,
  That it was all for that unhappy hart.

What thoughts must through the creature's brain have
        passed !
  Even from the topmost stone, upon the steep,
Are but three bounds—and look, Sir, at this last—
  O Master ! it has been a cruel leap.

For thirteen hours he ran a desperate race ;
  And in my simple mind we cannot tell
What cause the hart might have to love this place,
  And come and make his death-bed near the well.

Here on the grass perhaps asleep he sank,
  Lulled by this fountain in the summer-tide ;
This water was perhaps the first he drank
  When he had wandered from his mother's side.

In April here beneath the scented thorn
 He heard the birds their morning carols sing ;
And he, perhaps, for aught we know, was born
 Not half a furlong from that self-same spring.

But now here's neither grass nor pleasant shade ;
 The sun on drearier hollow never shone ;
So will it be, as I have often said,
 Till trees, and stones, and fountain all are gone.'

' Grey-headed Shepherd, thou hast spoken well ;
 Small difference lies between thy creed and mine :
This beast not unobserved by Nature fell ;
 His death was mourned by sympathy divine.

The Being that is in the clouds and air,
 That is in the green leaves among the groves,
Maintains a deep and reverential care
 For the unoffending creatures whom he loves.

The pleasure-house is dust :—behind, before,
 This is no common waste, no common gloom ;
But Nature, in due course of time, once more
 Shall here put on her beauty and her bloom.

She leaves these objects to a slow decay,
 That what we are, and have been, may be known ;
But, at the coming of the milder day,
 These monuments shall all be overgrown.

One lesson, Shepherd, let us two divide,
 Taught both by what she shows, and what conceals,
Never to blend our pleasure or our pride
 With sorrow of the meanest thing that feels.' "

Mr. Wordsworth is at the head of that
which has been denominated the Lake school

of poetry; a school which, with all my respect for it, I do not think sacred from
criticism or exempt from faults, of some of
which faults I shall speak with becoming
frankness; for I do not see that the liberty
of the press ought to be shackled, or freedom
of speech curtailed, to screen either its revo-
lutionary or renegado extravagances. This
school of poetry had its origin in the French
revolution, or rather in those sentiments and
opinions which produced that revolution; and
which sentiments and opinions were indirectly
imported into this country in translations from
the German about that period. Our poetical
literature had, towards the close of the last
century, degenerated into the most trite, insipid, and mechanical of all things, in the
hands of the followers of Pope and the old
French school of poetry. It wanted something to stir it up, and it found that something in the principles and events of the
French revolution. From the impulse it thus
received, it rose at once from the most servile
imitation and tamest common-place to the
utmost pitch of singularity and paradox. The
change in the belles-lettres was as complete,
and to many persons as startling, as the change
in politics with which it went hand in hand.
There was a mighty ferment in the heads of

statesmen and poets, kings and people. —
According to the prevailing notions, all was
to be natural and new. Nothing that was
established was to be tolerated. All the
common-place figures of poetry, tropes, alle-
gories, personifications, with the whole heathen mythology, were instantly discarded ; a
classical allusion was considered as a piece of
antiquated foppery ; capital letters were no
more allowed in print than letters - patent
of nobility were permitted in real life ; kings
and queens were dethroned from their rank
and station in legitimate tragedy or epic
poetry, as they were decapitated elsewhere ;
rhyme was looked upon as a relic of the
feudal system, and regular metre was abo-
lished along with regular government. —
Authority and fashion, elegance or arrange-
ment, were hooted out of countenance, as
pedantry and prejudice. Every one did that
which was good in his own eyes. The object
was to reduce all things to an absolute level ;
and a singularly affected and outrageous simplicity prevailed in dress and manners, in
style and sentiment. A striking effect produced where it was least expected, something
new and original, no matter whether good,
bad, or indifferent, whether mean or lofty,
extravagant or childish, was all that was aimed

at, or considered as compatible with sound
philosophy and an age of reason.   The licentiousness grew extreme : Coryate's Crudities
were nothing to it.   The world was to be
turned topsy-turvy ; and poetry, by the good-
will of our Adam-wits, was to share its fate,
and begin *de novo*.   It was a time of promise,
a renewal of the world and of letters ; and
the Deucalions, who were to perform this
feat of regeneration, were the present poet-
laureat and the two authors of the Lyrical
Ballads.   The Germans, who made heroes
of robbers, and honest women of cast-off
mistresses, had already exhausted the extravagant and marvellous in sentiment and situation ; our native writers adopted a wonderful
simplicity of style and matter.   The paradox
they set out with was that all things are by
nature equally fit subjects for poetry ; or that,
if there is any preference to be given, those
that are the meanest and most unpromising
are the best, as they leave the greatest scope
for the unbounded stores of thought and
fancy in the writer's own mind.   Poetry had
with them " neither buttress nor coigne of
vantage to make its pendant bed and pro-
creant cradle."   It was not " born so high :
its aiery buildeth in the cedar's top, and dallies
with the wind, and scorns the sun."   It grew

like a mushroom out of the ground; or was
hidden in it like a truffle, which it required
a particular sagacity and industry to find out
and dig up.   They founded the new school
on a principle of sheer humanity, on pure
nature void of art.   It could not be said of
these sweeping reformers and dictators in the
republic of letters, that " in their train walked
crowns and crownets; that realms and islands,
like plates, dropt from their pockets :" but
they were surrounded, in company with the
Muses, by a mixed rabble of idle apprentices
and Botany Bay convicts, female vagrants,
gipsies, meek daughters in the family of
Christ, of idiot boys and mad mothers, and
after them " owls and night-ravens flew."—
They scorned " degrees, priority, and place,
insisture, course, proportion, season, form,
office, and custom, in all line of order :"—
the distinctions of birth, the vicissitudes of
fortune, did not enter into their abstracted,
lofty, and levelling calculation of human
nature.   He who was more than man with
them was none.   They claimed kindred only
with the commonest of the people : peasants,
pedlars, and village-barbers were their oracles
and bosom friends.   Their poetry, in the
extreme to which it professedly tended, and
was in effect carried, levels all distinctions of

nature and society ; has " no figures nor no
fantasies," which the prejudices of superstition
or the customs of the world draw in the
brains of men ; " no trivial fond records " of
all that has existed in the history of past ages;
it has no adventitious pride, pomp, or circumstance, to set it off; " the marshal's truncheon,
nor the judge's robe ;" neither tradition, reverence, nor ceremony, " that to great ones
'longs :" it breaks in pieces the golden images
of poetry, and defaces its armorial bearings,
to melt them down in the mould of common
humanity or of its own upstart self-sufficiency.
They took the same method in their new-
fangled " metre ballad-mongering " scheme,
which Rousseau did in his prose paradoxes—
of exciting attention by reversing the established standards of opinion and estimation in
the world.   They were for bringing poetry
back to its primitive simplicity and state of
nature, as he was for bringing society back to
the savage state : so that the only thing remarkable left in the world by this change
would be the persons who had produced it.
A thorough adept in this school of poetry
and philanthropy is jealous of all excellence
but his own.   He does not even like to share
his reputation with his subject ; for he would
have it all to proceed from his own power and

originality of mind. Such a one is slow to admire any thing that is admirable; feels no interest in what is most interesting to others, no grandeur in any thing grand, no beauty in any thing beautiful. He tolerates only what he himself creates; he sympathizes only with what can enter into no competition with him, with " the bare trees and mountains bare, and grass in the green field." He sees nothing but himself and the universe. He hates all greatness and all pretensions to it, whether well or ill founded. His egotism is in some respects a madness; for he scorns even the admiration of himself, thinking it a presumption in any one to suppose that he has taste or sense enough to understand him. He hates all science and all art; he hates chemistry, he hates conchology; he hates Voltaire; he hates Sir Isaac Newton; he hates wisdom; he hates wit; he hates metaphysics, which, he says, are unintelligible, and yet he would be thought to understand them; he hates prose; he hates all poetry but his own; he hates the dialogues in Shakspeare; he hates music, dancing, and painting; he hates Rubens, he hates Rembrandt; he hates Raphael, he hates Titian; he hates Vandyke; he hates the antique; he hates the Apollo Belvidere · he hates the Venus of Medicis. This is the

reason that so few people take an interest in
his writings, because he takes an interest in
nothing that others do !—The effect has been
perceived as something odd ; but the cause or
principle has never been distinctly traced to
its source before, as far as I know.   The
proofs are to be found every where—in Mr.
Southey's Botany Bay Eclogues, in his book
of Songs and Sonnets, his Odes and Inscrip-
tions, so well parodied in the Anti-Jacobin
Review, in his Joan of Arc, and last, though
not least, in his Wat Tyler :

> " When Adam delved, and Eve span,
> Where was then the gentleman ?"—

(or the poet laureate either, we may ask ?)—
in Mr. Coleridge's Ode to an Ass's Foal, in
his lines to Sarah, his Religious Musings ;
and in his and Mr. Wordsworth's Lyrical
Ballads, *passim*.

Of Mr. Southey's larger epics, I have but
a faint recollection at this distance of time,
but all that I remember of them is mechanical
and extravagant, heavy and superficial.   His
affected, disjointed style is well imitated in
the Rejected Addresses.   The difference between him and Sir Richard Blackmore seems
to be that the one is heavy and the other
light, the one solemn and the other prag-

matical, the one phlegmatic and the other
flippant ; and that there is no Gay in the
present time to give a Catalogue Raisonné of
the performances of the living undertaker of
epics. Kehama is a loose sprawling figure,
such as we see cut out of wood or paper, and
pulled or jerked with wire or thread, to make
sudden and surprising motions, without meaning, grace, or nature in them. By far the
best of his works are some of his shorter
personal compositions, in which there is an
ironical mixture of the quaint and serious,
such as his lines on a picture of Gaspar
Poussin, the fine tale of Gualberto, his Description of a Pig, and the Holly-tree, which
is an affecting, beautiful, and modest retro-
spect on his own character. May the aspiration with which it concludes be fulfilled ! * —

---

* " O reader ! hast thou ever stood to see
　　The Holly Tree ?
　The eye that contemplates it well perceives
　　Its glossy leaves,
　Ordered by an intelligence so wise
　As might confound the Atheist's sophistries.

　Below, a circling fence, its leaves are seen
　　Wrinkled and keen ;
　No grazing cattle through their prickly round
　　Can reach to wound ;
　But as they grow where nothing is to fear,
　Smooth and unarm'd the pointless leaves appear.

But the little he has done of true and sterling excellence is overloaded by the quantity of indifferent matter which he turns out every

---

I love to view these things with curious eyes,
    And moralize;
And in the wisdom of the Holly Tree
    Can emblems see
Wherewith perchance to make a pleasant rhyme,
Such as may profit in the after time.

So, though abroad perchance I might appear
    Harsh and austere,
To those who on my leisure would intrude
    Reserved and rude,
Gentle at home amid my friends I'd be,
Like the high leaves upon the Holly Tree.

And should my youth, as youth is apt, I know,
    Some harshness show,
All vain asperities I day by day
    Would wear away,
Till the smooth temper of my age should be
Like the high leaves upon the Holly Tree.

And as when all the summer trees are seen
    So bright and green,
The Holly leaves their fadeless hues display
    Less bright than they,
But when the bare and wintry woods we see,
What then so cheerful as the Holly Tree?

So serious should my youth appear among
    The thoughtless throng,
So would I seem amid the young and gay
    More grave than they,
That in my age as cheerful I might be
As the green winter of the Holly Tree."—

year, " prosing or versing," with equally mechanical and irresistible facility.   His Essays,
or political and moral disquisitions, are *not* so
full of original matter as Montaigne's.   They
are second or third rate compositions in that
class.

It remains that I should say a few words of
Mr. Coleridge ;   and there is no one who has
a better right to say what he thinks of him
than I have.   " Is there here any dear friend
of Cæsar ?   To him I say, that Brutus's love
to Cæsar was no less than his."   But no matter.—His Ancient Mariner is his most remarkable performance, and the only one that
I could point out to any one as giving an
adequate idea of his great natural powers.   It
is high German, however, and in it he seems
to " conceive of poetry but as a drunken
dream, reckless, careless, and heedless, of
past, present, and to come."   His tragedies
(for he has written two) are not answerable to
it ; they are, except a few poetical passages,
drawling sentiment and metaphysical jargon.
He has no genuine dramatic talent.   There is
one fine passage in his Christabel, that which
contains the description of the quarrel between
Sir Leoline and Sir Roland de Vaux of
Tryermaine, who had been friends in youth.

" Alas ! they had been friends in youth,
But whispering tongues can poison truth ;
And constancy lives in realms above !
And life is thorny ! and youth is vain ;
And to be wroth with one we love,
Doth work like madness in the brain :
And thus it chanc'd as I divine,
With Roland and Sir Leoline.

Each spake words of high disdain
And insult to his heart's best brother,
And parted ne'er to meet again !
But neither ever found another
To free the hollow heart from paining—

They stood aloof, the scars remaining,
Like cliffs which had been rent asunder :
A dreary sea now flows between,
But neither heat, nor frost, nor thunder,
Shall wholly do away I ween
The marks of that which once hath been.

Sir Leoline a moment's space
Stood gazing on the damsel's face ;
And the youthful lord of Tryermaine
Came back upon his heart again."

It might seem insidious if I were to praise
his ode entitled Fire, Famine, and Slaughter,
as an effusion of high poetical enthnsiasm,
and strong political feeling. His Sonnet to
Schiller conveys a fine compliment to the
author of the Robbers, and an equally fine
idea of the state of youthful enthusiasm in
which he composed it.

" Schiller ! that hour I would have wish'd to die,
  If through the shudd'ring midnight I had sent
  From the dark dungeon of the tower time-rent,
That fearful voice, a famish'd father's cry—

That in no after moment aught less vast
  Might stamp me mortal ! A triumphant shout
  Black Horror scream'd, and all her goblin rout
From the more with'ring scene diminish'd pass'd.

Ah ! Bard tremendous in sublimity !
  Could I behold thee in thy loftier mood,
Wand'ring at eve, with finely frenzied eye,
  Beneath some vast old tempest-swinging wood !
  Awhile, with mute awe gazing, I would brood,
Then weep aloud in a wild ecstacy !"—

His *Conciones ad Populum,* Watchman,
&c. are dreary trash. Of his Friend, I have
spoken the truth elsewhere. But I may say
of him here, that he is the only person I ever
knew who answered to the idea of a man of
genius. He is the only person from whom I
ever learnt any thing. There is only one thing
he could learn from me in return, but *that* he
has not. He was the first poet I ever knew.
His genius at that time had angelic wings,
and fed on manna. He talked on for ever ;
and you wished him to talk on for ever. His
thoughts did not seem to come with labour
and effort ; but as if borne on the gusts of
genius, and as if the wings of his imagination
lifted him from off his feet. His voice rolled

on the ear like the pealing organ, and its
sound alone was the music of thought. His
mind was clothed with wings; and raised on
them, he lifted philosophy to heaven. In his
descriptions, you then saw the progress of
numan happiness and liberty in bright and
never - ending succession, like the steps of
Jacob's ladder, with airy shapes ascending
and descending, and with the voice of God
at the top of the ladder. And shall I, who
heard him then, listen to him now? Not
I! That spell is broke; that time is gone
for ever; that voice is heard no more: but
still the recollection comes rushing by with
thoughts of long-past years, and rings in my
ears with never-dying sound.

> " What though the radiance which was once so bright,
> Be now for ever vanish'd from my sight,
> Though nothing can bring back the hour
> Of glory in the grass, of splendour in the flow'r;
>   I do not grieve, but rather find
>   Strength in what remains behind;
>   In the primal sympathy,
>   Which having been, must ever be;
>   In the soothing thoughts that spring
>   Out of human suffering;
> In years that bring the philosophic mind !"—

I have thus gone through the task I intended, and have come at last to the level ground.
I have felt my subject gradually sinking from

under me as I advanced, and have been afraid
of ending in nothing. The interest has unavoidably decreased at almost every successive
step of the progress, like a play that has its
catastrophe in the first or second act. This,
however, I could not help. I have done as
well as I could.

THE END.

APPENDIX.

I.

ON MILTON'S LYCIDAS.

" At last he rose, and twitched his mantle blue .
To-morrow to fresh woods and pastures new."

OF all Milton's smaller poems, *Lycidas* is the
greatest favourite with me. I cannot agree to
the charge which Dr. Johnson has brought against
it of pedantry and want of feeling. It is the fine
emanation of classical sentiment in a youthful
scholar—" most musical, most melancholy." A
certain tender gloom overspreads it, a wayward
abstraction, a forgetfulness of his subject in the
serious reflections that arise out of it. The gusts
of passion come and go like the sounds of music
borne on the wind. The loss of the friend whose
death he laments seems to have recalled, with
double force, the reality of those speculations
which they had indulged together ; we are transported to classic ground, and a mysterious strain
steals responsive on the ear, while we listen to
the poet,

" With eager thought warbling his Doric lay."

I shall proceed to give a few passages at length
in support of my opinion.   The first I shall
quote is as remarkable for the truth and sweetness
of the natural descriptions as for the characteristic elegance of the allusions.

> ———" Together both, ere the high lawn appear'd
> Under the opening eye-lids of the morn,
> We drove a-field ; and both together heard
> What time the gray-fly winds her sultry horn,
> Battening our flocks with the fresh dews of night,
> Oft still the star that rose at evening bright
> Towards Heaven's descent had sloped his westering wheel.
> Meanwhile the rural ditties were not mute,
> Temper'd to the oaten flute :
> Rough satyrs danced, and fauns with cloven heel
> From the glad sound would not be absent long,
> And old Dametas loved to hear our song.
> But oh ! the heavy change, now thou art gone,
> Now thou art gone, and never must return !
> Thee, shepherd, thee the woods and desert caves
> With wild thyme and the gadding vine o'ergrown,
> And all their echoes mourn.
> The willows and the hazel copses green
> Shall now no more be seen
> Fanning their joyous leaves to thy soft lays.
> As killing as the canker to the rose,
> Or taint-worm to the weanling herds that graze,
> Or frost to flowers that their gay wardrobe wear,
> When first the white-thorn blows ;
> Such, Lycidas, thy loss to shepherd's ear !"

After the fine apostrophe on Fame which Phœ-
bus is invoked to utter, the poet proceeds :—

> " Oh fountain Arethuse, and thou honour'd flood,
> Smooth sliding Mincius, crown'd with vocal reeds,

That strain I heard was of a higher mood ;
But now my oat proceeds,
And listens to the herald of the sea
That came in Neptune's plea.
He ask'd the waves, and ask'd the felon winds,
What hard mishap hath doom'd this gentle swain ?
And question'd every gust of rugged winds
That blows from off each beaked promontory.
They knew not of his story :
And sage Hippotades their answer brings,
That not a blast was from his dungeon stray'd,
The air was calm, and on the level brine
Sleek Panope with all her sisters play'd."

If this is art, it is perfect art ; nor do we wish
for any thing better. The measure of the verse,
the very sound of the names, would almost produce the effect here described.   To ask the poet
not to make use of such allusions as these is to
ask the painter not to dip in the colours of the
rainbow, if he could.—In fact, it is the common
cant of criticism to consider every allusion to the
classics, and particularly in a mind like Milton's,
as pedantry and affectation.   Habit is a second
nature ; and, in this sense, the pedantry (if it is
to be so called) of the scholastic enthusiast, who
is constantly referring to images of which his
mind is full, is as graceful as it is natural.   It is
not affectation in him to recur to ideas and modes
of expression with which he has the strongest
associations, and in which he takes the greatest
delight. Milton was as conversant with the world

of genius before him as with the world of nature
about him; the fables of the ancient mythology
were as familiar to him as his dreams. To be a
pedant is to see neither the beauties of nature
nor of art. Milton saw both; and he made use of
the one only to adorn and give new interest to
the other. He was a passionate admirer of nature; and, in a single couplet of his, describing
the moon,—

> " Like one that had been led astray
>   Through the heaven's wide pathless way,"—

there is more intense observation, and intense
feeling of nature (as if he had gazed himself blind
in looking at her), than in twenty volumes of descriptive poetry. But he added in his own observation of nature the splendid fictions of ancient
genius, enshrined her in the mysteries of ancient
religion, and celebrated her with the pomp of
ancient names.

> " Next Camus, reverend sire, went footing slow,
>   His mantle airy, and his bonnet sedge,
>   Inwrought with figures dim, and on the edge
>   Like to that sanguine flower inscrib'd with woe.
>   Oh! who hath reft (quoth he) my dearest pledge?
>   Last came and last did go,
>   The pilot of the Galilean lake."—

There is a wonderful correspondence in the
rhythm of these lines to the ideas which they
convey. This passage, which alludes to the clerical character of *Lycidas,* has been found fault

with, as combining the truths of the Christian religion with the fiction of the Heathen mythology. I conceive there is very little foundation for this objection, either in reason or good taste. I will not go so far as to defend Camoens, who, in his *Lusiad*, makes Jupiter send Mercury with a dream to propagate the Catholic religion ; nor do I know that it is generally proper to introduce the two things in the same poem, though I see no objection to it here ; but of this I am quite sure, that there is no inconsistency or natural repugnance between this poetical and religious faith in the same mind. To the understanding, the belief of the one is incompatible with that of the other ; but, in the imagination, they not only may, but do constantly, co-exist. I will venture to go farther, and maintain that every classical scholar, however orthodox a Christian he may be, is an honest Heathen at heart. This requires explanation.—Whoever, then, attaches a reality to any idea beyond the mere name, has, to a certain extent (though not an abstract), an habitual and practical belief in it. Now, to any one familiar with the names of the personages of the Heathen mythology, they convey a positive identity beyond the mere name. We refer them to something out of ourselves. It is only by an effort of abstraction that we divest ourselves of the idea of their reality; all our involuntary prejudices are on their side. This is enough for the poet. They impose on the imagination by all the attractions of beauty and

grandeur. They come down to us in sculpture
and in song. We have the same associations with
them as if they had really been : for the belief of
the fiction in ancient times has produced all the
same effects as the reality could have done. It
was a reality to the minds of the ancient Greeks
and Romans, and through them it is reflected to
us. And, as we shape towers, and men, and armed
steeds, out of the broken clouds that glitter in
the distant horizon, so, throned above the ruins of
the ancient world, Jupiter still nods sublime on
the top of blue Olympus, Hercules leans upon
his club, Apollo has not laid aside his bow, nor
Neptune his trident ; the sea-gods ride upon the
the sounding waves, the long procession of heroes and demi - gods passes in endless review
before us, and still we hear

> " The muses in a ring
> Aye round about Jove's altar sing :
> . . . .
> Have sight of Proteus coming from the sea,
> And hear old Triton blow his wreathed horn."

If all these mighty fictions had really existed,
they could have done no more for us !—I shall
only give one other passage from *Lycidas ;* but
I flatter myself that it will be a treat to my
readers, if they are not already familiar with it.
It is the passage which contains that exquisite
description of the flowers :

> " Return, Alpheus ; the dread voice is past
> That shrunk thy streams ; return, Sicilian Muse,
> And call the vales, and bid them hither cast

Their bells and flow'rets of a thousand hues.
Ye valleys low, where the mild whispers use
Of shades and wanton winds and gushing brooks,
On whose fresh lap the swart-star sparely looks,
Throw hither all your quaint enamell'd eyes,
That on the green turf suck the honeyed showers,
And purple all the ground with vernal flowers;
Bring the rathe primrose that forsaken dies,
The tufted crow-toe, and pale jessamine,
The white pink, and the pansy freaked with jet,
The glowing violet,
The musk-rose, and the well-attired woodbine,
With cowslips wan, that hang the pensive head,
And every flower, that sad embroidery wears;
Bid amaranthus all his beauty shed.
And daffadillies fill their cups with tears,
To strew the laureat herse where Lycid lies.
For so to interpose a little cause,
Let our frail thoughts dally with false surmise.
Ah me! Whilst thee the shores and sounding seas
Waft far away, where'er thy bones are hurl'd,
Whether beyond the stormy Hebrides,
Where thou perhaps under the whelming tide
Visit'st the bottom of the monstrous world;
Or whether thou to our moist vows denied,
Sleep'st by the fables of Bellerus old,
Where the great vision of the guarded mount
Looks towards Namancos and Bayona's hold
Look homeward, Angel, now, and melt with ruth,
And, O ye Dolphins, waft the hapless youth."

Dr. Johnson is very much offended at the introduction of these Dolphins; and indeed, if he
had had to guide them through the waves, he
would have made much the same figure as his
old friend Dr. Burney does, swimming in the

Thames with his wig on, with the water-nymphs,
in the picture of Barry, at the Adelphi.

There is a description of flowers in the *Winter's Tale,* which I shall give as a parallel to Milton's. I shall leave my readers to decide which is the finest; for I dare not give the preference. *Perdita* says,—

> " Here's flowers for you,
> Hot lavender, mints, savoury, marjoram,
> The marygold that goes to bed with the sun,
> And with him rises, weeping; these are flowers
> Of middle summer, and I think they are given
> To men of middle age. Y' are welcome.
> " *Camillo.* I should leave grazing, were I of your flock,
> And only live by gazing.
> " *Perdita.* Out, alas!
> You'd be so lean that blasts of January
> Would blow you through and through. Now, my fairest
>   friends,
> I would I had some flowers o' th' spring, that might
> Become your time of day: O Proserpina,
> For the flowers now that, frighted, you let fall
> From Dis's waggon! daffodils,
> That come before the swallow dares, and take
> The winds of March with beauty; violets dim,
> But sweeter than the lids of Juno's eyes,
> Or Cytherea's breath; pale primroses,
> That die unmarried, ere they can behold
> Bright Phœbus in his strength, a malady
> Most incident to maids; bold oxlips, and
> The crown imperial; lilies of all kinds,
> The flower de lis being one. O these I lack
> To make you garlands of, and my sweet friend
> To strew him o'er and o'er."

Dr. Johnson's general remark, that Milton's genius had not room to shew itself in his smaller pieces, is not well-founded.   Not to mention *Lycidas*, the *Allegro*, and *Penseroso*, it proceeds on a false estimate of the merits of his great work, which is not more distinguished by strength and sublimity than by tenderness and beauty.—The last were as essential qualities of Milton's mind as the first.   The battle of the angels, which has been commonly considered as the best part of the *Paradise Lost*, is the worst.

II.

ON THE CHARACTER OF MILTON'S EVE.

THE difference between the character of *Eve* in Milton, and Shakspeare's female characters is very striking, and it appears to me to be this :—Milton describes *Eve* not only as full of love and tenderness for *Adam*, but as the constant object of admiration in herself. She is the idol of the poet's imagination, and he paints her whole person with a studied profusion of charms. She is the wife, but she is still as much as ever the mistress, of *Adam*. She is represented, indeed, as devoted to her husband, as twining round him for support, " as the vine curls her tendrils," but her own grace

and beauty are never lost sight of in the picture
of conjugal felicity. *Adam's* attention and regard
are as much turned to her as hers to him ; for
" in the first garden of their innocence," he had
no other objects or pursuits to distract his attention; she was both his business and his pleasure.
Shakspeare's females, on the contrary, seem to
exist only in their attachment to others. They are
pure abstractions of the affections. Their features are not painted, nor the colour of their hair.
Their hearts only are laid open. We are acquainted with *Imogen, Miranda, Ophelia*, or *Desdemona*, by what they thought and felt, but we
cannot tell whether they were black, brown, or
fair. But Milton's *Eve* is all of ivory and gold.
Shakspeare seldom tantalizes the reader with a
luxurious display of the personal charms of his
heroines, with a curious inventory of particular
beauties, except indirectly, and for some other
purpose, as where *Iachimo* describes *Imogen*
asleep, or the old men in the *Winter's Tale* vie
with each other in invidious praise of *Perdita*.
Even in *Juliet,* the most voluptuous and glowing
of the class of characters here spoken of, we are
reminded chiefly of circumstances connected with
the physiognomy of passion, as in her leaning
with her cheek upon her arm, or which only convey the general impression of enthusiasm made
on her lover's brain. One thing may be said, that
Shakspeare had not the same opportunities as
Milton : for his women were clothed, and it can

not be denied that Milton took *Eve* at a considerable disadvantage in this respect. He has
accordingly described her in all the loveliness of
nature, tempting to sight as the fruit of the Hes-
perides guarded by that Dragon old, herself the
fairest among the flowers of Paradise !

The figures of both *Adam* and *Eve* are very
prominent in this poem. As there is little action
in it, the interest is constantly kept up by the
beauty and grandeur of the images. They are
thus introduced :

" Two of far nobler shape, erect and tall,
  Godlike erect, with native honour clad,
  In naked majesty seemed lords of all,
  And worthy seemed ; for in their looks divine
  The image of their glorious Maker shone :
* * * * * * * * * * * * * *
                    Though both
  Not equal, as their sex not equal seem'd ;
  For contemplation he and valour form'd,
  For softness she and sweet attractive grace ;
  He for God only, she for God in him.
  His fair large front and eye sublime declar'd
  Absolute rule ; and hyacinthine locks
  Round from his parted forelock manly hung
  Clust'ring, but not beneath his shoulders broad ;
  She as a veil down to the slender waist
  Her unadorned golden tresses wore
  Dishevell'd, but in wanton ringlets wav'd
  As the vine curls her tendrils, which implied
  Subjection, but required with gentle sway,
  And by her yielded, by him best receiv'd,
  Yielded with coy submission, modest pride,
  And sweet reluctant amorous delay."

Eve is not only represented as beautiful, but with conscious beauty. Shakspeare's heroines are almost insensible of their charms, and wound without knowing it. They are not coquets. If the salvation of mankind had depended upon one of them, we don't know—but the devil might have been baulked. This is but a conjecture ! *Eve* has a great idea of herself, and there is some difficulty in prevailing on her to quit her own image, the first time she discovers its reflection in the water. She gives the following account of herself to *Adam :*—

> " That day I oft remember, when from sleep
> I first awak'd, and found myself repos'd
> Under a shade of flow'rs, much wond'ring where
> And what I was, whence thither brought and how.
> Not distant far from thence a murmuring sound
> Of waters issued from a cave, and spread
> Into a liquid plain, then stood unmov'd
> Pure as the expanse of Heav'n ; I thither went
> With unexperienc'd thought, and laid me down
> On the green bank, to look into the clear
> Smooth lake, that to me seem'd another sky :
> As I bent down to look just opposite
> A shape within the wat'ry gleam appear'd,
> Bending to look on me ; I started back,
> It started back ; but pleas'd I soon return'd,
> Pleas'd it return'd as soon with answ'ring looks
> Of sympathy and love."

The poet afterwards adds :—

> " So spake our general mother, and with eyes
> Of conjugal attraction unreprov'd,
> And meek surrender, half embracing lean'd

On our first father ; half her swelling breast
Naked met his under the flowing gold
Of her loose tresses hid : he in delight
Both of her beauty and submissive charms
Smil'd with superior love, as Jupiter
On Juno smiles, when he impregns the clouds
That shed the May flowers."

The same thought is repeated with greater
simplicity, and perhaps even beauty, in the beginning of the Fifth Book :—

" So much the more
His wonder was to find unwaken'd Eve
With tresses discompos'd and glowing cheek,
As through unquiet rest : he, on his side,
Leaning half-rais'd, with looks of cordial love
Hung over her enamour'd, and beheld
Beauty, which, whether waking or asleep,
Shot forth peculiar graces; then with voice
Mild, as when Zephyrus on Flora breathes,
Her hand soft touching, whisper'd thus : Awake
My fairest, my espous'd, my latest found,
Heav'n's last best gift, my ever new delight,
Awake." . . . .

The general style, indeed, in which *Eve* is ad-
dressed by *Adam*, or described by the poet, is in
the highest strain of compliment :—

" When Adam thus to Eve.   Fair consort, the hour
Of night approaches."
" To whom thus Eve, with perfect beauty adorned."
" To whom our general ancestor replied,
Daughter of God and Man, accomplish'd Eve."

Eve is herself so well convinced that these
epithets are her due that the idea follows her in

her sleep, and she dreams of herself as the para-
gon of nature, the wonder of the universe :—

> " Methought
> Close at mine ear, one call'd me forth to walk,
> With gentle voice, I thought it thine; it said,
> Why sleep'st thou, Eve ? now is the pleasant time,
> The cool, the silent, save where silence yields
> To the night-warbling bird, that now awake
> Tunes sweetest his love-labour'd song; now reigns
> Full-orb'd the moon, and with more pleasing light
> Shadowy sets off the face of things; in vain
> If none regard ; Heav'n wakes with all his eyes,
> Whom to behold but thee, Nature's desire ?
> In whose sight all things joy, with ravishment
> Attracted by thy beauty still to gaze."

This is the very topic, too, on which the Serpent afterwards enlarges with so much artful
insinuation and fatal consequences of success.
" So talked the spirited sly snake."—The conclusion of the foregoing scene, in which *Eve* relates
her dream and *Adam* comforts her, is such an
exquisite piece of description that, though not
to my immediate purpose, I cannot refrain from
quoting it :—

> " So cheer'd he his fair spouse, and she was cheer'd;
> But silently a gentle tear let fal'
> From either eye, and wip'd them with her hair ;
> Two other precious drops that ready stood,
> Each in their crystal sluice, he ere they fell
> Kiss'd, as the gracious signs of sweet remorse
> And pious awe, that fear'd to have offended."

The formal eulogy on *Eve* which *Adam* addresses to the Angel, in giving an account of

his own creation and hers, is full of elaborate
grace :—

> " Under his forming hand a creature grew,
> —————————so lovely fair
> That what seem'd fair in all the world seem'd now
> Mean, or in her summ'd up, in her contain'd
> And in her looks, which from that time infus'd
> Sweetness into my heart, unfelt before,
> And into all things from her air inspir'd
> The spirit of love and amorous delight."

That which distinguishes Milton from the
other poets, who have pampered the eye and fed
the imagination with exuberant descriptions of
female beauty, is the moral severity with which
he has tempered them. There is not a line in
his works which tends to licentiousness, or the
impression of which, if it has such a tendency,
is not effectually checked by thought and sentiment. The following are two remarkable
instances :—

> " In shadier bower
> More secret and sequester'd, though but feign'd,
> Pan or Sylvanus never slept, nor Nymph,
> Nor Faunus haunted. Here in close recess,
> With flowers, garlands, and sweet smelling herbs,
> Espoused Eve deck'd first her nuptial bed,
> And heavenly quires the hymenæan sung,
> What day the genial Angel to our sire
> Brought her in naked beauty more adorn'd,
> More lovely than Pandora, whom the Gods
> Endow'd with all their gifts, and O too like
> In sad event, when to th' unwiser son

Of Japhet brought by Hermes, she ensnar'd
Mankind by her fair looks, to be aveng'd
On him who had stole Jove's authentic fire."

The other is a passage of extreme beauty and pathos blended. It is the one in which the Angel is described as the guest of our first ancestors :—

"Meanwhile at table Eve
Minister'd naked, and their flowing cups
With pleasant liquors crown'd : O innocence
Deserving Paradise! if ever, then,
Then had the sons of God excuse to have been
Enamour'd at that sight : but in those hearts
Love unlibidinous reigned, nor jealousy
Was understood, the injur'd lover's Hell."

The character which a living poet has given of Spenser would be much more true of Milton :—

"Yet not more sweet
Than pure was he, and not more pure than wise ;
High Priest of all the Muses' mysteries."

Spenser, on the contrary, is very apt to pry into mysteries which do not belong to the Muses. Milton's voluptuousness is not lascivious nor sensual. He describes beautiful objects for their own sakes. Spenser has an eye to the consequences, and steeps every thing in pleasure, often not of the purest kind. The want of passion has been brought as an objection against Milton, and his *Adam* and *Eve* have been considered as rather insipid personages, wrapped up in one another,

and who excite but little sympathy in any one
else. I do not feel this objection myself :
I am content to be spectator in such scenes.
without any other excitement. In general the
interest in Milton is essentially epic, and not dramatic ; and the difference between the epic and
the dramatic is this, that in the former the imagination produces the passion, and in the latter
the passion produces the imagination. The
interest of epic poetry arises from the contemplation of certain objects in themselves grand
and beautiful ; the interest of dramatic poetry
from sympathy with the passions and pursuits of
others ; that is, from the practical relations of
certain persons to certain objects, as depending
on accident or will.

The Pyramids of Egypt are epic objects : the
imagination of them is necessarily attended with
passion ; but they have no dramatic interest ;
till circumstances connect them with some human catastrophe. Now a poem might be constructed almost entirely of such images, of the
highest intellectual passion, with little dramatic
interest ; and it is in this way that Milton has in
a great measure constructed his poem. That is
not its fault, but its excellence. The fault is
in those who have no idea but of one kind of
interest. But this question would lead to a longer
discussion than I have room for at present. I
shall conclude these extracts from Milton with
two passages, which have always appeared to

me to be highly affecting, and to contain a fine discrimination of character :—

> " O unexpected stroke, worse than of Death !
> Must I thus leave thee, Paradise ? thus leave
> Thee, native soil, these happy walks and shades,
> Fit haunt of Gods ? Where I had hope to spend,
> Quiet, though sad, the respite of that day
> That must be mortal to us both. O flowers,
> That never will in other climate grow,
> My early visitation and my last
> At even, which I bred up with tender hand
> From the first opening bud, and gave ye names,
> Who now shall rear ye to the sun, or rank
> Your tribes, and water from th' ambrosial fount ?
> Thee, lastly, nuptial bow'r, by me adorn'd
> With what to sight or smell was sweet, from thee
> How shall I part, and whither wander down
> Into a lower world, to this obscure
> And wild ? how shall we breathe in other air
> Less pure, accustom'd to immortal fruits ?"

This is the lamentation of *Eve* on being driven out of Paradise. *Adam's* reflections are in a different strain, and still finer. After expressing his submission to the will of his Maker, he says—

> " This most afflicts me, that departing hence
> As from his face I shall be hid, depriv'd
> His blessed countenance ; here I could frequent
> With worship place by place where he vouchsaf'd
> Presence divine, and to my sons relate,
> On this mount he appeared, under this tree
> Stood visible, among these pines his voice
> I heard, here with him at this fountain talk'd :

So many grateful altars I would rear
Of grassy turf, and pile up every stone
Of lustre from the brook, in memory
Or monument to ages, and thereon
Offer sweet-smelling gums and fruits and flowers ·
In yonder nether world where shall I seek
His bright appearances, or footstep trace ?
For though I fled him angry, yet, recall'd
To life prolong'd and promis'd race, I now
Gladly behold though but his utmost skirts
Of glory, and far off his steps adore."

III.

ON MR. WORDSWORTH'S POEM,
"THE EXCURSION."

In power of intellect, in lofty conception, in the depth of feeling, at once simple and sublime, which pervades every part of it, and which gives to every object an almost preternatural and preterhuman interest, this work has seldom been surpassed. The poem of the *Excursion* resembles that part of the country in which the scene is laid. It has the same vastness and magnificence, with the same nakedness and confusion. It has the same overwhelming, oppressive power. It excites or recals the same sensations which those who have traversed that wonderful scenery must have felt. We are surrounded with the constant sense and superstitious awe of the collective power of matter, of the gigantic and eternal forms of nature, on which, from the beginning of time, the hand of man has made no impression. Here are no dotted lines, no hedge-row beauties, no box-tree borders, no gravel walks, no square mechanic inclosures; all is left loose and irregular in the rude chaos of aboriginal nature. The boundaries of hill and valley are the poet's only geography, where we wander with him incessantly over deep beds of moss and waving fern, amidst the troops of red-deer and wild animals. Such is the severe simplicity of Mr. Wordsworth's taste that I doubt whether he would not reject a druidical temple, or time-hallowed ruin, as too modern and artificial for his purpose. He only familiarizes himself or his readers with a stone, covered with lichens, which has slept in the same spot of ground from the creation of the world, or with the rocky fissure between two mountains caused by thunder, or with a cavern scooped out by the sea. His mind is, as it were, coeval with the primary forms of things; his imagination holds immediately from nature, and "owes no allegiance" but "to the elements."

The *Excursion* may be considered as a philosophical pastoral poem, — as a scholastic romance. It is less a poem on the country than on the love of the country. It is not so much a description of natural objects as of the feel-

ings associated with them; not an account of
the manners of rural life, but the result of the
poet's reflections on it. He does not present
the reader with a lively succession of images or
incidents, but paints the outgoings of his own
heart, the shapings of his own fancy. He may
be said to create his own materials; his
thoughts are his real subject. His understanding broods over that which is "without form
and void," and "makes it pregnant." He sees
all things in himself. He hardly ever avails
himself of remarkable objects or situations,
but, in general, rejects them as interfering with
the workings of his own mind, as disturbing
the smooth, deep, majestic current of his own
feelings. Thus his descriptions of natural
scenery are not brought home distinctly to the
naked eye by forms and circumstances, but
every object is seen through the medium of
innumerable recollections, is clothed with the
haze of imagination like a glittering vapour, is
obscured with the excess of glory, has the
shadowy brightness of a waking dream. The
image is lost in the sentiment, as sound in the
multiplication of echoes,

> " And visions, as prophetic eyes avow,
>   Hang on each leaf, and cling to every bough."

In describing human nature, Mr. Wordsworth
equally shuns the common 'vantage-grounds of
popular story, of striking incident, or fatal

catastrophe, as cheap and vulgar modes of producing an effect. He scans the human race as
the naturalist measures the earth's zone, without attending to the picturesque points of view,
the abrupt inequalities of surface. He contemplates the passions and habits of men, not in
their extremes, but in the first elements ; their
follies and vices, not at their height, with all
their embossed evils upon their heads, but as
lurking in embryo,—the seeds of the disorder
inwoven with our very constitution. He only
sympathizes with those simple forms of feeling
which mingle at once with his own identity, or
with the stream of general humanity. To him
the great and the small are the same ; the near
and the remote; what appears, and what only
is. The general and the permanent, like the
Platonic ideas, are his only realities. All accidental varieties and individual contrasts are lost
in an endless continuity of feeling; like drops
of water in the ocean-stream ! An intense intellectual egotism swallows up every thing.
Even the dialogues introduced in the present
volume are soliloquies of the same character,
taking different views of the subject. The recluse, the pastor, and the pedlar, are three persons in one poet. I myself disapprove of
these "interlocutions between Lucius and Caius"
as impertinent babbling, where there is no dramatic distinction of character. But the evident
scope and tendency of Mr. Wodwortrh's mind

is the reverse of dramatic. It resists all change of character, all variety of scenery, all the bustle, machinery, and pantomime of the stage, or of real life,—whatever might relieve, or relax, or change the direction of its own activity, jealous of all competition. The power of his mind preys upon itself. It is as if there were nothing but himself and the universe. He lives in the busy solitude of his own heart; in the deep silence of thought. His imagination lends life and feeling only to "the bare trees and mountains bare;" peoples the viewless tracts of air, and converses with the silent clouds!

I could have wished that our author had given to his work the form of a didactic poem altogether, with only occasional digressions or allusions to particular instances. But he has chosen to encumber himself with a load of narrative and description, which sometimes hinders the progress and effect of the general reasoning, and which, instead of being inwoven with the text, would have come in better in plain prose as notes at the end of the volume. Mr. Wordsworth, indeed, says finely, and perhaps as truly as finely:—

> "Exchange the shepherd's frock of native grey
> For robes with regal purple tinged; convert
> The crook into a sceptre; give the pomp
> Of circumstance; and here the tragic Muse
> Shall find apt subjects for her highest art.
> Amid the groves, beneath the shadowy hills,

> The generations are prepared ; the pangs,
> The internal pangs are ready ; the dread strife
> Of poor humanity's afflicted will
> Struggling in vain with ruthless destiny."

But he immediately declines availing himself of these resources of the rustic moralist : for the priest, who officiates as "the sad historian of the pensive plain," says in reply :—

> " Our system is not fashioned to preclude
> That sympathy which you for others ask :
> And I could tell, not travelling for my theme
> Beyond the limits of these humble graves,
> Of strange disasters ; but I pass them by,
> Loth to disturb what Heaven hath hushed to peace."

There is, in fact, in Mr. Wordsworth's mind an evident repugnance to admit any thing that tells for itself without the interpretation of the poet,—a fastidious antipathy to immediate effect, —a systematic unwillingness to share the palm with his subject. Where, however, he has a subject presented to him, "such as the meeting soul may pierce," and to which he does not grudge to lend the aid of his fine genius, his powers of description and fancy seem to be little inferior to those of his classical predecessor, Akenside. Among several others which I might select, I give the following passage, describing the religion of ancient Greece :—

> " In that fair clime, the lonely herdsman, stretch'd
> On the soft grass through half a summer's day,

With music lulled his indolent repose :
And in some fit of weariness, if he,
When his own breath was silent, chanced to hear
A distant strain, far sweeter than the sounds
Which his poor skill could make, his fancy fetch'd
Even from the blazing chariot of the sun,
A beardless youth, who touched a golden lute,
And filled the illumined groves with ravishment.
The nightly hunter, lifting up his eyes
Towards the crescent moon, with grateful heart
Called on the lovely wanderer, who bestowed
That timely light, to share his joyous sport :
And hence, a beaming Goddess with her Nymphs
Across the lawn and through the darksome grove,
(Nor unaccompanied with tuneful notes
By echo multiplied from rock or cave,)
Swept in the storm of chase, as moon and stars
Glance rapidly along the clouded heavens,
When winds are blowing strong. The traveller slaked
His thirst from rill, or gushing fount, and thanked
The Naiad.—Sun-beams, upon distant hills
Gliding apace, with shadows in their train,
Might, with small help from fancy, be transformed
Into fleet Oreads, sporting visibly.
The zephyrs fanning as they passed their wings,
Lacked not for love, fair objects, whom they wooed
With gentle whisper. Withered boughs grotesque,
Stripped of their leaves and twigs by hoary age,
From depth of shaggy covert peeping forth
In the low vale, or on steep mountain side :
And sometimes intermixed with stirring horns
Of the live deer, or goat's depending beard ;
These were the lurking satyrs, a wild brood
Of gamesome Deities ! or Pan himself,
The simple shepherd's awe-inspiring God.

The foregoing is one of a succession of splendid passages equally enriched with philosophy

and poetry, tracing the fictions of Eastern mythology to the immediate intercourse of the imagination with Nature, and to the habitual propensity of the human mind to endow the outward forms of being with life and conscious motion. With this expansive and animating principle, Mr. Wordsworth has forcibly, but somewhat severely, contrasted the cold, narrow, lifeless spirit of modern philosophy :—

> " How, shall our great discoverers obtain
> From sense and reason less than these obtained,
> Though far misled ? Shall men for whom our age
> Unbaffled powers of vision hath prepared,
> To explore the world without, and world within,
> Be joyless as the blind ? Ambitious souls——
> Whom earth at this late season hath produced
> To regulate the moving spheres, and weigh
> The planets in the hollow of their hand ;
> And they who rather dive than soar, whose pains
> Have solved the elements, or analyzed
> The thinking principle—shall they in fact
> Prove a degradèd race ? And what avails
> Renown, if their presumption make them such ?
> Inquire of ancient wisdom ; go, demand
> Of mighty nature, if 'twas ever meant
> That we should pry far off, yet be unraised :
> That we should pore, and dwindle as we pore,
> Viewing all objects unremittingly
> In disconnection dead and spiritless ;
> And still dividing and dividing still
> Break down all grandeur, still unsatisfied
> With the perverse attempt, while littleness
> May yet become more little ; waging thus
> An impious warfare with the very life
> Of our own souls !—And if indeed there be

An all-pervading spirit, upon whom
Our dark foundations rest, could he design,
That this magnificent effect of power,
The earth we tread, the sky which we behold
By day, and all the pomp which night reveals,
That these—and that superior mystery,
Our vital frame, so fearfully devised,
And the dread soul within it—should exist
Only to be examined, pondered, searched,
Probed, vexed, and criticised—to be prized
No more than as a mirror that reflects
To proud self-love her own intelligence ?"

From the chemists and metaphysicians our
author turns to the laughing sage of France,
Voltaire. "Poor gentleman, it fares no better
with him, for he's a wit." We cannot, however, agree with Mr. Wordsworth, that *Candide*
is *dull*. It is, if our author pleases, "the production of a scoffer's pen," or it is any thing
but dull. It may not be proper in a grave, dis-
creet, orthodox, promising young divine, who
studies his opinions in the contraction or dis-
tension of his patron's brow, to allow any merit
to a work like *Candide*; but I conceive that it
would have been more manly in Mr. Wordsworth, nor do I think it would have hurt the
cause he espouses, if he had blotted out the
epithet, after it had peevishly escaped him.
Whatsoever savours of a little, narrow, in-
quisitorial spirit, does not sit well on a poet and
a man of genius. The prejudices of a philosopher are not natural. There is a frankness

and sincerity of opinion, which is a paramount obligation in all questions of intellect, though it may not govern the decisions of the spiritual courts, who may, however, be safely left to take care of their own interests. There is a plain directness and simplicity of understanding, which is the only security against the evils of levity, on the one hand, or of hypocrisy, on the other. A speculative bigot is a solecism in the intellectual world. I can assure Mr. Wordsworth that I should not have bestowed so much serious consideration on a single voluntary perversion of language, but that my respect for his character makes me jealous of his smallest faults !

With regard to his general philippic against the contractedness and egotism of philosophical pursuits, I only object to its not being carried farther. I shall not affirm with Rousseau (his authority would perhaps have little weight with Mr. Wordsworth)—*Tout homme refiechi est mechant;* but I conceive that the same reasoning which Mr. Wordsworth applies so eloquently and justly to the natural philosopher and metaphysician may be extended to the moralist, the divine, the politician, the orator, the artist, and even the poet. And why so? Because wherever an intense activity is given to any one faculty, it necessarily prevents the due and natural exercise of others. Hence all those professions or pursuits where the mind is ex-

clusively occupied with the ideas of things as
they exist in the imagination or understanding,
as they call for the exercise of intellectual
activity, and not as they are connected with
practical good or evil, must check the genial
expansion of the moral sentiments and social
affections ; must lead to a cold and dry abstraction, as they are found to suspend the animal
functions and relax the bodily frame. Hence
the complaint of the want of natural sensibility
and constitutional warmth of attachment in
those persons who have been devoted to the
pursuit of any art or science,—of their restless
morbidity of temperament, and indifference to
everything that does not furnish an occasion for
the display of their mental superiority and the
gratification of their vanity. The philosophical
poet himself, perhaps, owes some of his love of
nature to the opportunity it affords him of
analysing his own feelings and contemplating
his own powers,—of making every object about
him a whole-length mirror to reflect his favourite thoughts, and of looking down on the frailties
of others in undisturbed leisure, and from a
more dignified height.

One of the most interesting parts of this work
is that in which the author treats of the French
Revolution, and of the feelings connected with
it, in ingenuous minds, in its commencement
and its progress. The *solitary*,* who, by domes-

* This word is not English.

tic calamities and disappointments, had been cut
off from society, and almost from himself, gives
the following account of the manner in which
he was roused from his melancholy:—

> " From that abstraction I was roused—and how?
> Even as a thoughtful shepherd by a flash
> Of lightning, startled in a gloomy cave
> Of these wild hills. For, lo! the dread Bastile,
> With all the chambers in its horrid towers,
> Fell to the ground: by violence o'erthrown
> Of indignation; and with shouts that drowned
> The crash it made in falling! From the wreck
> A golden palace rose, or seemed to rise,
> The appointed seat of equitable law
> And mild paternal sway. The potent shock
> I felt; the transformation I perceived,
> As marvellously seized as in that moment
> When, from the blind mist issuing, I beheld
> Glory—beyond all glory ever seen,
> Dazzling the soul! Meanwhile prophetic harps
> In every grove were ringing, 'War shall cease:
> Did ye not hear that conquest is abjured?
> Bring garlands, bring forth choicest flowers, to deck
> The tree of liberty!'—My heart rebounded:
> My melancholy voice the chorus joined.
> Thus was I re-converted to the world;
> Society became my glittering bride,
> And airy hopes my children. From the depths
> Of natural passion seemingly escaped,
> My soul diffused itself in wide embrace
> Of institutions and the forms of things.
> ————————————If with noise
> And acclamation, crowds in open air
> Expressed the tumult of their minds, my voice
> There mingled, heard or not. And in still groves,
> Where mild enthusiasts tuned a pensive lay

Of thanks and expectation, in accord
With their belief, I sang Saturnian rule
Returned—a progeny of golden years
Permitted to descend, and bless mankind.

* * * * * *

Scorn and contempt forbid me to proceed !
But history, time's slavish scribe, will tell
How rapidly the zealots of the cause
Disbanded—or in hostile ranks appeared :
Some, tired of honest service ; these outdone,
Disgusted, therefore, or appalled, by aims
Of fiercer zealots.—So confusion reigned,
And the more faithful were compelled to exclaim,
As Brutus did to virtue, ' Liberty,
I worshipped thee, and find thee but a shade.'
SUCH RECANTATION HAD FOR ME NO CHARM,
NOR WOULD I BEND TO IT."

The subject is afterwards resumed, with the
same magnanimity and philosophical firmness:—

————————— " For that other loss,
The loss of confidence in social man,
By the unexpected transports of our age
Carried so high, that every thought—which looked
Beyond the temporal destiny of the kind—
To many seemed superfluous ; as no cause
For such exalted confidence could e'er
Exist ; so, none is now for such despair.
The two extremes are equally remote
From truth and reason ;—do not, then, confound
One with the other, but reject them both ;
And choose the middle point, whereon to build
Sound expectations. This doth he advise
Who shared at first the illusion. At this day,
When a Tartarian darkness overspreads
The groaning nations ; when the impious rule,
By will, or by established ordinance,

> Their own dire agents, and constrain the good
> To acts which they abhor; though I bewail
> This triumph, yet the pity of my heart
> Prevents me not from owning that the law,
> By which mankind now suffers, is most just.
> For by superior energies; more strict
> Affiance in each other; faith more firm
> In their unhallowed principles; the bad
> Have fairly earned a victory o'er the weak,
> The vacillating, inconsistent good."

In the application of these memorable lines, I should, perhaps, differ a little from Mr. Wordsworth; nor can I indulge with him in the fond conclusion afterwards hinted at, that one day *our* triumph, the triumph of humanity and liberty, may be complete. For this purpose, I think several things necessary which are impossible. It is a consummation which cannot happen till the nature of things is changed, till the many become as united as the *one*, till romantic generosity shall be as common as gross selfishness, till reason shall have acquired the obstinate blindness of prejudice, till the love of power and of change shall no longer goad man on to restless action, till passion and will, hope and fear, love and hatred, and the objects proper to excite them, that is, alternate good and evil, shall no longer sway the bosoms and businesses of men. All things move, not in progress, but in a ceaseless round; our strength lies in our weakness; our virtues are built on our vices; our faculties are as limited as our being; nor

can we lift man above his nature more than
above the earth he treads. But though I cannot weave over again the airy, unsubstantial
dream, which reason and experience have dis-
pelled,

" What though the radiance, which was once so bright,
    Be now for ever taken from my sight,
    Though nothing can bring back the hour
    Of glory in the grass, of splendour in the flower :"—

yet I will never cease, nor be prevented from
returning on the wings of imagination to that
bright dream of my youth ; that glad dawn of
the day-star of liberty ; that spring time of the
world, in which the hopes and expectations of
the human race seemed opening in the same gay
career with my own ; when France called her
children to partake her equal blessings beneath
her laughing skies ; when the stranger was met
in all her villages with dance and festive songs,
in celebration of a new and golden era ; and
when, to the retired and contemplative student,
the prospects of human happiness and glory were
seen ascending like the steps of Jacob's ladder,
in bright and never-ending succession. The
dawn of that day was suddenly overcast ; that
season of hope is past ; it is fled with the other
dreams of my youth, which I cannot recal,
but has left behind it traces, which are not to be
effaced by Birth-day and Thanksgiving odes, or
the chaunting of *Te Deums* in all the churches

of Christendom. To those hopes eternal regrets
are due; to those who maliciously and wilfully
blasted them, in the fear that they might be ac-
complished, I feel no less what I owe—hatred
and scorn as lasting!

Mr. Wordsworth's writings exhibit all the
internal power, without the external form, of
poetry. He has scarcely any of the pomp and
decoration and scenic effect of poetry : no gorgeous palaces, nor solemn temples, awe the
imagination; no cities rise " with glistering spires
and pinnacles adorned;" we meet with no knights
pricked forth on airy steeds; no hair-breadth
'scapes and perilous accidents by flood or field.
Either from the predominant habit of his mind
not requiring the stimulus of outward impressions, or from the want of an imagination teeming
with various forms, he takes the common every
day events and objects of nature, or rather seeks
those that are the most simple and barren of
effect ; but he adds to them a weight of interest
from the resources of his own mind, which makes
the most insignificant things serious and even
formidable. All other interests are absorbed in
the deeper interest of his own thoughts, and find
the same level. His mind magnifies the littleness
of his subject, and raises its meanness; lends it
his strength, and clothes it with borrowed grandeur. With him, a mole-hill, covered with wild
thyme, assumes the importance of " the great
vision of the guarded mount :" a puddle is filled

with preternatural faces, and agitated with the
fiercest storms of passion.

The extreme simplicity which some persons
have objected to in Mr. Wordsworth's poetry, is
to be found only in the subject and the style : the
sentiments are subtle and profound. In the
latter respect, his poetry is as much above the
common standard or capacity, as in the other it
is below it. His poems bear a distant resemblance to some of Rembrandt's landscapes, who,
more than any other painter, created the medium
through which he saw nature, and out of the
stump of an old tree, a break in the sky, and a
bit of water, could produce an effect almost
miraculous.

Mr. Wordsworth s poems in general are the
history of a refined and contemplative mind, conversant only with itself and nature. An intense
feeling of the associations of this kind is the peculiar and characteristic feature of all his productions. He has described the love of nature
better than any other poet. This sentiment, inly
felt in all its force, and sometimes carried to an
excess, is the source both of his strength and of
his weakness. — However I may sympathize
with Mr. Wordsworth in his attachment to groves
and fields, I cannot extend the same admiration
to their inhabitants, or to the manners of a
country life in general. I go along with him,
while he is the subject of his own narrative, but
I take leave of him when he makes pedlars

and ploughmen his heroes and the interpreters of his sentiments. It is, I think, getting into low company, and company, besides, that I do not like. I take Mr. Wordsworth himself for a great poet, a fine moralist, and a deep philosopher; but if he insists on introducing me to a friend of his, a parish clerk, or the barber of the village, who is as wise as himself, I must be excused if I draw back with some little want of cordial faith. I am satisfied with the friendship which subsisted between *Parson Adams* and *Joseph Andrews.*—The author himself lets out occasional hints that all is not as it should be among these northern Arcadians. Though, in general, he professes to soften the harsher features of rustic vice, he has given us one picture of depraved and inveterate selfishness, which I apprehend could only be found among the inhabitants of these boasted mountain districts. The account of one of his heroines concludes as follows:

" A sudden illness seized her in the strength
   Of life's autumnal season.—Shall I tell
   How on her bed of death the matron lay,
   To Providence submissive, so she thought;
   But fretted, vexed, and wrought upon—almost
   To anger, by the malady that griped
   Her prostrate frame with unrelaxing power,
   As the fierce eagle fastens on the lamb.
   She prayed, she moaned—her husband's sister watched
   Her dreary pillow, waited on her needs ;
   And yet the very sound of that kind foot

Was anguish to her ears !—' And must she rule
Sole mistress of this house when I am gone ?
Sit by my fire—possess what I possessed—
Tend what I tended—calling it her own !'
Enough ;—I fear too much.—Of nobler feeling
Take this example :—One autumnal evening,
While she was yet in prime of health and strength,
I well remember, while I passed her door,
Musing with loitering step, and upward eye
Turned tow'rds the planet Jupiter, that hung
Above the centre of the vale, a voice
Roused me, her voice ;—it said, ' That glorious star
In its untroubled element will shine
As now it shines, when we are laid in earth,
And safe from all our sorrows.'—She is safe,
And her uncharitable acts, I trust,
And harsh unkindnesses, are all forgiven ;
Though, in this vale, remembeied with deep awe !"

I think it is pushing our love of the admiration of natural objects a good deal too far
to make it a set-off against a story like the
preceding.

All country people hate each other. They
have so little comfort that they envy their neighbours the smallest pleasure or advantage, and
nearly grudge themselves the necessaries of life.
From not being accustomed to enjoyment, they
become hardened and averse to it—stupid, for
want of thought—selfish, for want of society.
There is nothing good to be had in the country,
or, if there is, they will not let you have it. They
had rather injure themselves than oblige any one
else. Their common mode of life is a system of

wretchedness and self-denial, like what we read
of among barbarous tribes. You live out of the
world. You cannot get your tea and sugar without sending to the next town for it: you pay
double, and have it of the worst quality. The
small-beer is sure to be sour—the milk skimmed
—the meat bad, or spoiled in the cooking. You
cannot do a single thing you like; you cannot
walk out or sit at home, or write or read, or think
or look as if you did, without being subject to
impertinent curiosity. The apothecary annoys
you with his complaisance; the parson with his
superciliousness. If you are poor,·you are despised; if you are rich, you are feared and hated.
If you do any one a favour, the whole neighbourhood is up in arms; the clamour is like
that of a rookery; and the person himself, it is
ten to one, laughs at you for your pains, and
takes the first opportunity of shewing you that
he labours under no uneasy sense of obligation.
There is a perpetual round of mischief-making
and backbiting, for want of any better amusement. There are no shops, no taverns, no
theatres, no opera, no concerts, no pictures, no
public buildings, no crowded streets, no noise
of coaches, or of courts of law,—neither cour-
tiers nor courtesans, no literary parties, no
fashionable routs, no society, no books, or knowledge of books. Vanity and luxury are the civi-
lizers of the world, and sweeteners of human life.
Without objects either of pleasure or action, it

grows harsh and crabbed : the mind becomes stagnant, the affections callous, and the eye dull. Man left to himself soon degenerates into a very disagreeable person. Ignorance is always bad enough ; but rustic ignorance is intolerable. Aristotle has observed that tragedy purifies the affections by terror and pity. If so, a company of tragedians should be established at the public expense, in every village or hundred, as a better mode of education than either Bell's or Lancaster's. The benefits of knowledge are never so well understood as from seeing the effects of ignorance, in their naked, undisguised state, upon the common country people. Their selfishness and insensibility are perhaps less owing to the hardships and privations, which make them, like people out at sea in a boat, ready to devour one another, than to their having no idea of any thing beyond themselves and their immediate sphere of action. They have no knowledge of, and consequently can take no interest in, any thing which is not an object of their senses, and of their daily pursuits. They hate all strangers, and have generally a nickname for the inhabitants of the next village. The two young noblemen in Guzman d'Alfarache, who went to visit their mistresses only a league out of Madrid, were set upon by the peasants, who came round them calling out, "*a wolf.*" Those who have no enlarged or liberal ideas can have no disinterested or generous sentiments.

Persons who are in the habit of reading novels and romances are compelled to take a deep interest, and to have their affections strongly excited by fictitious characters and imaginary situations; their thoughts and feelings are constantly carried out of themselves, to persons they never saw, and things that never existed: history enlarges the mind, by familiarizing us with the great vicissitudes of human affairs, and the catastrophes of states and kingdoms ; the study of morals accustoms us to refer our actions to a general standard of right and wrong; and abstract reasoning, in general, strengthens the love of truth, and produces an inflexibility of principle which cannot stoop to low trick and cunning.   Books, in Lord Bacon's phrase, are "a discipline of humanity."   Country people have none of these advantages, nor any others to supply the place of them.   Having no circulating libraries to exhaust their love of the marvellous, they amuse themselves with fancying the disasters and disgraces of their particular acquaintance.   Having no hump-backed *Richard* to excite their wonder and abhorrence, they make themselves a bug-bear of their own, out of the first obnoxious person they can lay their hands on.   Not having the fictitious distresses and gigantic crimes of poetry to stimulate their imagination and their passions, they vent their whole stock of spleen, malice, and invention, on their friends and next-door neighbours.   They get up a little pastoral drama at home, with fancied events, but real characters. All their spare time is spent in manufacturing and propagating the lie for the day, which does its office, and expires. The next day is spent in the same manner. It is thus that they embellish the simplicity of rural life! The common people in civilized countries are a kind of domesticated savages. They have not the wild imagination, the passions, the fierce energies, or dreadful vicissitudes of the savage tribes, nor have they the leisure, the indolent enjoyments and romantic superstitions, which belonged to the pastoral life in milder climates, and more remote periods of society. They are taken out of a state of nature, without being put in possession of the refinements of art. The customs and institutions of society cramp their imaginations without giving them knowledge. If the inhabitants of the mountainous districts described by Mr. Wordsworth are less gross and sensual than others, they are more selfish. Their egotism becomes more concentrated, as they are more insulated, and their purposes more inveterate, as they have less competition to struggle with. The weight of matter which surrounds them crushes the finer sympathies. Their minds become hard and cold, like the rocks which they cultivate. The immensity of their mountains makes the human form appear little and insignificant. Men are seen crawling between heaven and earth, like insects to their graves. Nor do they regard one another any more than flies on a wall. Their physiognomy expresses the materialism of their character, which has only one principle—rigid self-will. They move on with their eyes and foreheads fixed, looking neither to the right nor to the left, with a heavy slouch in their gait, and seeming as if nothing would divert them from their path. I do not admire this plodding pertinacity, always directed to the main chance. There is nothing which excites so little sympathy, in my mind, as exclusive selfishness.—If my theory is wrong, at least it is taken from pretty close observation, and is, I think, confirmed by Mr. Wordsworth's own account.

Of the stories contained in the latter part of the volume, I like that of the Whig and Jacobite friends and of the good knight, Sir Alfred Irthing, the best. The last reminded me of a fine sketch of a similar character in the beautiful poem of *Hart Leap Well*. To conclude,—If the skill with which the poet had chosen his materials had been equal to the power which he has undeniably exerted over them; if the objects (whether persons or things) which he makes use of as the vehicle of his sentiments, had been such as to convey them in all their depth and force; then the production before me might indeed "have proved a monument," as he himself wishes it, worthy of the author, and of his country.

Whether, as it is, this very original and powerful performance may not rather remain like one
of those stupendous, but half-finished structures,
which have been suffered to moulder into decay,
because the cost and labour attending them exceeded their use or beauty, I feel that it would
be presumptuous in me to determine.

———◆———

IV.

POPE, LORD BYRON, AND MR. BOWLES.*

THIS is a very proper letter for a lord to write
to his bookseller, and for Mr. Murray to show
about among his friends, as it contains some
dry rubs at Mr. Bowles, and some good hits at
Mr. Southey and his " invariable principles."
There is some good *hating* and some good
writing in it, some coarse jests and some dog-
matical assertions; but that it is by any means
a *settler* of the question is what we are in all
due form inclined to doubt. His Lordship, as
a poet, is a little headstrong and self-willed, a
spoiled child of nature and fortune: his philosophy and criticism have a tincture of the
same spirit: he doles out his opinions with a

---

* Letter to *** ***** on the Rev. W. L. Bowles's
Strictures on the Life and Writings of Pope. By the
Right Hon. Lord Byron. Third Edition. Murray.

great deal of frankness and spleen, saying,
" This I like, that I loathe!" but he does not
trouble himself, or the reader, with his reasons,
any more than he accounts to his servants for
the directions he gives them. This might seem
too great a compliment in his Lordship to the
public.

All this *pribble-prabble* about Pope, and Milton,
and Shakspeare, and what foreigners say of us,
and the Venus, and Antinöus, and the Acropolis,
and the Grand Canal at Venice, and the Turkish
fleet, and Falconer's Shipwreck, and ethics, and
ethical poetry (with the single exception of some
bold picturesque sketches in the poet's best prose
style) is what might be talked by any Bond-street
lounger of them all, after a last night's debauch,
in the intervals between the splashings of the
soda-water and the acid taste of the port wine
rising in the mouth. It is no better than that.
If his Lordship had sent it in from Long's, or
the Albany, to be handed about in Albemarle-
street, in slips as he wrote it, it would have
been very well. But all the way from Ravenna,
cannot he contrive to send us something better
than his own ill humour and our own common-
places—than the discovery that Pope was a
poet, and that Cowper was none ; and the old
story that Canova, in forming a statue, takes a
hand from one, a foot from another, and a nose
from a third, and so makes out the idea of perfect beauty ! (I would advise his Lordship to

say less about this subject of *virtu*, for he knows
little about it; and, besides, his perceptions are
at variance with his theories.) In truth, his
Lordship has the worst of this controversy.
though he throws out a number of pert, smart,
flashy things, with the air of a man who sees
company on subjects of taste, while his reverend
antagonist, who is the better critic and logician
of the two, goes prosing on in a tone of ob-
sequious pertinacity and sore pleasantry, as if
he were sitting (an unwelcome guest) at his
lordship's table, and were awed, yet galled, by
the cavalier assumption of patrician manners.
I cannot understand these startling *voluntaries*,
played off before the public on the ground of
personal rank, nor the controversial under-song,
like the drone of a bag-pipe, that forms a
tedious accompaniment to them. As Jem
Belcher, when asked if he did not feel a little
awkward at facing Gamble, the tall Irishman,
made answer, " An' please ye, sir, when I am
stript to my shirt, I am afraid of no man;"—so
I would advise Mr. Bowles, in a question of
naked argument, to fear no man, and to let no
man bite his thumb at him. If his Lordship
were to invite his brother-poet to his house, and
to eke out a sour jest by the flavour of Monte-
Pulciano or Frontiniac,—if in the dearth of
argument he were to ply his friend's weak side
with rich sauces and well-seasoned hospitality,
" *Ah! ça est bon, ah! goutez ça!*"—if he were

to point, in illustration of Pope's style, to the marble pillars, the verandas, the pier glasses, the classic busts, the flowering dessert, and were to exclaim, " You see, my dear Bowles, the superiority of art over nature, the triumph of polished life over Gothic barbarism ; we have here neither the ghosts nor fairies of Shakspeare, nor Milton's Heaven, nor *his* Hell, yet we contrive to do without them ;"—it might require Parson Supple's command of countenance to smile off this uncourteous address ; but the divine would not have to digest such awkward raillery on an empty stomach — he would have his *quid pro quo :* his Lordship would have paid for the liberty of using his privilege of peerage. But why any man should carry the *rôle* of his Lordship's chaplain out of his Lordship's house, is what I see no reason for.

Lord Byron, in the Preface to his Tragedy, complains that Horace Walpole has had hard measure dealt him by the critics, " firstly, because he was a lord, and secondly, because he was a gentleman." I do not know how the case may stand between the public and a dead nobleman ; but a living lord has every reasonable allowance made him, and can do what no one else can. If Lord Byron chooses to make a bad joke, by means of an ill-spent pun, it is a condescension in his Lordship :—if he puts off a set of smart assertions and school-boy instances for pithy proofs, it is not because he is not able, but because he cannot be at the pains of going deeper into the question :—if he is rude to an antagonist, it is construed into agreeable familiarity ; any notice from so great a man appears like a favour :—if he tells or recommends " a tale of bawdry," he is not to be tied down by the petty rules which restrict common men :— if he publishes a work which is thought of too equivocal a description for the delicate air of Albemarle-street, his Lordship's own name in the title-page is sufficient to back it without the formality of a bookseller's ; if a wire-drawn tragedy of his is acted, in spite of his protestations against such an appeal to the taste of a vulgar audience, the storm of pitiless damnation is not let loose upon it, because it is felt that it would fall harmless on so high and proud a head ; the gilded coronet serves as a conductor to carry off the lightning of popular criticism, which might blast the merely laurelled bard ; the blame, the disappointment, the flat effect, is thrown upon the manager, upon the actors— upon anybody but the noble poet ! This sounding title swells the mouth of Fame, and lends her voice a thousand circling echoes : the rank of the author, and the public charity extended to him, as he does not want it, cover a multitude of sins. What does his lordship mean, then, by this whining over the neglect of Horace Walpole, — this uncalled-for sympathy with the faded lustre of patrician and gentlemanly pretensions? Has *he* had only half his fame?—or does he already feel, with morbid anticipation, the retiring ebb of that overwhelming tide of popularity which, having been raised too high by adventitious circumstances, is lost in flats and shallows, as soon as their influence is withdrawn? Lord Byron has been twice as much talked of as he would have been had he not been Lord Byron. His rank and genius have been happily placed " each other's beams to share," and both together, by their mutually reflected splendour, may be said to have melted the public coldness into the very wantonness of praise : the faults of the man (real or supposed) have only given a dramatic interest to his works.

Whence, then, this repining, this ungracious cavilling, this *got-up* ill-humour? We load his Lordship with ecstatic admiration, with unqualified ostentatious eulogies ; and he throws them stifling back in our face : he thanks us with cool, cutting contempt: he asks us for our voices, " our sweet voices," like Coriolanus ; and, like Coriolanus, disdains us for the unwholesome gift. Why, then, does he ask for it? If, as a lord, he holds in contempt and abhorrence the willing, delighted homage, which the public pay to the poet, let him retire and feed the pride of birth in stately solitude, or take his place among his equals : but if he does not find this enough, and wants our wondering tribute of applause to satisfy his craving vanity, and make him something more than a mere vulgar lord among hundreds of other lords, why dash the cup of delicious poison which, at his uneasy request, we tender him, to the ground, with indignant reckless hands, and tell us that he scorns equally our censure or our praise? If he looks upon both as equal impertinence, he can easily escape out of the reach of both by ceasing to write; we shall in that case soon cease to think of his Lordship: but if he cannot do without our good opinion, why affect all this coyness, coldness, and contempt? If he says he writes not to please us, but to live by us, that only alters the nature of the obligation, and he might still be civil to Mr. Murray's customers. Whether he is independent of public opinion, or dependent on it, he need not be always sending his readers to Coventry. When we come to offer him our demonstrations of good will, he should not kick us down stairs. If he persists in this humour, the distaste may in time " become mutual."

Before we proceed, there is one thing in which we must say we heartily agree with Lord Byron; and that is the ridicule with which he treats Mr. Bowles's editorial inquisition into the moral character of Pope. It is a pure piece of clerical priggism. If Pope was not free from vice, we should like to know who is. He was one of the most faultless of poets, both in his life and in his writings. We should not care to throw the first stone at him. We do not wonder at Lord Byron's laughing outright at Mr. Bowles's hysterical horrors at poor Pope's platonic peccadillos, nor at his being a little impatient of the other's attempt to make himself a *make-believe* character of perfection out of the "most small faults" he could rake up against the reputation of an author, whom he was bound either not to edit or not to injure. But we think his Lordship turns the tables upon the divine, and gets up into the reading-desk himself, without the proper canonical credentials when he makes such a fuss as he does about didactic or moral poetry as the highest of all others, because moral truth and moral conduct are of such vast and paramount concernment in human life. But because they are such good things in themselves, does it follow that they are the better for being put into rhyme? We see no connexion between "ends of verse, and sayings of philosophers." This reasoning reminds us of the critic who said that the only poetry he knew of, good for any thing, was the four lines, beginning "Thirty days hath September, April, June, and November," for that these were really of some use in finding out the number of days in the different months of the year. The rules of arithmetic are important in many respects, but we do not know that they are the fittest subjects of poetry. Besides, Pope

was not the only moral poet, nor are we sure
that we understand his moral system, or that
Lord Byron understands it, or that he understood it himself.   Addison paraphrased the
Psalms. and Blackmore sung the Creation : yet
Pope has written a lampoon upon the one, and
put the other in his Dunciad.   Mr. Bowles has
numbers of manuscript sermons by him, the
morality of which, we will venture to say, is
quite as pure, as orthodox, as that of the un-
published cantos of Don Juan ; yet we doubt
whether Mr. Murray, the Mæcenas of poetry
and orthodoxy, would give as much for the one
as for the other.   We do not look for the
flowers of fancy in moral treatises, nor for a
homily in his Lordship's irregular stanzas.   The
Decalogue, as a practical prose composition, or
as a body of moral laws and precepts, is of
sufficient weight and authority ; but we should
not regard the putting of this into heroic verse
as an effort of the highest poetry. That " Stern-
hold and Hopkins had great qualms" is no imputation on the pious raptures of the Hebrew
bard : and we suspect his Lordship himself
would object to the allegory in Spenser, as a
drawback on the poetry, if it is in other respects to his Lordship's taste, which is more
than we can pretend to determine.   The Noble
Letter-writer thus moralizes on this subject, and
transposes the ordinary critical canons somewhat arbitrarily and sophistically.

" The depreciation of Pope is partly founded
upon a false idea of the dignity of his order of
poetry, to which he has partly contributed by
the ingenuous boast,

> That not in Fancy's maze he wandered long,
> But *stoop'd* to Truth, and moraliz'd his song.

He should have written 'rose to truth.' In my
mind the highest of all poetry is ethical poetry,
as the highest of all earthly objects must be
moral truth. Religion does not make a part
of my subject; it is something beyond human
powers, and has failed in all human hands except
Milton's and Dante's, and even Dante's powers
are involved in his delineation of human passions, though in supernatural circumstances.
What made Socrates the greatest of men? His
moral truth—his ethics. What proved Jesus
Christ the Son of God hardly less than his
miracles? His moral precepts. And if ethics
have made a philosopher the first of men, and
have not been disdained as an adjunct to his
Gospel by the Deity himself, are we to be told
that ethical poetry, or didactic poetry, or by
whatever name you term it, whose object is to
make men better and wiser, is not the *very first
order* of poetry; and are we to be told this too
by one of the priesthood? It requires more
mind, more wisdom, more power, than all the
'forests' that ever were 'walked' for their
'de cription' and all the epics that ever were

founded upon fields of battle. The Georgics are indisputably, and, I believe, *undisputedly*, even a finer poem than the Æneid. Virgil knew this : he did not order *them* to be burnt.

The proper study of mankind is man.

" It is the fashion of the day to lay great stress upon what they call ' imagination' and ' invention,'—the two commonest of qualities : an Irish peasant, with a little whiskey in his head, will imagine and invent more than would furnish forth a modern poem. If Lucretius had not been spoiled by the Epicurean system, we should have had a far superior poem to any now in existence. As mere poetry, it is the first of Latin poems. What then has ruined it ? His ethics. Pope has not this defect : his moral is as pure as his poetry is glorious." p. 42.

Really this is very inconsequential, incongruous reasoning. An Irish peasant, with a little whiskey in his head, would not fall upon more blunders, contradictions, and defective conclusions. Lord Byron talks of the ethical systems of Socrates and Jesus Christ. What made the former the great man he supposes?—The invention of his system—the discovery of sublime moral truths. Does Lord Byron mean to say that the mere repetition of the same precepts in prose, or the turning of them into verse, will make others as great, or will make a great man at all ? The two things compared are wholly disparates. The finding out the 48th proposition in Euclid made Pythagoras a great man. Shall we say that the putting this into a grave, didactic distich would make either a great mathematician or a great poet? It would do neither the one nor the other; though, according to Lord Byron, this distich would belong to the highest class of poetry, "because it would do that in verse which one of the greatest of men had wished to accomplish in prose." Such is the way in which his Lordship transposes the common sense of the question,—because it is his humour! The value of any moral truth depends on the philosophic invention implied in it. But this rests with the first author, and the general idea, which forms the basis of didactic poetry, remains the same, through all its mechanical transmissions afterwards. The merit of the ethical poet must therefore consist in his manner of adorning and illustrating a number of these general truths which are not his own, that is, in the poetical invention and imagination he brings to the subject, as Mr. Bowles has well shown, with respect to the episodes in the Essay on Man, the description of the poor Indian, and the lamb doomed to death, which are all the unsophisticated reader ever remembers of that much-talked-of production. Lord Byron clownishly chooses to consider all poetry but what relates to this ethical or didactic truth as "a lie." Is Lear a lie? Or does his Lordship prefer the story, or the moral, in Æsop's Fables? He asks " why must the *poet* mean the *liar,* the *feigner,* the *tale-teller?* A man may make and create better things than these."— He may make and create better things than a common - place, and he who does not makes and creates nothing. The ethical or didactic poet necessarily repeats after others, because general truths and maxims are limited. The individual instances and illustrations, which his Lordship qualifies as " lies," " feigning," and " tale-telling," are infinite, and give endless scope to the genius of the true poet. The rank of poetry is to be judged of by the truth and purity of the moral—so we find it "in the bond,"—and yet Cowper, we are told, was no poet. Is there any keeping in this, or is it merely an air? Again, we are given to understand that didactic poetry " requires more mind, more power than all the descriptive or epic poetry that ever was written :" and as a proof of this, his Lordship lays it down that the Georgics are a finer poem than the Æneid. We do not perceive the inference here. " Virgil knew this: he did not order *them* to be burnt.

The proper study of mankind is man."

Does our author mean that this was Virgil's reason for liking his pastoral poetry better than his description of Dido and Æneas ? But farther, there is a Latin poem (that of Lucretius) supe-

rior even to the Georgics; nay, it would have
been so to any poem now in existence, but for
one unlucky circumstance. And what is that?
"Its ethics!" So that ethics have spoiled the
finest poem in the world. This is the rub that
makes didactic poetry come in such a question-
able shape. If original, like Lucretius, there
will be a difference of opinion about it. If trite
and acknowledged, like Pope, however pure,
there will be little valuable in it. It is the glory
and the privilege of poetry to be conversant
about those truths of nature and the heart that
are at once original and self-evident. His Lordship ought to *have known this*. In the same passage, he speaks of imagination and invention as
" the two commonest of qualities." We will tell
his Lordship what is commoner—the want of
them. "An Irish peasant," he adds, " with a
little whiskey in his head, will imagine and invent
more than"—(What? Homer, Spenser, and
Ariosto? No: but than)—" would furnish forth
a modern poem." That we will not dispute. But
at any rate, when sober the next morning, he
would be as " full of wise saws and modern instances" as his Lordship; and in either case,
equally positive, tetchy, and absurd!

His Lordship, throughout his pamphlet, makes
a point of contradicting Mr. Bowles, and, it
would seem, of contradicting himself. He cannot be said to have any opinions of his own,
but whatever any one else advances, he denies

out of mere spleen and rashness. " He hates
the word *invariable*," and not without reason.
" What is there of human, be it poetry, philosophy, wit, wisdom, science, power, glory, mind,
matter, life, or death, which is invariable ?"—
There is one of the particulars in this enumera-
tion which seems pretty invariable, which is
death. One would think that the principles of
poetry are so too, notwithstanding his peevish
disclaimer : for towards the conclusion of this
letter he sets up Pope as a classic model, and
considers all modern deviations from it as
grotesque and barbarous.

" They have raised a mosque by the side of a
Grecian temple of the purest architecture ; and,
more barbarous than the barbarians from whose
practice I have borrowed the figure, they are not
contented with their own grotesque edifice, unless
they destroy *the prior and purely beautiful fabric
which preceded*,* and which shames them and
theirs for ever and ever."

Lord Byron has here substituted his own invariable principles for Mr. Bowles's, which he
hates as bad as Mr. Southey's variable politics.
Will nothing please his Lordship—neither dull
fixtures nor shining weather-cocks ?—We might
multiply instances of a want of continuous rea-

---

* We have " purest architecture" just before ; and " the
prior fabric which preceded," is rather more than an
inelegant pleonasm.

soning, if we were fond of this sort of petty
cavilling. Yet we do not know that there is
any better quarry in the book. Why does his
Lordship tells us that "ethical poetry is the
highest of all poetry," and yet that "Petrarch
the sonnetteer" is esteemed by good judges the
very highest poet of Italy? Mr. Bowles is a
sonnetteer, and a very good one. Why does he
assert that " the poet who executes the best is
the highest, whatever his department," and then
affirm in the next page that didactic poetry " requires more mind, more wisdom, more power,
than all the forests that ever were walked for
their description ;" and then again, two pages
after, that " a good poet can make a silk purse
of a sow's ear:" that is, as he interprets it,
" can imbue a pack of cards with more poetry
than inhabits the forests of America ?" That's
a *Non Sequitur*, as Partridge has it. Why, contending that all subjects are alike indifferent to
the genuine poet, does he turn round upon himself, and assume that " the sun shining upon a
warming pan cannot be made sublime or poetical?" Why does he say that " there is nothing
in nature like the bust of the Antinöus, except
the Venus," which is not in nature ?* Why does
he call the first " that wonderful *creation* of perfect beauty," when it is a mere portrait, and on
that account so superior to his favourite coxcomb

---

* See Mr. Bowles's Two Letters.

the Apollo? Why does he state that "more poetry cannot be gathered into existence" than we here see, and yet that this poetry arises neither from nature nor moral exaltedness; Mr. Bowles and he being at issue on this very point, viz. the one affirming that the essence of poetry is derived from nature, and his Lordship, that it consists in moral truth? Why does he consider a shipwreck as an artificial incident? Why does he make the excellence of Falconer's Shipwreck consist in its technicalities, and not in its faithful description of common feelings and inevitable calamity? Why does he say all this, and much more, which he should not? Why does he write prose at all? Yet, in spite of all this trash, there is one passage for which we forgive him, and here it is.

"The truth is, that in these days the grand *primum mobile* of England is *cant*; cant political, cant poetical, cant religious, cant moral; but always cant, multiplied through all the varieties of life. It is the fashion, and, while it lasts, will be too powerful for those who can only exist by taking the tone of the times. I say *cant*, because it is a thing of words, without the smallest influence upon human actions; the English being no wiser, no better, and much poorer, and more divided among themselves, as well as far less moral, than they were before the prevalence of this verbal decorum." These words should be written in letters of gold, as the testimony of a

lofty poet to a great moral truth, and we can
hardly have a quarrel with the writer of them.

There are three questions which form the
subject of the present pamphlet; viz. What is
poetical? What is natural? What is artificial?
And we get an answer to none of them. The
controversy, as it is carried on between the chief
combatants, is much like a dispute between two
artists, one of whom should maintain that blue
is the only colour fit to paint with, and the other
that yellow alone ought ever to be used. Much
might be said on both sides, but little to the
purpose. Mr. Campbell leads off the dance, and
launches a ship as a beautiful and poetical artificial object. But he so loads it with patriotic,
natural, and foreign associations, and the sails
are " so perfumed that the winds are love-sick,"
that Mr. Bowles darts upon and seizes it as con-
traband to art, swearing that it is no longer
the work of the shipwright, but of Mr. Campbell's lofty poetic imagination; and dedicates its
stolen beauty to the right owners, the sun, the
winds, and the waves. Mr. Campbell, in his
eagerness to make all sure, having overstepped
the literal mark, presses no farther into the
controversy ; but Lord Byron, who is "like an
Irishman in a row, *any body's customer*," carries
it on with good polemical hardihood, and runs
a very edifying parallel between the ship without
the sun, the winds and waves,—and the sun, the
winds, and waves without the ship. " The sun,"

says Mr. Bowles, " is poetical, by your Lordship's admission." We think it would have been so without it. But his Lordship contends that " the sun would no longer be poetical, if it did not shine on ships, or pyramids, or fortresses, and other works of art," (he expressly excludes " footmen's liveries" and " brass warming-pans" from among those artificial objects that reflect new splendour on the eye of Heaven)—to which Mr. Bowles replies, that let the sun but shine, and " it is poetical *per se,*" in which we think him right. His Lordship decompounds the wind into a *caput mortuum* of poetry, by making it howl through a pig-stye, instead of

> Roaming the illimitable ocean wide ;

and turns a water-fall, or a clear spring, into a slop-bason, to prove that nature owes its elegance to art. His Lordship is " ill at these numbers." Again, he affirms that the ruined temple of the Parthenon is poetical, and the coast of Attica, with Cape Colonna, and the recollection of Falconer's Shipwreck, classical. Who ever doubted it ? What then ? Does this prove that the Rape of the Lock is not a mock-heroic poem ? He assures us that a storm with cock-boats scudding before it is interesting, particularly if this happens to take place in the Hellespont, over which the noble critic swam ; and makes it a question whether the dark cypress groves, or the white towers and minarets of Constantinople, are more impressive to the imagination? What has this to do with Pope's grotto at Twickenham, or the boat in which he paddled across the Thames to Kew? Lord Byron tells us (and he should know) that the Grand Canal at Venice is a muddy ditch, without the stately palaces by its side; but then it is a natural, not an artificial, canal; and finally, he asks, what would the desert of Tadmor be without the ruins of Palmyra, or Salisbury Plain without Stone-Henge? Mr. Bowles, who, though tedious and teazing, has "damnable iteration in him," and has read the Fathers, answers very properly, by saying that a desert alone "conveys ideas of immeasurable distance, of profound silence, of solitude;" and that Salisbury Plain has the advantage of Hounslow Heath, chiefly in getting rid of the ideas of artificial life, "carts, caravans, raree-showmen, butchers' boys, coaches with coronets, and livery servants behind them," even though Stone-Henge did not lift its pale head above its barren bosom. Indeed, Lord Byron's notions of art and poetry are sufficiently wild, romantic, far-fetched, obsolete: his taste is Oriental, Gothic; his Muse is not domesticated; there is nothing *mimminee - pimminee,* modern, polished, light, fluttering, in his standard of the sublime and beautiful: if his thoughts are proud, pampered, gorgeous, and disdain to mingle with the objects of humble, unadorned nature, his lordly

eye at least " keeps distance due" from the
vulgar vanities of fashionable life; from drawing-
rooms, from card-parties, and from courts.   He
is not a carpet poet.   He does not sing the
sofa, like poor Cowper.   He is qualified neither
for poet-laureate nor court-newsman.   He is at
issue with the Morning Post and Fashionable
World on what constitutes the true pathos and
sublime of human life.   He hardly thinks Lady
Charlemont so good as the Venus, or as an
Albanian girl that he saw mending the road in
the mountains.   If he does not like flowers and
forests, he cares as little for stars, garters, and
princes' feathers, for diamond necklaces and
paste buckles.   If his Lordship cannot make
up his mind to the quiet, the innocence, the
simple, unalterable grandeur of nature, we are
sure that he hates the frippery, the foppery, and
pert grimace of art, quite as much.   His Lordship likes the poetry, the imaginative part of
art, and so do we; and so we believe did the
late Mr. John Scott.   He likes the *sombre* part
of it, the thoughtful, the decayed, the ideal, the
spectral shadow of human greatness, the departed
spirit of human power.   He sympathizes not
with art as a display of ingenuity, as the
triumph of vanity or luxury, as it is connected
with the idiot, superficial, petty self-complacency
of the individual and the moment (these are
to him not " luscious as locusts, but bitter as
coloquintida"); but he sympathizes with the

triumphs of Time and Fate over the proudest
works of man—with the crumbling monuments
of human glory — with the dim vestiges of
countless generations of men—with that which
claims alliance with the grave, or kindred with
the elements of nature. This is what he calls
art and artificial poetry. But this is not what
anybody else understands by the terms, commonly or critically speaking. There is as little
connection between the two things as between
the grand-daughters of Mr. Coutts, who appeared at court the other day, and Lady Godiva
—as there is between a reigning toast and an
Egyptian mummy. Lord Byron, through the
whole of the argument, pelts his reverend op-
ponent with instances, like throwing a stone at
a dog, which the incensed animal runs after,
picks up, mumbles between his teeth, and tries
to see what it is made of. The question is,
however, too tough for Mr. Bowles's powers of
mastication, and, though the fray is amusing,
nothing comes of it. Between the Editor of
Pope and the Editor of the New Monthly
Magazine, his Lordship sits

> ———— high arbiter,
> And by decision more embroils the fray.

What is the use of taking a work of art,
from which " all the art of art is flown," a
mouldering statue, or a fallen column in Tadmor's marble waste, that staggers and overawes

the mind, and gives birth to a thousand dim
reflections, by seeing the power and pride of
man prostrate and laid low in the dust; what is
there in this to prove the self-sufficiency of the
upstart pride and power of man? A ruin is
poetical. Because it is a work of art, says
Lord Byron. No, but because it is a work of
art o'erthrown. In it we see, as in a mirror,
the life, the hopes, the labour of man defeated,
and crumbling away under the slow hand of
time; and all that he has done reduced to
nothing, or to a useless mockery. Or as one
of the bread-and-butter poets has described the
same thing a little differently, in his tale of
Peter Bell the potter,—

> The stones and tower
> Seem'd fading fast away
> From human thoughts and purposes,
> To yield to some transforming power,
> And blend with the surrounding trees.

If this is what Lord Byron means by artificial
objects, there is an end of the question, for he
will get no critic, no school to differ with him.
But a fairer instance would be a snug citizen's
box by the road-side, newly painted, plastered,
and furnished, with every thing in the newest
fashion and gloss, not an article the worse for
wear, and a lease of one-and-twenty years to
run, and then let us see what Lord Byron, or
his friend and " host of human life" will make

of it, compared with the desolation and the
waste of all these comforts, arts, and elegances.
Or let him take—not the pyramids of Egypt,
but the Pavilion at Brighton, and make a
poetical description of it in prose or verse. I
defy him. The poetical interest, in his Lordship's transposed cases, arises out of the imaginary interest. But the truth is that, where
art flourishes and attains its object, imagination
droops, and poetry along with it. It ceases, or
takes a different and ambiguous shape ; it may
be elegant, ingenious, pleasing, instructive, but
if it aspires to the semblance of a higher interest,
or the ornaments of the highest fancy, it necessarily becomes burlesque, as for instance in the
Rape of the Lock. As novels end with marriage,
poetry ends with the consummation and success
of art. And the reason (if Lord Byron would
attend to it) is pretty obvious. Where all the
wishes and wants are supplied, anticipated by art,
there can be no strong cravings after ideal good
nor dread of unimaginable evils ; the sources
of terror and pity must be dried up : where the
hand has done everything, nothing is left for
the imagination to do or to attempt : where all
is regulated by conventional indifference, the
full workings, the involuntary, uncontrollable
emotions of the heart cease: property is not a
poetical, but a practical prosaic idea, to those who
possess and clutch it, and cuts off others from
cordial sympathy ; but nature is common pro-

perty, the unenvied idol of all eyes, the fairy ground where fancy plays her tricks and feats ; and the passions, the workings of the heart (which Mr. Bowles very properly distinguishes from manners, inasmuch as they are not in the power of the will to regulate or satisfy), are still left as a subject for something very different from didactic or mock-heroic poetry. By *art* and *artificial*, as these terms are applied to poetry or human life, we mean those objects and feelings which depend for their subsistence and perfection on the will and arbitrary conventions of man and society; and by nature, and natural objects, we mean those objects which exist in the universe at large, without, or in spite of, the interference of human power and contrivance, and those interests and affections which are not amenable to the human will. That we are to exclude art, or the operation of the human will, from poetry altogether, is what we do not affirm ; but we mean to say that where this operation is the more complete and manifest, as in the creation of given objects, or regulation of certain feelings, there the spring of poetry, *i. e.* of passion and imagination, is proportionably and much impaired. We are masters of Art, Nature is our master ; and it is to this greater power that we find working above, without, and within us, that the genius of poetry bows and offers up its highest homage. If the infusion of art were not a natural dis-

qualifier for poetry, the most artificial objects
and manners would be the most poetical: on
the contrary, it is only the rude beginnings, or
the ruinous decay of objects of art, or the simplest modes of life and manners, that admit of
or harmonize kindly with, the tone and language
of poetry. To consider the question otherwise
is not to consider it too curiously, but not to
understand it all. Lord Byron talks of Ulysses
striking his horse Rhesus with his bow, as an
instance of the heroic in poetry. But does not
the poetical dignity of the instrument arise from
its very commonness and simplicity? A bow is
not a supererogation of the works of art. It
is almost peculiar to a state of nature, that is,
the first and rudest state of society. Lord
Byron might as well talk of a shepherd's crook,
or the garland of flowers with which he crowns
his mistress, as images borrowed from artificial
life. He cannot make a gentleman-usher's rod
poetical, though it is the pink of courtly and
gentlemanly refinement. Will the bold stickler
for the artificial essence of poetry translate
Pope's description of Sir Plume,—

> Of amber-headed snuff-box justly vain,
> And the nice conduct of a clouded cane,—

into the same sort of poetry as Homer's description of the bow of Ulysses? It is out of
the question. The very mention of the last has
a sound with it like the twang of the bow it-

self; whereas the others, the snuff-box and clouded-cane, are of the very essence of effeminate impertinence. Pope says, in Spence's Anecdotes, that "a lady of fashion would admire a star, because it would remind her of the twinkling of a lamp on a ball-night." This is a much better account of his own poetry than his noble critic has given. It is a clue to a real solution of the difficulty. What is the difference between the feeling with which we contemplate a gas-light in one of the squares, and the crescent moon beside it, but this—that though the brightness, the beauty perhaps, to the mere sense, is the same or greater, yet we know that when we are out of the square, we shall lose sight of the lamp, but that the moon will lend us its tributary light wherever we go; it streams over green valley or blue ocean alike; it is hung up in air, a part of the pageant of the universe; it steals with gradual, softened state into the soul, and hovers, a fairy-apparition, over our existence! It is this which makes it a more poetical object than a patent-lamp, or a Chinese lanthorn, or the chandelier at Coventgarden, brilliant as it is, and which, though it were made ten times more so, would still only dazzle and scorch the sight so much the more; it would not be attended with a mild train of reflected glory; it would "denote no foregone conclusion," would touch no chord of imagination or the heart; it would have nothing ro-

mantic about it.—A man can make any thing
but he cannot make a sentiment! It is a thing
of inveterate prejudice, of old association, of
common feeling, and so is poetry, as far as it is
serious. A "pack of cards," a silver bodkin,
a paste buckle, "may be imbued" with as much
mock poetry as you please, by lending false
associations to it; but real poetry, or poetry of
the highest order, can only be produced by un-
ravelling the real web of associations, which
have been wound round any subject by nature,
and the unavoidable conditions of humanity.
Not to admit this distinction at the threshold
is to confound the style of Tom Thumb with
that of the Moor of Venice, or Hurlothrumbo
with the Doge of Venice. It is to mistake jest
for earnest, and one thing for another.

> How far that little candle throws its beams!
> So shines a good deed in a naughty world.

The image here is one of artificial life; but
it is connected with natural circumstances and
romantic interests, with darkness, with silence,
with distance, with privation, and uncertain
danger : it is common, obvious, without pretension or boast, and therefore the poetry founded upon it is natural, because the feelings are
so. It is not the splendour of the candle itself,
but the contrast to the gloom without,—the
comfort, the relief it holds out from afar to the
benighted traveller,—the conflict between nature

and the first and cheapest resources of art, that
constitutes the romantic and imaginary, that is,
the poetical interest, in that familiar but striking image. There is more art in the lamp or
chandelier; but, for that very reason, there is
less poetry. A light in a watch-tower, a beacon
at sea, is sublime for the same cause; because
the natural circumstances and associations set
it off; it warns us against danger, it reminds
us of common calamity, it promises safety and
hope: it has to do with the broad feelings and
circumstances of human life, and its interest
does not assuredly turn upon the vanity or pretensions of the maker or proprietor of it. This
sort of art is co-ordinate with nature, and
comes into the first class of poetry, but no one
ever dreamt of the contrary. The features of
nature are great leading land-marks, not near
and little, or confined to a spot, or an individual
claimant; they are spread out everywhere the
same, and are of universal interest. The true
poet has therefore been described as

Creation's tenant, he is nature's heir.

What has been thus said of the man of
genius might be said of the man of no genius.
The spirit of poetry and the spirit of humanity
are the same. The productions of nature are
not locked up in the cabinets of the curious,
but spread out on the green lap of earth. The
flowers return with the cuckoo in the spring:

the daisy for ever looks bright in the sun; the
rainbow still lifts its head above the storm to
the eye of infancy or age—

> So was it when my life began;
> So is it now I am a man,
> So shall it be till I grow old and die;

but Lord Byron does not understand this, for he
does not understand Mr. Wordsworth's poetry,
and we cannot make him.   His Lordship's nature, as well as his poetry, is something arabes-
que and outlandish.—Again, once more, what,
we would ask, makes the difference between an
opera of Mozart's, and the singing of a thrush
confined in a wooden cage at the corner of the
street in which we live? The one is nature, and
the other is art: the one is paid for, and the
other is not.   Madame Fodor sings the air of
Vedrai Carino in *Don Giovanni* so divinely because she is hired to sing it; she sings it to
please the audience, not herself, and does not
always like to be *encored* in it; but the thrush
that awakes us at day-break with its song does
not sing because it is paid to sing, or to please
others, or to be admired or criticised: it sings
because it is happy: it pours the thrilling
sounds from its throat, to relieve the overflow-
ings of its own breast—the liquid notes come
from, and go to, the heart, dropping balm into
it, as the gushing spring revives the traveller's
parched and fainting lips.   That stream of joy
comes pure and fresh to the longing sense, free

from art and affectation; the same that rises
over vernal groves, mingled with the breath of
morning, and the perfumes of the wild hyacinth;
that waits for no audience, that wants no re-
hearsing, that exhausts its raptures, and is
still—

Hymns its good God, and carols sweet of love.

There is this great difference between nature
and art, that the one *is* what the other *seems*,
and gives all the pleasure it expresses, because
it feels it itself. Madame Fodor sings, as a
musical instrument may be made to play a tune,
and perhaps with no more real delight: but it
is not so with the linnet or the thrush, that
sings because God pleases, and pours out its
little soul in pleasure. This is the reason why
its singing is (so far) so much better than me-
lody or harmony, than bass or treble, than the
Italian or the German school, than quavers or
crotchets, or half-notes, or canzonets, or quar-
tetts, or any thing in the world but truth and
nature!

To give one more instance or two of what we
understand by a natural interest ingrafted on
artificial objects, and of the principle that still
keeps them distinct. Amelia's "hashed mutton" in Fielding is one that we might mention.
Hashed mutton is an article in cookery, homely
enough in the scale of art, though far removed
from the simple products of nature; yet we

should say that this common delicacy which
Amelia provided for her husband's supper, and
then waited so long in vain for his return, is the
foundation of one of the most natural and affecting incidents in one of the most natural and
affecting books in the world.—No description of
the most splendid and luxurious banquet could
come up to it. It will be remembered, when
the *Almanach des Gourmands,* and even the
article on it in the last Edinburgh Review, are
forgotten. Did Lord Byron never read Boccaccio? We wish he would learn refinement
from him, and get rid of his hard *bravura* taste,
and swash-buckler conclusions. What makes
the charm of the story of the Falcon? Is it
properly art or nature? The tale is one of artificial life, and elegant manners, and chivalrous
pretensions; but it is the fall from these, the
decline into the vale of low and obscure poverty,—the having but one last loop left to
hang life on, and the sacrifice of that to a feeling still more precious, and which could only
give way with life itself,—that elevates the
sentiment, and has made it find its way into all
hearts. Had Federigo Alberigi had an aviary
of hawks, and preserves of pheasants without
end, he and his poor bird would never have been
heard of. It is not the expense and ostentation
of the entertainment he sets before his mistress,
but the prodigality of affection, squandering
away the last remains of his once proud for-

tunes, that stamps this beautiful incident on the
remembrance of all who have ever read it. We
wish Lord Byron would look it over again, and
see whether it does not most touch the chords
of pathos and sentiment in those places where
we feel the absence of all the pomp and vanities
of art. Mr. Campbell talks of a ship as a
sublime and beautiful object in art. We will
confess we always stop to look at the mail-
coaches with no slight emotion, and, perhaps,
extend our hands after some of them, in sign of
gratulation. They carry the letters of friends,
of relations; they keep up the communication
between the heart of a country. We do not
admire them for their workmanship, for their
speed, for their livery—there is something more
in it than this. Perhaps we can explain it by
saying, that we once heard a person observe—
" I always look at the Shrewsbury mail, and
sometimes with tears in my eyes : that is the
coach that will bring me the news of the death
of my father and mother." His Lordship will
say, the mail-coach is an artificial object. Yet
we think the interest here was not founded upon
that circumstance. There was a finer and
deeper link of affection that did not depend on
the red painted pannels, or the *dyed garments* of
the coachman and guard. At least it strikes
us so.

This is not an easy subject to illustrate, and
it is still more difficult to define. Yet we shall

attempt something of the sort. 1. Natural objects are common and obvious, and are imbued
with an habitual and universal interest, without
being vulgar. Familiarity in them does not
breed contempt, as it does in the works of man.
They form an ideal class; their repeated impression on the mind, in so many different circumstances, grows up into a sentiment. The
reason is, that we refer them generally and col-
lectively to ourselves, as links and mementos of
our various being; whereas, we refer the works
of art respectively to those by whom they are
made or to whom they belong. This distracts
the mind in looking at them, and gives a petty
and unpoetical character to what we feel relating to them. When the works of art become
poetical, it is when they are emancipated from
this state of " circumscription and confine," by
some circumstance that sets aside the idea of
property and individual distinction. The sound
of village bells,—

——The poor man's only music,*

excites as lively an interest in the mind as the
warbling of a thrush: the sight of a village
spire presents nothing discordant with the surrounding scenery.

2. Natural objects are more akin to poetry
and the imagination, partly because they are
not our own handy-work, but start up spon-

* Coleridge

taneously, like a visionary creation, of their own accord, without our knowledge or connivance—

> The earth hath bubbles, as the water hath,
> And these are of them;—

and farther, they have this advantage over the works of art, that the latter either fall short of their pre-conceived intention, and excite our disgust and disappointment by their defects; or, if they completely answer their end, they then leave nothing to the imagination, and so excite little or no romantic interest that way. A Count Rumford stove, or a Dutch oven, are useful for the purposes of warmth or culinary dispatch. Gray's purring favourite would find great comfort in warming its nose before the one, or dipping its whiskers in the other; and so does the artificial animal, man: but the poetry of Rumford grates or Dutch ovens it would puzzle even Lord Byron to explain. Cowper has made something of the "loud-hissing urn," though Mr. Southey, as being one of the more refined "naturals," still prefers "the song of the kettle." The more our senses, our self-love, our eyes and ears, are surrounded, and, as it were, saturated with artifical enjoyments and costly decorations, the more the avenues to the imagination and the heart are unavoidably blocked up. We do not say that this may not be an advantage to the individual; we say it is a disadvantage to the poet. Even

"Mine Host of Human Life" has felt its palsying, enervating influence. Let any one (after ten years old) take shelter from a shower of rain in Exeter Change, and see how he will amuse the time with looking over the trinkets, the chains, the seals, the curious works of art. Compare this with the description of Una and the Red Cross Knight in Spenser:

> Enforc'd to seek some covert nigh at hand,
> A shady grove not far away they spied,
> That promis'd aid the tempest to withstand :
> Whose lofty trees, yclad with summer's pride,
> Did spread so broad that heaven's light did hide,
> Not pierceable with power of any star ;
> And all within were paths and alleys wide,
> With footing worn, and leading inward far ;
> Far harbour that them seems ; so in they enter'd are.
>
> And forth they pass, with pleasure forward led,
> Joying to hear the birds' sweet harmony,
> Which therein shrowded from the tempest's dread,
> Seem'd in their song to scorn the cruel sky.
> Much can they praise the trees so straight and high,
> The sailing pine, the cedar proud and tall,
> The vine-prop elm, the poplar never dry,
> The builder oak, sole king of forests all,
> The aspen good for staves, the cypress funeral.*

---

* Most people have felt the *ennui* of being detained under a gateway in a shower of rain. Happy is he who has an umbrella, and can escape when the first fury of the storm has abated. Turn this gateway into a broker's shop, full of second-hand furniture—tables, chairs, bedsteads, bolsters, and all the accommodations of man's life,—the case will not be mended. On the other hand, convert it

Artificial flowers look pretty in a lady's head-dress; but they will not do to stick into lofty verse. On the contrary, a crocus bursting out of the ground seems to blush with its own golden light—" a thing of life." So a greater authority than Lord Byron has given his testimony on this subject : " Behold the lilies of the field, they toil not, neither do they spin ; yet I say unto you, that even Solomon in all his glory was not arrayed like one of these." Shakspeare speaks of

———————Daffodils,
That come before the swallow dares, and take
The winds of March with beauty.

All this play of fancy and dramatic interest could not be transferred to a description of hot-

---

into a wild natural cave, and we may idle away whole hours in it, marking a streak in the rock, or a flower that grows on the sides, without feeling time hang heavy on us. The reason is that, where we are surrounded with the works of man—the sympathy with the art and purposes of man, as it were, irritates our own will, and makes us impatient of whatever interferes with it : while, on the contrary, the presence of nature, of objects existing without our intervention and controul, disarms the will of its restless activity, and disposes us to submit to accidents that we cannot help, and the course of outward events, without repining. We are thrown into the hands of nature, and become converts to her power. Thus the idea of the artificial, the conventional, the voluntary, is fatal to the romantic and imaginary. To us it seems that the free spirit of nature rushes through the soul, like a stream with a murmuring sound, the echo of which is poetry.

house plants, regulated by a thermometer. Lord Byron unfairly enlists into the service of his argument those artificial objects which are direct imitations of nature, such as statuary, &c. This is an oversight. At this rate, all poetry would be artificial poetry. Dr. Darwin is among those who have endeavoured to confound the distinctions of natural and artificial poetry, and, indeed, he is, perhaps, the only one who has gone the whole length of Lord Byron's hypercritical and super-artificial theory. Here are some of his lines, which have been greatly admired :

Apostrophe to Steel.

Hail, adamantine steel ! magnetic lord,
King of the prow, the ploughshare, and the sword !
True to the pole, by thee the pilot guides
His steady course amid the struggling tides,
Braves with broad sail the immeasurable sea,
Cleaves the dark air, and asks no star but thee !

This is the true false gallop of the sublime. Yet steel is a very useful metal, and doubtless performs all these wonders. But it has not, among so many others, the virtue of amalgamating with the imagination. We might quote also his description of the spinning-jenny, which is pronounced by Dr. Aikin to be as ingenious a piece of mechanism as the object it describes ; and, according to Lord Byron, this last is as well suited to the manufacture of verses as of cotton-twist without end.

3. Natural interests are those which are real
and inevitable, and are so far contradistinguished
from the artificial, which are factitious and affected. If Lord Byron cannot understand the
difference, he may find it explained by contrast-
ing some of Chaucer's characters and incidents
with those in the Rape of the Lock, for instance.
Custance, floating in her boat on the wide sea, is
different from Pope's heroine,

> Launched on the bosom of the silver Thames.

Griselda's loss of her children, one by one,
of her *all*, does not belong to the same class of
incidents, nor of subjects for poetry, as Belinda's
loss of her favourite curl. A sentiment that has
rooted itself in the heart, and can only be torn
from it with life, is not like the caprice of the
moment—the putting on of paint and patches,
or the pulling off a glove. The inbred character is not like a masquerade dress. There is a
difference between the theatrical and natural,
which is important to the determination of the
present question, and which has been overlooked
by his Lordship. Mr. Bowles, however, formally
insists (and with the best right in the world) on
the distinction between passion and manners.
But he agrees with Lord Byron that the Epistle
to Abelard is the height of the pathetic.

> Strange that such difference should be
> 'Twixt tweedledum and tweedledee.

That it is in a great degree pathetic, I should

be among the last to dispute ; but its character is more properly rhetorical and voluptuous. That its interest is of the highest or deepest order is what I should wonder to hear any one affirm who is intimate with Shakspeare, Chaucer, Boccaccio, our own early dramatists, or the Greek tragedians. There is more true, unfeigned, unspeakable, heartfelt distress in one line of Chaucer's tale just mentioned,

> Let me not like a worm go by the way,

than in all Pope's writings put together ; and I say it without any disrespect to him, too Didactic poetry has to do with manners, as they are regulated, not by fashion or caprice, but by abstract reason and grave opinion, and is equally remote from the dramatic, which describes the involuntary and unpremeditated impulses of nature. As Lord Byron refers to the Bible, I would just ask him here, which he thinks the most poetical parts of it, the Law of the twelve tables, the book of Leviticus, &c. ; or the Book of Job, Jacob's dream, the story of Ruth, &c. ?

4. Supernatural poetry is, in the sense here insisted on, allied to nature, not to art, because it relates to the impressions made upon the mind by unknown objects and powers, out of the reach both of the cognizance and will of man, and still more able to startle and confound his imagination, while he supposes them to exist,

than either those of nature or art. The Witches in Macbeth, the Furies in Æschylus, are so far artificial objects that they are creatures of the poet's brain ; but their impression on the mind depends on their possessing attributes which baffle and set at nought all human pretence, and laugh at all human efforts to tamper with them. Satan in Milton is an artificial or ideal character : but would any one call this artificial poetry ? It is, in Lord Byron's phrase, super-artificial, as well as super-human poetry. But it is serious business. Fate, if not Nature, is its ruling genius. The Pandemonium is not a baby-house of the fancy, and it is ranked (ordinarily) with natural, *i. e.* with the highest and most important order of poetry, and above the Rape of the Lock. I intended a definition, and have run again into examples. Lord Byron's *concretions* have spoiled me for philosophy.

THE END.